THE ALLITERATIVE REVIVAL

THE ALLITERATIVE REVIVAL

THORLAC TURVILLE-PETRE

D. S. BREWER · ROWMAN & LITTLEFIELD

© Thorlac Turville-Petre 1977

Published by D. S. Brewer Ltd
240 Hills Road, Cambridge, England
and by Rowman and Littlefield
81 Adams Drive, Totowa, New Jersey 07512, U.S.A.

UK ISBN 0 85991 019 9
US ISBN 0-87471-955-0

Printed and bound in Great Britain
by Redwood Burn Limited,
Trowbridge & Esher

ACKNOWLEDGEMENTS

For advice on aspects of vocabulary, in particular topographical terms, I should like to thank Professor Kenneth Cameron; for help on Dunbar I am grateful to Professor James Kinsley. Professor John Burrow and Joan Turville-Petre have been generous with advice and encouragement at every stage. I am greatly indebted to both, and also to Dr. Derek Brewer from whose valuable criticisms I hope I have profited.

Grateful acknowledgements are due to Faber and Faber Ltd. and Random House Inc. for permission to quote copyright material from *Collected Longer Poems* by W. H. Auden.

Nottingham   July, 1976

CONTENTS

ABBREVIATIONS

E.E.T.S., E.S.	Early English Text Society, Extra Series.
E. Sts.	*English Studies.*
J.E.G.P.	*Journal of English and Germanic Philology.*
M.Æ.	*Medium Ævum.*
L.S.E.	*Leeds Studies in English and Kindred Languages.*
M.E.D.	*Middle English Dictionary.*
M.L.N.	*Modern Language Notes.*
M.L.R.	*Modern Language Review.*
M.P.	*Modern Philology.*
M.S.	*Mediaeval Studies.*
N. & Q.	*Notes and Queries.*
N.M.	*Neuphilologische Mitteilungen.*
OE.	Old English.
O.E.D.	*Oxford English Dictionary.*
OFr.	Old French.
ON.	Old Norse.
P.B.A.	*Proceedings of the British Academy.*
R.E.S.	*Review of English Studies.*
S.T.S.	Scottish Text Society.

Chapter 1

THE ORIGINS OF THE ALLITERATIVE REVIVAL

Wynnere and Wastoure

The poem *Wynnere and Wastoure* describes a debate between two bitter enemies, one representing the principle of saving and the other of spending. It is, first and foremost, a topical satire directed at fourteenth-century conditions. Closer study will show that it has a deeper level of significance than the merely topical, but the references to people and events of the time focus attention on particular political and social issues. The references are also of great help in dating the poem. Edward III, who has reigned for twenty-five years, is the arbiter of the dispute, Sir William Shareshull, Chief Justice from 1350 to 1361 is mentioned scathingly, the Order of the Garter (instituted in 1349) and the Statute of Treasons of 1352 are both alluded to. From these and other topical references it is reasonably safe to conclude that the poem was composed in 1352–3.[1]

It is the earliest datable poem of the Alliterative Revival. An enquiry into the origins and early history of the Revival must pay close attention to *Wynnere and Wastoure*. What is the quality and the character of the work? What information can it give about the author's attitude to writing this sort of poetry, and about his view of the position and the function of poetry in society?

The author emphasises the contemporary significance of his poem at the outset, by introducing in a prologue the theme of the corruption and dissension all around him. Many strange events, he begins, have taken place since the founding of Britain by Brutus after the Fall of Troy, but these have been nothing in comparison to the strange and terrible events of today. The whole social order seems to be collapsing; indeed all the signs are that Doomsday is fast approaching. He looks back fondly to one aspect of the Golden Age that as a poet he misses most painfully:

> Whylome were lordes in londe þat loued in thaire hertis
> To here makers of myrthes þat matirs couthe fynde.　　　　　(20–1)
>
> [Whylome – *once*; makers of myrthes – *authors of delightful poems*; matirs – *topics*.]

But in the present times of degeneracy poets who have a serious message to tell are neglected in favour of mere children:

> Bot now a childe appon chere, withowtten chyn-wedys,
> Þat neuer wroghte thurgh witt three wordes togedire,
> Fro he can jangle als a jaye, and japes telle,
> He schall be leuede and louede and lett of a while
> Wele more þan þe man that made it hymseluen　　　　　(24–8)
>
> [appon chere – *in appearance*; chyn-wedys – *beard*; Fro – *as soon as*; leuede – *believed*; lett of – *highly regarded*; made it – *composed a poem*.]

Taking this prologue as a starting point, the debate itself becomes an illustration of the symptoms, and an explanation of the causes, of the sickness destroying English society. The author relates that as he wanders in the west he comes to a pleasant spot where the birds are singing and the stream babbles along. Here he lies down and finally falls asleep. In his dream he sees two armies ready to attack one another. On the top of a cliff is a pavilion adorned with the device of the Order of the Garter. Looking into the tent he sees the King (Edward III) dressed in the finest and brightest robes. Even his belt is extravagantly adorned:

> Full gayly was that grete lorde girde in the myddis,
> A brighte belte of ble, broudirde with fewles,
> With drakes and with dukkes, daderande þam semede
> For ferdnes of fawcons fete, lesse fawked þay were.   (95–8)
>
> [ble – *colour*; broudirde – *embroidered*; daderande – *trembling*; ferdnes – *fear*;
> lesse – *lest*; fawked – *captured by the falcons*.]

The King turns to a young knight at his side and orders him to prevent the two armies meeting. The knight buckles on his armour and rides down to survey the opposing forces. He sees soldiers from all over Europe, from France, Lorraine, Lombardy, Spain and Westphalia, and he sees in one army a forest of waving banners, representing the Pope, the lawyers, the Franciscans, Dominicans, Carmelites and Austin Friars, as well as wool and wine sellers and numerous merchants. The banners are described with biting sarcasm. Here the sandalled Franciscans are represented:

> The thirde banere one bent es of blee whitte,
> With sexe galegs, I see, of sable withinn,
> And iche one has a brown brase with bokels twayne.
> Thies are Sayn Franceys folke, þat sayen alle schall fey worthe;
> They aren so ferse and so fresche, þay feghtyn bot seldom.
> I wote wele for wynnynge thay wentten fro home;
> His purse weghethe full wele that wanne thaym all hedire.   (156–62)
>
> [one bent – *on the battlefield*; blee – *colour*; galegs – *sandals*; sable – *black*; brase –
> *strap*; fey worthe – *die*; wote – *know*; wynnynge – *gain*; wanne – *persuaded*.]

In the other army, described only briefly, he sees the nobility and the professional soldiers. A representative from each army, the first named Winner and the second Waster, steps forward to present his case before the King, who listens indulgently as the two opponents argue it out.

Winner complains that everything he saves is dissipated by Waster:

> I gedir, I glene, and he lattys goo sone,
> I pryke and I pryne, and he the purse opynes.   (231–2)
>
> [gedir – *gather*; pryke and pryne – *tidy up*.]

Waster counters with the powerful argument that what Winner regards as good husbandry is more truly seen as a reprehensible amassing of wealth:

> The bemys benden at the rofe, siche bakone there hynges,
> Stuffed are sterlynges vndere stelen bowndes.   (251–2)
>
> [sterlynges – *coins*; bowndes – *bands*.]

While Winner hoards, the poor starve:

> Let be thy cramynge of thi kystes, for Cristis lufe of heuen!
> Late the peple and the pore hafe parte of thi siluere,
> For if thou wydwhare scholde walke, and waytten the sothe,
> Thou scholdeste reme for rewthe, in siche ryfe bene the pore.   (255–8)
>
> [kystes – *chests*; wydwhare – *round and about*; waytten – *look for*; reme for rewthe –
> *weep for sorrow*; ryfe – *large numbers*.]

For this sinfulness Winner will go to Hell.

Winner replies that Waster has indeed sold all he has, but there is no virtue in that since he has frittered it away on his followers and in the tavern, and for this wickedness God will condemn him at the Last Day. Waster then puts forward the somewhat specious argument that his feasts feed the poor by keeping money in circulation, and that this is 'plesynge to the Prynce þat Paradise wroghte'. Quite carried away by the thought of the social benefits conferred by his feasting, he goes even further and wishes an end to days of fasting imposed by the Church – ember days, eves of saints' days, Fridays and all. But Winner sets Waster's lavish feasts in sharper focus by describing, with quite extraordinarily elaborate detail, the bill of fare, a small part of which consists of:

> Roste with the riche sewes and the ryalle spyces,
> Kiddes cleuen by þe rigge, quarterd swannes,
> Tartes of ten ynche, þat tenys myn hert
> To see þe borde ouerbrade with blasande disches,
> Als it were a rayled rode with rynges and stones. (339–43)

[sewes – *sauces*; ryalle – *rich*; cleuen – *split*; rigge – *back*; tenys – *angers*; ouerbrade – *covered*; blasande – *shining*; rayled rode – *adorned crucifix*.]

Waster maintains that this is as it should be. The social hierarchy must be preserved; indeed, the narrator himself had complained in the prologue that it was crumbling. Lords must live richly, lads humbly and yet comfortably, so that everybody will be content. What is produced must be consumed, otherwise there will be such an abundance of cheap food that no-one will work and the social order will go awry.

However, Winner paints a sad picture of the destruction of the social order caused by Waster's extravagance. Estates have been sold to pay for pretty clothes for the ladies:

> ʒour forfadirs were fayne, when any frende come,
> For to schake to þe schawe and schewe hym þe estres,
> In iche holt þat þay had ane hare for to fynde,
> Bryng to þe brode lande bukkes ynewe,
> To lache and to late goo, to lightten þaire hertis.
> Now es it sett and solde, my sorowe es þe more,
> Wastes alle wilfully, ʒour wyfes to paye. (402–8)

[schake – *go*; schawe – *wood*; estres – *estates*; ynewe – *enough*; lache – *catch*; sett – *leased*; paye – *please*.]

He goes on to give the example of the Virgin Mary who dressed so simply, as a reminder of the vanity of fashionable clothes. A man must care for his sweetheart, answers Waster romantically, for love inspires many a man to courageous behaviour, and that is a better course of life than ceaseless anxiety over one's possessions. Winner will go to Hell for his scrimping and saving, and the Devil will distribute his goods.

The King stills the dispute, but condemns neither side. He orders Winner to make his way to the Pope and the cardinals for the time being, because they know Winner well and will care for him fittingly. Waster is to live in London, waylaying any passing stranger:

> Teche hym to þe tauerne till he tayte worthe,
> Doo hym drynk al nyʒte þat he dry be at morow,
> Sythen ken hym to the crete to comforth his vaynes. (477–9)[2]

[Teche – *direct*; tayte worthe – *gets drunk*; Doo – *make*; Sythen – *then*; ken – *introduce*; crete – *Cretan wine*.]

When the King goes on his wars abroad, then he will again have need of Winner by his side. With this statement the poem ends incomplete, but it is not likely that much has been lost, though it is possible that the few remaining lines would have made the significance of the King's judgement clearer.

As the poem stands, the King seems to endorse the viewpoints of both Winner and Waster, and to suggest that both are necessary to a smooth running of society. What are we to make of this judgement? However skilfully the contestants have deployed their arguments, it has emerged that both are motivated by self-interest, by greed on the one hand and by pleasure-seeking on the other. Each adopts a pose of moral gravity, claiming frequently that his own activities are pleasing to God whereas his opponent's will lead him to eternal damnation. But these repeated appeals to God's judgement have the effect of adding another dimension to the poem. Waster maintains his feasting is in accordance with God's will, while Winner likens Waster's groaning feast-table to a jewelled cross; here and elsewhere in the poem the purpose of the reference is to set this topical satire in the context of Christian morality. In this way the questions posed by the poem concern not merely the benefits to society of saving and spending, but also the moral justification for these activities – is it *right* (rather than socially advantageous) for a man to hoard his wealth, is it *right* for him to spend it frivolously? Certainly, judged in the light of Christian morality there is something sadly amiss in the moral standards of Winner and Waster, and therefore something wrong too with the benign approval of Edward III. The arbitration of this temporal ruler is gravely flawed; however, as the poet reminds us at the beginning of the poem, the disputants will be summoned before an even higher court in the not too distant future:

> Thene dredfull domesdaye it draweth neghe aftir.
> Bot who-so sadly will see and the sothe telle
> Say it newely will neghe, or es neghe here. (17–19)

> [sadly – *seriously*; newely will neghe – *will soon approach*.]

Winner and Waster may both prosper in this world, but their greed and selfishness will condemn them in the next.

It can be seen that *Wynnere and Wastoure* is a thoroughly sophisticated attack on social abuses. The author is a practised poet, self-confident enough to include the whole of society from the King downwards in his satire, and confident also of his ability to handle the alliterative line. At no time does the reader sense that the poet is uncertain of the direction in which he is going, nor at any time does he feel that the writer is unaware of the potentialities of his verse-form. This is quite remarkable when we remember that this is the earliest poem of the Alliterative Revival to which we can with some confidence assign a date. In every respect *Wynnere and Wastoure* is a characteristic alliterative poem; it shares the verbal resources, the stylistic techniques and the preoccupations that are the hall-marks of the poems of the Alliterative Revival. There are parallels with later works, and some of them may possibly be the result of borrowing, for nothing is more probable than that writers working within the same stylistic tradition should imitate one another at times. However, the *general* similarities of style between *Wynnere and Wastoure* and later poems are more striking and significant than the occasional direct parallels, for they indicate that the author of *Wynnere and Wastoure* was writing in a style that already by his time had established its norms and its characteristic forms of expression.

How sharply can the relationships between *Wynnere and Wastoure* and later alliterative poems be defined? There are interesting similarities with the two most famous alliterative poems, *Piers Plowman* and *Sir Gawain and the Green Knight*. With the former *Wynnere and Wastoure* shares the device of the dream-vision, the concern with contemporary conditions and the urge to see deeper moral implications in the degeneracy of the times. For both the poets one of the abuses of the age (though it is an abuse of every age) is the corrupt and improper use of money and the injustices in society that result from this. The opening of *Piers Plowman* has its Wasters and also its Winners, though the latter are honourable characters who:

> In settyng and in sowying swonken ful harde
> And wonnen that wastours with glotonye destruyeth. (Prol. 21–2)

The scene of Glutton in the tavern (*Piers Plowman*, v. 304 ff.) is reminiscent of Waster in the tavern – not that there are particular parallels of verbal detail, but rather similarities of general treatment and attitude. It is possible, and it has been argued,[3] that William Langland knew *Wynnere and Wastoure*, but the parallels between the poems may equally well be the result of a common approach to certain themes and ideas and an alliterative 'mode of expression'.

With *Sir Gawain and the Green Knight* the most striking parallel is an almost identical opening, as both poets introduce their account of marvels by remarking on the strange events that have taken place in Britain since the ending of the Siege of Troy by 'tresoun' and the founding of Britain by Brutus. Here there are some verbal echoes which could indicate borrowing, but we will discover that tracing verbal parallels between the alliterative poems is a profitless task.

Two lesser-known alliterative poems show close structural and thematic similarities to *Wynnere and Wastoure*, and in this case there is more convincing evidence for arguing that the early work was used as a model. Both *The Parlement of the Thre Ages* and *Death and Liffe* are dream-vision debates on the same scale as *Wynnere and Wastoure*, and they too present a dispute between allegorical figures.[4] The three poems open with descriptions of spring which have in common not only the general atmosphere but also some of the details, for example:

> The throstills full throly they threpen togedire   (*Wynnere*, 37)
> And the throstills full throly threpen in the bankes   (*Parlement*, 14)
>
> [throly – *fiercely*; threpen – *vie with one another*.]

It is possible to view the three debate-poems as a progression. *Wynnere and Wastoure* opposes two possible ways of living – sparing and spending, and neither is portrayed in a very favourable light. In the *Parlement* the spokesmen for these two courses are Middle Age and Youth, but the argument is raised to another plane by the intervention of Old Age, who claims that the inevitability of death, as illustrated by the lives of the Nine Worthies, makes nonsense of the viewpoints of the two younger men. *Death and Liffe* takes the argument yet a stage further, for here the two arch-enemies are finally brought face-to-face, and Life – Eternal Life – shows that the might of Death is not invincible. The dating of the two later poems is quite uncertain. The *Parlement* is probably from the late fourteenth century, and *Death and Liffe* is generally thought – though on quite insufficient evidence – to be a mid fifteenth-century work. The probability that they are both related in some way to *Wynnere and Wastoure* must be regarded as strong.

We can in this way make out something of the particular relationship of *Wynnere and Wastoure* to other poems, but it is equally to the point to notice the common approach to writing poetry that this poet shares with the other alliterative writers. We may say that he belongs to the same school of writers. He uses the same distinctive vocabulary that they use, words found abundantly in alliterative verse but rarely elsewhere. It is true that the range of this alliterative vocabulary is not so extensive in *Wynnere and Wastoure* as it is in some of the later works, such as *Sir Gawain and the Green Knight* or *The Wars of Alexander*, but it is conspicuous enough.[5] To take only one group of synonyms, those for 'man'; in his 500 lines the author of *Wynnere and Wastoure* uses the following characteristic alliterative words all ultimately derived from the Old English vocabulary and used abundantly in fourteenth-century alliterative works: *beryn, freke, gome, hathell, lede, renke, schalke, segge* and *wy*. All the alliterative poets show a delight in richness and profusion, in richness of vocabulary and also in richness of description. Descriptions are most characteristically enumerative: we know exactly what birds Waster eats for dinner, just as we know the precise menu for the feast King Arthur prepares for the Roman ambassadors in the alliterative *Morte Arthure*; Edward III's spokesman buckles on his armour piece by piece just as Sir Gawain does; the elaborate clothes that King Edward wears are described with the same particularising detail as Youth's bejewelled clothing in *The Parlement of the Thre Ages*. Most obvious of all, the author of *Wynnere and Wastoure* uses the same metrical techniques, the same predominant alliterative pattern, as well as the same metrical licences; there is not the hesitation and irregularity – nor, for that matter, the over-rigid adherence to a single arrangement – to suggest that the author had incomplete command over his verse-form.[6]

It seems most improbable that the author of *Wynnere and Wastoure* was himself the initiator of so well-defined a style handled with such sophistication. Although this is the earliest datable poem of the Alliterative Revival, it must itself have been preceded by other works within the same tradition. But was this an ancient tradition? The narrator's own statement, already quoted, that 'makers of myrthes' were in former days supported by 'lordes in londe' might be interpreted as suggesting this. It might equally well be a standard piece of wishful thinking, a lament for a Golden Age along the same lines as 'there are no longer kings or emperors or gold-givers such as there previously were' from *The Seafarer*.[7] Although it has usually been taken as a reference to a venerable tradition of alliterative verse composed at the behest of aristocratic patrons, is there any sound evidence for the existence of such a tradition? I am going to suggest that there is not. To explore this question, and to examine possible ideas about the origins of the Alliterative Revival, we shall follow the developments of alliterative writing from the last records of the strict Old English poetic line to the new flowering of alliterative poetry in the fourteenth century.

Early Middle English Alliterative Works

An extremely important record of the development of the alliterative line in late Old English is provided by the Anglo-Saxon Chronicle.[8] Here, arranged by date, are examples of a number of different styles of writing. By far the most common, naturally, is straightforward narrative prose, recounting, sometimes in the baldest fashion, the chief events of the year. For more lyrical or impassioned descriptions the writers had other styles to choose from.[9] Prose could be heightened by the use of a number of the techniques of verse, in particular alliteration, rhyme, parallelism of syntax and the grouping of words and phrases so as to form regular rhythmic units. Two of the entries in this rhythmic prose, for the years 959 and 975 (in the 'D' version), are very much in the style of the known works of Archbishop Wulfstan, and may have been composed by him.

Alternatively the writers of the Chronicle might use verse. For events that were especially solemn and noteworthy, verse conforming strictly to the traditional patterns of Old English poetry might be considered appropriate. The first of such entries describes the Battle of Brunanburh of 937; the last one (in the 'C' and 'D' versions) commemorates the death of Edward the Confessor in 1065, less than one year before the Conquest. Even in this late piece the rhythms of 'classical' Old English verse are preserved with remarkable fidelity:

> Eadward se æðela eðel bewerode,
> Land and leode, oðþæt lungre becom
> Deað se bitera, and swa deore genam
> Æþelne of eorðan; englas feredon
> Soþfæste sawle innan swegles leoht. (24–8)

[*The noble Edward guarded his native land, his country and his people, until suddenly bitter death came, and took from the earth a lord so dear. Angels bore his righteous soul to the light of Heaven.*]

This is poetry that performs its function admirably; it commemorates an honoured king with due solemnity and with the traditional phraseology that will bring to mind the deaths of other heroes from both the historical and the legendary past.

Side by side with such sonorous poetry there is verse of a very different style. The entry in the 'C' and 'D' versions under the year 1036, describing the arrest of Alfred son of King Ethelred, is an instance of this:

> Se æþeling lyfode þa gyt, ælc yfel man him gehet,
> Oðþæt man geradde þæt man hine lædde
> To Eligbyrig swa gebundenne.
> Sona swa he lende, on scype man hine blende,
> And hine swa blindne brohte to ðam munecon,
> And he þar wunode ða hwile þe he lyfode.
> Syððan hine man byrigde, swa him wel gebyrede,
> Ful wurðlice, swa he wyrðe wæs,
> Æt þam west ende, þam styple ful gehende,
> On þam suð portice. Seo saul is mid Criste. (16–25)

[*The prince was still alive; he was threatened with every evil, until it was decided that he should be led to Ely bound up in this way. As soon as he arrived he was blinded on the ship and, thus blinded, was brought to the monks, with whom he remained as long as he was alive. Afterwards he was buried as well befitted him, very worthily as he deserved, at the west end of the church, near the steeple, in the south chapel. His soul is with Christ.*]

A second example in this style may be found in the entry for the year 1086 in the 'E' version of the Chronicle (which is the only version to be continued so late). For the years 1067 (in the 'D' version) and 1075 (in the 'D' and 'E' versions) there are two snatches in a rather similar vein, but they are too short to be analysed with confidence.

Various insulting names have been given to this type of verse. The term 'popular' verse (always, strangely enough, a pejorative term) is most widely current, but it is quite unsuitable because of its unjustifiable implication that this verse was regarded with greater fondness by the uninitiated or uneducated than 'classical' Old English verse was. Another term used, 'debased' verse,[10] is even more unfortunate, with its suggestion that this verse-form is an unsuccessful attempt at 'classical' Old English verse by writers capable of nothing better. If we are to understand this sort of verse at all, it is important to realise that the authors are not trying to ape their elders – it is the author of the lines on Edward the Confessor who is doing this – but on the contrary they have decided to abandon the tight controls of the traditional style. For this reason the purely descriptive term 'loose alliterative verse' is what I shall use.

In so far as this loose alliterative verse can be analysed, it will be seen that it makes use of some of the techniques of regular Old English verse and ignores others. Each line falls into two half-lines, and the half-line is generally of two stresses. Some half-lines are bound together by alliteration, although the alliterative and stress patterns do not necessarily correspond to those of regular verse. Alliteration is, however, sometimes supplemented or replaced by rhyme or assonance, as in the first two lines of the extract, and this is a device which is found very rarely in traditional Old English verse. In general, rhythmic patterns are most irregular, and cannot usefully be classified on the basis of 'Sievers' five types'.

There are differences, too, in the syntactical arrangement and in the vocabulary. The syntactic unit is the line, and the technique so characteristic of traditional verse of having the sense-pause in the middle of the line, with consequent enjambment, is rarer in this loose alliterative style. As the syntax becomes less tightly organised, the line itself becomes much full. The vocabulary is no longer characterised by poeticisms, by words and phrases which by their associations bring with them certain traditional attitudes to life and death; it is a prose vocabulary.

The breakdown and eventual abandonment of the strict Old English style were probably inevitable in any case, given the huge changes that were taking place in the language itself, with the decay of inflectional endings and the consequent increase in the importance of functional words.[11] In such circumstances the tightness and density of the Old English alliterative style became more and more difficult to achieve, and even a poem as traditional in style and theme as *The Battle of Maldon* shows occasional examples of diffuseness not evident in earlier poems.[12] However, changes in the language were a purely negative force, with power to destroy an old style but not to develop a new one. The creation of this new style should be associated with other literary movements of the late Anglo-Saxon period. The most significant of these is the prose style used by Ælfric, particularly in his *Lives of Saints*. While there is not enough evidence to suggest that Ælfric's prose inspired the writers of loose alliterative verse, the two styles have many features in common. Ælfric used many of the techniques of Old English verse to enhance his prose style, with the result that his phrases fall fairly regularly into four-stress patterns, often linked by alliteration. An authoritative study of Ælfric's rhythmic style describes it as 'the introduction of metrical controls similar to, though much looser than, those of the alliterative poets: the linking of roughly equivalent, normally two-stress phrases in pairs by a nearly constant use of phonetic correspondences, chiefly alliteration'.[13] However, Ælfric very rarely uses rhyme, which is frequent in loose alliterative verse.

The comparison of Ælfric's prose with loose alliterative verse makes the point that the distinction between prose and verse is not always a sharp one; indeed, when we are presented with a tightly organised prose style and a loosely controlled verse style it is often difficult, in fact unnecessary, to decide which is prose and which verse.[14] This point will have to be borne in mind when we examine the alliterative styles in the period that follows.

'Classical' Old English verse died quickly after the Conquest. Probably the last poem written in the traditional style is *Durham*, composed before 1109.[15] With great care the author of this short piece reproduces the rhythms of traditional verse as well as he is able, but a detailed analysis of the language and metre[16] suggests that this is a brave, but not entirely successful attempt at embalming a dead verse-form. Another reason for thinking that *Durham* is an exercise in antiquarianism is that its praise of Durham's beauties and its celebration of the saints associated with the town follow strictly a rhetorical tradition of *encomium urbis* that was a set piece in medieval Latin poetry and was derived from classical models.[17] To judge from *Durham*, the traditional style was dead, though not quite buried, by the end of the eleventh century.

Other alliterative works of the early Middle English period are composed in a much looser style, and they are to be associated with the entries in loose alliterative verse in the Anglo-Saxon Chronicle. Unfortunately there are too few examples of pieces in this style to enable us to chart the poetic development or discern a 'school' of poets. The style was in any case so loosely organised that each writer tailored it to suit himself. It is likely, therefore, that the differences in style between such early Middle English works as *The Worcester Fragments*, *The Proverbs of Alfred* and Laȝamon's *Brut* are not milestones in a developing tradition, but examples of individual modifications to a fluid and imprecise verse-form.

Perhaps the earliest of the Middle English works in this style is a short and impressive poem, *The Grave*, which is preserved in a manuscript containing homilies (many by Ælfric) copied down during the second half of the twelfth century. *The Grave* was added on a blank leaf not many years after the manuscript was compiled.[18] There is some evidence to indicate that the manuscript was in the West Midlands in the thirteenth century, and the dialect of *The Grave* suggests that it was composed in the south of that region.[19] The poet plays imaginatively upon the conceit of the grave as a house – the dead man has left his rich hall for a more lowly, and more permanent, dwelling:

Ne bið nu þin hus healice itinbred;
Hit bið unheh and lah, þonne þu list þerinne.
Ðe helewaȝes beoð laȝe, sidewaȝes unheȝe,
Þe rof bið ibyld þire broste ful neh.
Swa ðu scealt on molde wunien ful calde,
Dimme and deorcæ. Þet den fulæt on honde.
Dureleas is þet hus, and dearc hit is wiðinnen,
Ðær þu bist feste bidytt, and dæð hefð þa cæȝe.   (7–14)

[*And now your house is not loftily built. It is short and low, when you are lying in it. The end-walls are low, the side-walls are not high, the roof is built very near your breast. Thus you will dwell in the earth, cold, dim and dark. That den will soon become foul. The house is doorless and dark inside, where you are firmly shut up – and Death has the key.*]

As this extract shows, the lines alliterate in a fairly regular manner, though occasionally, as in the line 'Swa ðu scealt on molde wunien ful calde', alliteration is replaced by assonance at the end of the half-line.

This macabre little poem attracted two lesser poets. One of these was Longfellow, who made a barely comprehensible modernisation of it. The other was the author of *The Departing Soul's Address to the Body*,[20] who late in the twelfth century incorporated into his much longer and more diffuse poem all of the most vivid details from *The Grave*, padding them out with material borrowed from earlier homiletic treatment of the same topic.[21] The approach taken by this writer may be illustrated by the following passage, in which are embedded some of the details from the section of *The Grave* quoted above. The soul reproaches the dead body:

Noldest þu on þine huse herborwen þeo wrecchen,
Ne mihten heo under þine roue none reste finden.
Noldest þu nefre helpen þam orlease wrecchen,
Ac þu sete on þine benche, underleid mid þine bolstre;
Þu wurpe cneow ofer cneow, ne icneowe þu þe sulfen
Þet þu scoldest mid wurmen wunien in eorþan.
Nu þu hauest neowe hus, inne beþrungen,
Lowe beoþ þe helewowes, unheiȝe beoþ þe sidwowes,
Þin rof liiþ on þine breoste ful neih.
Colde is þe ibedded, cloþes bideled;
Nulleþ þine hinen cloþes þe senden,
For heom þuncheþ al to lut þet þu heom bilefdest.   (Fragment C, 23–34)

[*You would not give shelter in your house to the poor, and they were not able to find rest under your roof. You would never help the humble wretches, but you sat on your bench, propped up on your cushion; you cast one knee over the other, not realising that you yourself would dwell with worms in the earth. Now you have a new house, very cramped inside. The end-walls are low, the side-walls are not high, and the roof lies very near your breast. You are provided with a cold bed, without clothes; your servants will not send you clothes, for they think that what you bequeathed to them is much too little.*]

Only fragments of this poem are preserved, but it is remarkable that anything at all remains. The manuscript was cut up and glued together to form the binding of a book in Worcester Cathedral. As a result, seven sections of the poem are preserved, totalling 342 lines. Although rather repetitive, and at times gruesomely morbid, it is a work of some power to judge from what remains. The author uses the alliterative line with a little more freedom than the author of *The Grave*, and in a few passages he abandons the accentual alliterative line altogether in favour of balanced rhymed lines with a more regularly syllabic rhythm:

Forloren þu hauest þeo ece blisse,
  binumen þu hauest þe paradis;
Binumen þe is þet holi lond,
  þen deofle þu bist isold on hond.   (Fragment D, 37–8)

[*You have lost eternal bliss, you have deprived yourself of Paradise; you are deprived of that Holy Land, you are sold into the hands of the Devil.*]

Another fragment of the same manuscript gives a poem in a similar style but on a different subject. In this *First Worcester Fragment*[22] the author laments that since the Conquest the Anglo-Saxon writers who instructed the people *in English* have been replaced by foreigners. After mentioning Bede and Ælfric, and listing thirteen Anglo-Saxon bishops, the poet continues:

Þeos lærden ure leodan on Englisc.
Næs deorc heore liht, ac hit fæire glod.
Nu is þeo leore forleten and þet folc is forloren,
Nu beoþ oþre leoden þeo læreþ ure folc.   (15–18)

[*These taught our people in English. Their light was not dark, but glowed brightly. Now this learning is abandoned and the people forsaken, now there are other men who teach our people.*]

For once we know something of the scribe who copied this nostalgic lament and also *The Departing Soul's Address*. He was a man who was hard at work in Worcester in the early thirteenth century, who had a special interest in Old English compositions. He copied out Ælfric's grammar (originally designed to help those who spoke Old English to learn Latin, but now used in reverse as a guide to Old English), and he also glossed many Old English homilies and other works of instruction, as well as Old English translations of Gregory and Bede. Obviously his aim was to 'læren ure leodan' by means of the works of his English ancestors, and he must have sympathised strongly with the sentiments expressed in *The First Worcester Fragment*.[23]

In the same county, at about the same time,[24] lived another writer who was deeply interested in Britain's past. Laȝamon, as he tells us himself, was a priest at Areley Kings on the banks of the Severn, and he resolved to give an account of the glorious history of his country:

> An preost wes on leoden, Laȝamon wes ihoten,
> He wes Leouenaðes sone, liðe him beo Drihten.
> He wonede at Ernleȝe, at æðelen are chirechen,
> Vppen Seuarne staþe, sel þar him þuhte,
> On-fest Radestone, þer he bock radde.
> Hit com him on mode and on his mern þonke,
> Þet he wolde of Engle þa æðelæn tellen,
> Wat heo ihoten weoren and wonene heo comen
> Þa Englene londe ærest ahten.   (*Brut*, 1–9)[25]

[*There was a priest among the people, called Laȝamon, the son of Leovenath – may God be merciful to him. He lived at Areley at the noble church on the bank of the Severn; he thought it pleasant there, near Redstone, where he read the missal (i.e. celebrated Mass?). It occurred to him as an excellent idea that he should relate the origins of the English, what they were called and from where they came, those who first possessed England.*]

Laȝamon proceeds to relate the history of England in over 16,000 long-lines of alliterative verse. He takes much of his information from the *Roman de Brut* which the Norman poet Wace had translated in 1155 from Geoffrey of Monmouth's *Historia Regum Britanniae*. The story begins with the escape of Aeneas from Troy and the arrival of his descendant Brutus in Britain, and it goes on to give an account of the legendary kings of Britain, laying particular emphasis upon Arthur.

Laȝamon's *Brut* is the only work of major significance composed in the loose alliterative style. In essentials Laȝamon inherits the techniques used in *The Worcester Fragments* and, before that, in the lines from the Anglo-Saxon Chronicle, although he has very definitely impressed the mark of his own strange genius upon this amorphous style. He uses rhyme more frequently than his predecessors; metrical analysis shows that slightly less than half his lines have rhyme or assonance, while nearly one line in three lacks alliteration.[26] Alliteration, when it is used, may fall upon any stress, including the last stress of the line.

There is also some freedom in the number of stressed syllables in each half-line. The majority of half-lines are indubitably of two stresses:

> Þa Énglene lónde   ǽrest áhten.

A few half-lines (usually with rhyme) are certainly heavier than this, with as many as four stresses and with a more regularly syllabic rhythm:

> Swa féor swa hé for dǽðes káre   dúrsten ǽies wéies fáren.[27]

Lines like this last one should be compared with the rhymed lines from *The Departing Soul's Address* quoted earlier, where the pattern is very similar. It is, however, less easy to be dogmatic about many other half-lines in the *Brut*, for in these the rhythm is so unclearly signposted that they could be regarded as having two, three or four stresses.[28] In fact this uncertainty over stress-pattern is the great weakness of the loose alliterative style, and in all probability was the principal cause for its subsequent assimilation into rhythmic schemes of a firmer structure. Nevertheless, since the rhythm of Laȝamon's half-line is predominantly a two-stress pattern, it is natural to regard these uncertain half-lines also as two-stressed, even though, when read out of context, they could be of other patterns. An example of a line that might be stressed in a variety of ways is:

> And softe hine adun leiden and forð gunnen hine liðen.

When read in context, as I quote it below, the stresses seem to fall most naturally in this way:

> And sófte hine adun léiden   and fórð gunnen hine líðen.

Surprisingly often Laȝamon is able to overcome the weakness inherent in the loose alliterative style. In the following description of the departure of Arthur to Avalon, alliteration, rhyme and variations of rhythm combine to create a lyrical passage of great poetic power, in some ways untypical of the poem:

> Æfne þan worden þer com of se wenden
> Þet wes an sceort bat liðen, sceouen mid vðen,
> And twa wimmen þerinne wunderliche idihte,
> And heo nomen Arður anan and aneouste hine uereden,
> And softe hine adun leiden and forð gunnen hine liðen.
> Þa wes hit iwurðen þat Merlin seide whilen:
> Þat weore unimete care of Arðures forðfare.
> Bruttes ileueð ȝete þat he bon on liue
> And wunnien in Aualun mid fairest alre aluen;
> And lokieð euere Bruttes ȝete whan Arður cumen liðe.[29]

> [*With those words a small boat came sailing from the sea, driven by the waves, and in it were two women wonderfully arrayed. They took hold of Arthur at once and quickly carried him, and laid him down softly and sailed away. Then what Merlin had once said had come to pass, that there would be great sorrow when Arthur departed. The Britons still believe that he is alive and is dwelling in Avalon with the fairest of all elves, and they still look forward to the time when Arthur will return.*]

It is in his poetic diction that Laȝamon is strikingly different from the other writers in the loose alliterative style. The authors of *The Worcester Fragments* and of other Early Middle English alliterative works used, by and large, the vocabulary of prose; Laȝamon alone builds up for himself a specifically poetic vocabulary.[30] This vocabulary is in part inherited from Old English poetic usage. For example, words for 'man' or 'warrior', such as *beorn, guma, hæleð, rinc, secg* and *wer* are used widely in Old English poetry and reappear in Laȝamon's *Brut*. To judge from extant Middle English texts, these words were not part of the language of written prose, and were not in widespread use even in poetry. It seems from his use of these and many similar words that Laȝamon was choosing a vocabulary with a distinctive, even perhaps archaic, flavour.[31] In this respect it is noteworthy that even though he was translating from the French, Laȝamon seems to have deliberately avoided words of French origin.

Similar conclusions may be drawn from Laȝamon's fondness for compound nouns and adjectives. Compounds are a characteristic feature of the Old English poetic style, and by means of them the poet greatly extended his vocabulary. Laȝamon also uses a fairly wide range of compounds, many of which were common enough in Old and Middle English, but some of which are unique to his poem (although if more texts had been preserved the number of compounds unique to Laȝamon might be reduced).[32] As an example we may examine some of Laȝamon's compound nouns that have *here* 'army' as their first element. Compounds such as *hereburne* 'corslet' (OE. *herebyrne*), *hireȝeonge* 'military expedition' (OE. *heregang*), and *heretoȝe* 'commander' (OE. *heretoga*) are found in Old English and also (with the exception of *hereburne*) elsewhere in Middle English. However, other compounds formed in exactly the same way are found neither in Old English nor anywhere else in Middle English except in Laȝamon's *Brut*. Examples are *heredring* 'warrior' (OE. *here* + *dreng* 'soldier'), *herrefeng* 'plunder' (OE. *here* + *feng* 'booty'), and *hærescrud* 'armour' (OE. *here* + *scrud* 'garment'). It looks very much as though Laȝamon is here building up his own poetic vocabulary in a way that sets him apart from earlier writers of the loose alliterative style, and that he is doing this in order to give his work an unfamiliar and possibly archaic flavour. Features of the orthography of the text as we have it also provide some support for the belief that Laȝamon was deliberately archaising.[33]

However, Laȝamon's individualistic style did not win the approval of all his readers. The poem is preserved in two manuscripts, both copied in the second half of the thirteenth century. One of these, the Otho manuscript, presents what is in effect a revised version of Laȝamon's work. The length of the poem is somewhat reduced, and much of the distinctive vocabulary is discarded. It appears that this scribe considered Laȝamon's *Brut* to be in need of simplification and modernisation.

It may be that Laȝamon chose the loose alliterative line for his historical poem because it had the tang of distant antiquity about it. This raises the question of the immediate origins of Laȝamon's alliterative line. The suggestion which is sometimes made that Laȝamon was drawing on a tradition of heroic verse orally handed down has little to support it.[34] It is, however, probable that the poet knew at least the odd piece of Old English verse; for example *Cædmon's Hymn* and *Bede's Death Song* were still being copied out in texts of Bede's *Historia Ecclesiastica* which Laȝamon claims to have used.[35] He may well have known some of the homilies of Ælfric composed in rhythmic alliterative prose. He could therefore have read enough at least to recognise the antiquity and Englishness of the alliterative line, and even perhaps to observe its characteristic vocabulary. But Laȝamon learnt his metrical technique not from Old English poetry but from works such as *The Worcester Fragments*. It is with these and other examples of the loose alliterative line that the *Brut* is most closely connected, though we should also recognise that Laȝamon was aiming at very different effects from his predecessors, and for this reason remodelled the loose alliterative style.

Another literary movement in the South West Midlands during the late twelfth and early thirteenth centuries was the work of prose writers, who were centred apparently in Herefordshire, and who carried on the traditions of Old English prose in a number of different ways. With the most famous of these prose works, the *Ancrene Riwle*, we are not here concerned, but it is worth considering briefly a group of works which make use of alliteration as well as other devices to emphasise the rhythmic character of their mannered style.

The principal model for this rhetorical style of English prose was probably the work of Ælfric, whose homilies in rhythmic alliterative prose were still quite widely available, and additional impetus may have been provided by stylists who advocated similar rhetorical devices for Latin prose.[36] The authors (or author) of the so-called 'Katherine Group' of homilies which relate the lives of the virgin martyrs St. Katherine, St. Juliana and St. Margaret, rely heavily on alliterative patterning as an ornament to their incantatory prose style, a style which is seen at its most effective in the extraordinary description of the devil who comes to swallow up the unfortunate St. Margaret:

> His lockes and his longe berd blikeden al of golde, and his grisliche teð semden of swart irn. His twa ehnen steareden steappre þen þe steoren and ten ʒimstanes, brade ase bascins, in his ihurnde heaued on eiðer half on his heh hokede nease. Of his speatewile muð sperclede fur ut, and of his nease-þurles þreste smorðrinde smoke, smecche forcuðest. And lahte ut his tunge, se long þet he swong hire abuten his swire.... He strahte him and sturede toward tis meoke meiden, and geapede wið his genow upon hire ungeinliche, and bigon to crahien and crenge wið swire, as þe þe hire walde forswolhe mid alle.[37]

> [*His hair and his long beard shone entirely of gold, and his terrible teeth looked like black iron. His two eyes shone brighter than stars and precious stones, broad as basins, in his horned head on either side of his high, hooked nose. From his foul mouth fire sparkled out, and from his nostrils poured suffocating smoke, most horrible of tastes. He poked his tongue out so far that he wrapped it around his neck.... He moved and went towards this humble girl, and gaped at her terribly with his jaws, and began to bend and arch his neck as though he were about to swallow her up.*]

Works of a related group of texts, known as the 'Wooing Group', are also composed in elaborate rhetorical prose. Alliteration is here not always so prominent as in the works of the 'Katherine Group' and the tone is more lyrical. The pieces are rhapsodic addresses to Christ and the Virgin Mary, which are characterised all too often by fulsome endearments, as when Christ is thus apostrophised:

> Nu mi derewurðe druð, mi luue, mi lif, mi leof, mi luueleuest, mi heorte haliwej, mi sawle swetnesse; þu art lufsum on leor, þu art al schene.[38]

> [*Now my precious darling, my love, my life, my beloved, my dearest one, balm of my heart, sweetness of my soul, you are lovely of countenance, you are entirely beautiful.*]

At least two of the 'Wooing Group', *Þe Wohunge of ure Lauerd* and *The Ureisun of God Almihti* remained popular, for they were adapted in the fourteenth century and exercised a direct influence on fourteenth-century mystical writings, and, I shall suggest, an indirect influence on poems of the Alliterative Revival.

These early medieval alliterative works in prose as well as in verse are associated particularly with Worcestershire and Herefordshire. One or two poems come from other parts of the country. *The Proverbs of Alfred*, which is composed in an exceedingly loose mixture of alliterative and rhymed verse, was perhaps written in Sussex,[39] whereas *The Bestiary*, in which passages in the loose alliterative style (with and without rhyme) alternate with rhymed syllabic verse, seems to have been written in the East Midlands.[40] However, it was in the South West Midlands that the traditions of alliterative verse and prose flourished, and this is not surprising in view of the high regard in which the diocese of Worcester long held older traditions of writing.[41]

The Theory of Oral Tradition

We have traced the history of the loose alliterative style, in so far as it remains to us, from pre-Conquest entries in the Anglo-Saxon Chronicle up to Laʒamon's *Brut* and works contemporary with it. To all appearances the early thirteenth century witnessed the death of this particular style, although it is possible that some later examples have been lost. Probably it was too loosely organised to hold its own against the more regular syllabic metres in rhyming couplets and stanzas. Laȝamon's *Brut* and *The Bestiary* provide the last examples for over a hundred years of the unrhymed alliterative line, the line in which alliteration is an essential structural principle rather than (to a greater or lesser extent) a decorative feature. However, alliteration continued to be used throughout the thirteenth and fourteenth centuries in rhyming stanzas, and, perhaps more sporadically, for prose works. The *unrhymed* line emerged once more in the mid-fourteenth century in such poems as *Wynnere and Wastoure*, but the style of the poems of the Revival differs markedly from the loosely organised style of Laȝamon. Indeed in some ways fourteenth-century poetry, with its more tightly organised patterns of alliteration and rhythm and with its avoidance of rhyme, represents a return to the practices of Old English poets and a radical departure from the style of Laȝamon's *Brut*. At all events the poetry of the Alliterative Revival is not a direct descendant of Laȝamonic verse.

The reappearance of unrhymed alliterative poetry in the mid-fourteenth century, in a style so sharply dissimilar from the type of verse that had vanished more than a hundred years previously, has given rise to the theory that there must have existed from Anglo-Saxon times an uninterrupted oral tradition of alliterative verse, and this theory is now generally – if sometimes hesitantly – accepted. The idea was stated with most conviction, and with most romantic appeal, by R. W. Chambers in his valuable essay 'The Continuity of English Prose':

> There can be few stranger things in the history of literature than this sudden disappearance and reappearance of a school of poetry. It was kept alive by oral tradition through nine generations, appearing in writing very rarely, and then usually in a corrupt form, till it suddenly came forth, correct, vigorous, and bearing with it a whole tide of national feeling.[42]

This concept of an oral tradition of 'correct' alliterative poetry extending unrecorded over a huge period of three hundred years, from the Conquest to the middle of the fourteenth century, is hard to accept. Those who subscribe to the theory are often pardonably vague about its implications. First of all, what exactly is meant by an 'oral tradition'? In a stimulating book on *The Gawain-Poet*, A. C. Spearing suggests that alliterative verse may have 'survived largely by dropping to a popular, orally-transmitted level'.[43] As always, it is unclear what 'popular' means. 'Oral transmission' could include a variety of different activities. A poem originally written down by its author might subsequently be memorised and passed by word of mouth from the repertoire of one entertainer to another. There is possibly evidence that this sort of activity took place with lyrics and other relatively short poems where there is sometimes great disparity in the readings of different manuscripts. However, the great advantage of the alliterative line is its suitability for long narrative, and it would be a superhuman task to memorise a work of the length of Laȝamon's *Brut* or *The Destruction of Troy*, even for a memory not dulled by the technological advances of more recent centuries. Furthermore, if the theory of oral transmission implies no more than this, it does not account satisfactorily for the complete absence of manuscript evidence of such poems.

A second possibility that might be considered is that alliterative poems were not written works at any stage, but existed as spoken compositions. In other words, the act of composition would be taking place as the entertainer recited his poem. This form of oral composition is known in other cultures, but despite much speculation on the matter no firm evidence has been forthcoming to show that it took place in England.[44] It is also pertinent to observe that the great majority of surviving alliterative poems, from Laȝamon's *Brut* to *The Destruction of Troy* and *The Wars of Alexander*, are extremely 'bookish' compositions; they are translations or adaptations of long works in French or Latin, written by fairly learned men who had a text of the original in front of them.

Even if we were prepared to accept the possibility of some form of oral transmission, we should still expect to find some traces of the tradition. However, there is no evidence that such a tradition ever existed. It is just conceivable that, supposing such poems were sometimes written down, all the manuscripts of all these poems were lost without trace. Certainly a proportion of Early Middle English literature has perished, though painstaking research has managed to recover a surprising number of references by contemporary chroniclers and translators to works now lost, and a fair assortment of bits and pieces quoted in sermons and other far-flung sources.[45] But there has been discovered not one single witness to what must have been, if the theory is to be accepted, a flourishing tradition of alliterative poetry.[46] In this situation it is reasonable to ask whether dependence upon a poetic tradition for whose existence there is no evidence is the most satisfactory explanation of the Revival of the fourteenth century.

Nor does the written tradition of early Middle English alliterative verse require us to posit an oral tradition running side by side with it; in fact the existence of such works as *The Worcester Fragments* and Laȝamon's *Brut* is something of an argument *against* the oral tradition, since it is not easy to understand why all surviving written poetry should have been composed in the loose alliterative style if a tighter and more 'correct' style had still been flourishing in oral tradition. The written alliterative works do not reflect an oral tradition, but, as has been shown, they are developments of a written tradition going back to pre-Conquest times. It is strange logic on the part of Chambers to account for these, the only survivals of an alliterative tradition, as 'corrupt forms' of a tradition which has not itself survived!

The oral tradition has always been put forward to explain the similarities between Old English and fourteenth-century verse. It is true that both verse-lines are tightly constructed, in obvious contrast to the loose line as used by Laȝamon. But are the similarities great enough to demand an explanation so improbable? An alternative hypothesis which does away with the troublesome need for an unbroken line of descent over three centuries is that fourteenth-century writers, conscious of the lack of a well-organised verse form that was particularly suitable for long narrative, were able to construct such a form by adapting the various types of alliterative writing then current. A certain number of metrical and verbal similarities between a tightly constructed alliterative line of the tenth century and a tightly constructed line of the fourteenth are inevitable. They constitute the basis for the composition of alliterative verse in English. Actually, they are not as many as might at first appear, for the similarities between the two types of verse have understandably been exaggerated by critics who accept the theory of an unbroken oral tradition and who have made light of the vast differences that are equally significant.

My examination of the poetry of the Revival, particularly in the chapters on metre and vocabulary, will I hope contribute to an understanding of the differences in character and technique between this and Old English verse.

There is, however, one similarity shared by the two schools of poetry that is so striking that it deserves to be faced immediately. This is that in both *Beowulf* and in *Sir Gawain and the Green Knight* the standard pattern of alliteration does not involve the last stress of the line. There are logical, rather than historical, grounds to account for this. Alliteration in the standard pattern is functional, and one of its functions is to pick out the stressed syllables. If alliteration is used unnecessarily, it becomes not functional but decorative. Now alliteration on the fourth stress is not necessary and not functional, because the last stressed syllable of the line is very seldom in an ambiguous position. Even in *Gawain*, where the line is so much longer and looser than in *Beowulf*, the last stress falls generally on one of the last two syllables of the line and on the final word, the stress-pattern of which is predetermined. The reason why this alliterative scheme *works* as a norm in all Germanic languages is that there is a logical basis for it, the principle of which may be expressed as the 'minimum necessary guidance system'. This principle also explains why the practice of alliterating *both* stressed syllables in the first half-line, common in *Beowulf*, is quite standard in *Gawain*, because the need for guidance is so much greater in the longer line of the latter poem.

As a result of using a standard pattern, the non-alliterating last stress becomes in a regularly ordered alliterative style a line-end marker, signalling the completion of a metrical unit. The conclusion is not that the author of *Gawain* was continuing an ancient unbroken tradition – because a tradition is not kept for its own sake – but that in a regularly constructed alliterative line the alliteration operates most satisfactorily and most logically in this pattern.

In this view the fourteenth-century poets did not inherit a tradition of 'correct' verse miraculously preserved, but instead they consciously – and by gradual stages – remodelled a written tradition of alliterative composition that led back only by rather tortuous routes to Old English verse. The history of medieval English literature will make better sense if we accept that the tradition of 'classical' Old English poetry died out soon after the Conquest, and that for over one hundred years it was succeeded by a looser form of alliterative verse, which in its turn died out, though not before it had sown the seeds of the Alliterative Revival. An examination of the ways in which alliteration was used in the period from 1250 to 1350 will perhaps bear out this view of the origins of the Revival.

The Use of Alliteration 1250–1350

Although there are no records of the composition of the unrhymed alliterative line in the period between the verse of the early thirteenth century and the poems of the Alliterative Revival in the middle of the fourteenth century, it may be that verse of the type that Laȝamon composed continued to be written for a time. Even if it was no longer composed, it is certain that it was still known to some. The manuscript in which *The Bestiary* is preserved was copied perhaps as late as 1300,[47] while Laȝamon's *Brut* was transcribed at least twice after 1250,[48] and was presumably read for some time after that. In addition, alliterative verse of a different sort continued to be written throughout this century. It was not superseded by the rhymed syllabic line, but instead incorporated into it. An early example of this is *On Serving Christ*,[49] a thirteenth-century poem in which rough alliterative lines are grouped into irregular rhyming stanzas, and during the first half of the fourteenth century the alliterative line is found exclusively in rhyming stanzas.

The most important collection of rhymed alliterative verse is MS. Harley 2253. This is a large and diverse anthology assembled in Hereford round about 1340,[50] and it contains works in verse and prose in three languages, French, Latin and English. The English poems, many of which are very fine, are written in a wide variety of styles by a number of authors from different parts of the country, and they range quite widely in date. An early poem describes the Battle of Lewes of 1264, while a later one mentions the Battle of Bannockburn of 1314. Some poems use alliteration only sporadically or not at all, but in about seventeen of the lyrics alliteration occurs with marked regularity. Stanza patterns of all kinds are used, some simple, others highly complex. Even the most richly alliterating poems show a tendency towards a much greater rhythmic regularity than anything attempted by Laȝamon. What the Harley poets have brilliantly achieved is a fusion of the alliterative line with syllabic verse in rhyming stanzas. Readers who dislike this ornate style complain that alliteration is superfluous in these poems. Such criticism is wide of the mark. Alliteration is used in the *Harley Lyrics*, together with other stylistic devices, to achieve a number of different effects. These may be observed by examining the poem *The Poet's Repentance*, in which the poet confesses that he has been devoted to Eve instead of the Virgin Mary.[51] The poem combines many devices in a stanza of amazing intricacy, which is basically of twelve lines with alternating rhymes. The stanza is in two parts, the first of four-stress lines rhyming *ababab*, the second of three-stress lines rhyming *cdcd*. The alliteration runs through pairs of lines, so that the alliterative pattern, linking the lines in pairs, works in counterpoint to the alternating rhyme pattern. Furthermore, in the first and third stanza the first eight lines end on the same consonant, and since the lines alliterate in pairs the result is rhyme of the type 'wet – wit' (pararhyme). The poem is a worthy predecessor of later works in the ornate style, such as *Pearl* (which is also in twelve-line stanzas). It begins:

> Weping haueþ myn wonges wet
> For wikked werk ant wone of wyt,
> Vnbliþe y be til y ha bet
> Bruches broken, ase bok byt,
> Of leuedis loue, þat y ha let,
> Þat lemeþ al wiþ luefly lyt.
> Ofte in song y haue hem set,
> Þat is vnsemly þer hit syt.
>   Hit syt ant semeþ noht
>   Þer hit ys seid in song;
>   Þat y haue of hem wroht
>   Ywis hit is al wrong.   (1–12)

[*Weeping has wet my cheeks, for my evil behaviour and lack of sense; I will be unhappy until I have atoned – as the Book commands – for sins committed against the love of a Lady whom I have forsaken and who shines with lovely splendour. I have often written about ladies in song, which is not a suitable place. It is not right or proper when it is related in song. What I have written about them is wrong without a doubt.*]

The second stanza begins 'Al wrong y wrohte for a wyf' and is in this way linked to the first stanza by repetition and alliteration. The alliteration is part of the fabric of the verse, and is 'ornamental' only in the sense that any other poetic device is. Only in the narrowest of metrical senses does alliteration have no function here; that is to say that because the lines are linked by end-rhyme, alliteration is not the only feature holding them together, and because the rhythm is predominantly iambic, alliteration is not a necessary device for picking out the stressed syllables. Even this statement is occasionally untrue: without alliteration the stress pattern of the line 'Bruches broken ase bok byt' would be unintelligible. Other alliterative *Harley Lyrics*, such as *The Three Foes of Man* and *Annot and John*, also use alliteration in a line with more or less regular rhythm, though here again alliteration is used to pick out the stress in an irregular line.

Some *Harley Lyrics* depart further from syllabic regularity and approach more closely the accentual rhythm of unrhymed alliterative verse, so that in these poems alliteration may be said to have a more strictly metrical function. *On the Retinues of the Great*,[52] a satirically abusive attack on noblemen's servants, shows how constant alliteration may be used in a less regular rhythmic pattern to give emphasis to the words of mockery:

Of rybaudȝ y ryme ant rede o mi rolle,
Of gedelynges, gromes, of Colyn and of Colle,
Harlotes, hors-knaues, bi pate and bi polle
To deuel ich hem to-lyure ant take to tolle! (1–4)

[*I sing of rascals and read from my scroll, of low fellows, servants, of Colin and Colle, rogues and stable boys, every one of them I consign to the devil and hand them over as tribute.*]

Poems exhibiting a similar degree of syllabic irregularity are *The Man in the Moon*,[53] *The Satire on the Consistory Courts*[54] and, as this extract will show, *The Song of the Husbandman*:

Þus me pileþ þe pore and pykeþ ful clene,
Þe ryche men raymeþ wiþouten eny ryht,
Ar londes and ar leodes liggeþ fol lene
Þorh biddyng of baylyfs such harm hem haþ hiht.
Men of religioun me halt hem ful hene,
Baroun and bonde, þe clerc and þe knyht.
Þus wil walkeþ in lond, and wondred ys wene,
Falsshipe fatteþ and marreþ wyþ myht. (25–32)[55]

[*Thus the poor are robbed and picked clean, the rich take what they want without right. Their lands and their people remain with very little because of the demands of bailiffs who have threatened them with such trouble. Baron, bondman, cleric and knight have little regard for men of religion. Thus Will walks the land and hardship is to be expected, Falsehood grows fat and destroys with its power.*]

Even in these poems it may be noticed that the use of rhyming stanzas has the effect of encouraging a tendency towards syllabic regularity. In other ways, also, the use of end-rhyme in the *Harley Lyrics* alters the character of the alliterative line. Laȝamon had preserved the concept of the half-line, and both rhyme (at the half-line) and alliteration in the *Brut* have the function of linking one half-line to another. But end-rhyme links pairs or groups of lines, and the result is that the line is no longer so sharply divided into two halves that need to be bound together. For this reason the alliteration in the *Harley Lyrics* need not span the line: 'Of gedelynges, gromes, of Colyn and of Colle'. Even so, *The Song of the Husbandman* illustrates that the half-line has by no means disappeared.

The use of rhyme has another effect which is very much worth observing. In the *unrhymed* alliterative line as it appeared in Old English and was to appear again in the poems of the Revival, the last stressed syllable of the line does not share in the alliteration, for reasons outlined earlier. Because it is not marked by alliteration, it is the lightest of the four stresses. In rhymed verse, however, the chief weight of the line falls on the rhyming syllable, quite displacing the balance of the old alliterative line. In *rhymed* alliterative verse, therefore, there is no incongruity in the last syllable sharing in the alliteration, as it usually does in the *Harley Lyrics*. When rhyme was once more abandoned in the poems of the Revival, the emphasis shifted away from the last stress, and, as a more or less inevitable consequence, the practice of involving this syllable in the alliteration became a device used only occasionally and for special effect. Significantly enough, however, the last stress continued to be alliterated in the *rhymed* alliterative works of the late fourteenth and fifteenth centuries.

The *Harley Lyrics* provide evidence that the art of writing verse in what is basically an accentual alliterative line did not die out, even though the use of end-rhyme involves many modifications to the line. One more feature that they possess that is of interest in relation to the poems of the Revival is the vocabulary. A list of the words in the lyrics that later became part of the characteristic alliterative vocabulary would include the synonyms for 'man' – *aþel/haþel*, *bern*, *gome* and *lede* – as well as the commendatory adjectives *rekene* 'prompt' and *wlonke* 'splendid', the adverb *spaclyche* 'quickly' and the verb *blykyeþ* 'gleams'. In common with the works of the Revival, the *Harley Lyrics* display a great richness of vocabulary and a fondness for recondite words, a feature encouraged by the exigencies of alliteration. This important collection of lyrics contains poems that handle complex patterns of rhyme and alliteration with exuberance and inventiveness. In other manuscripts there are a few more examples of the rhymed alliterative line from about the same period,[56] but nowhere else are such brilliant effects achieved.

The lyrics of satire and complaint, such as *The Song of the Husbandman* quoted above, are in their style and subject-matter interesting precursors of *Wynnere and Wastoure*, but even more directly relevant in this respect is another piece from the Harley manuscript, *Thomas of Erceldoun's Prophecy*.[57] This prophecy is composed in a sort of incantatory alliterative prose. Thomas of Erceldoun, asked to predict when the war with the Scots will end, replies mysteriously:

> When man as mad a kyng of a capped man,
> When mon is leuere oþermones þyng þen is owen,
> When Londyon ys forest, ant forest ys felde,
> When hares kendles o þe herston,
> When wyt and wille werres togedere.... (1–5)

> [*When a capped man (i.e. a priest?) has been made king, when the things of another man are dearer than one's own, when London is forest, and forest is field, when hares give birth on the hearthstone, when Wit and Will fight together....*]

He foretells the conflict at Bannockburn, and ends:

> When laddes weddeþ leuedis;
> When scottes flen so faste þat for faute of ship hy drouneþ hemselue.
> Whenne shal þis be? Nouþer in þine tyme ne in myne,
> Ah comen and gon wiþinne twenty wynter ant on. (15–18)

> [*When lads marry ladies, when Scots flee so fast that for lack of ships they drown themselves. When shall this be? Neither in your time or in mine, but it will come and go within one and twenty winters.*]

Many of the elements of this mystifying prophecy were probably traditional, and some were certainly used in supposed predictions of other events. The author of *Wynnere and Wastoure* repeats two of them, that hares shall crouch on hearthstones and that ill-bred fellows shall marry noble ladies:

> When wawes waxen schall wilde, and walles bene doun,
> And hares appon herthe-stones schall hurcle in hire fourme,

And eke boyes of no blode, with boste and with pryde
Schall wedde ladyes in londe and lede þam at will,
Thene dredfull domesdaye it draweth neghe aftir.

(13–17)[58]

[wawes – *waves*; hurcle – *crouch*; fourme – *lair*; lede – *govern*.]

Since similar predictions are found elsewhere, these parallels do not demonstrate direct borrowing from the Harley text, but certainly the author of *Wynnere and Wastoure* drew on the same tradition of prophetic writing. Whether he knew the prophecy in the same form of rhythmic alliterative prose it is impossible to say.

There are other examples, besides this prophecy, of rhythmic alliterative prose in the fourteenth century. Similar techniques were used by those who inherited or revived the traditions of devotional alliterative prose that had flourished, as we have seen, a century earlier. A work that provides interesting information on the models, methods and aims of these fourteenth-century writers is *A Talkyng of the Love of God*, in the preface of which the author describes the nature of his prose style as follows:

Men schal fynden lihtliche þis tretys in cadence, after þe bigynninge, ʒif hit beo riht poynted, and rymed in sum stude, to beo more louesum to hem þat hit reden.[59]

[lihtliche – *easily*; poynted – *punctuated*; stude – *place*; louesum – *attractive*.]

On inspection *A Talkyng* proves to be a reworking, with some additional material, of two treatises of the early thirteenth-century 'Wooing Group' – *The Ureisun of God Almihti* and *Þe Wohunge of ure Lauerd*.[60] The rhythmic qualities or 'cadence' of the earlier treatises are preserved, indeed extended. *A Talkyng* thus carries on an English tradition of rhythmic prose stretching ultimately back to Old English times.

Also influenced by the 'Wooing Group' and the tradition of alliterative prose was Richard Rolle, the most famous of the fourteenth-century mystics.[61] Rolle was born at Thornton Dale in Yorkshire about the year 1300, and died at Hampole in the same county in 1349. At the age of eighteen he became a hermit, and he thereafter gained a great reputation for sanctity, so great, in fact, that after his death numerous works were quite falsely ascribed to him, with the result that it is not always easy to be certain which of the many works with which he is credited were actually written by him.[62]

Rolle's earliest works were composed in Latin. The most extraordinary of these, the *Melos Amoris*, is described in some of the manuscripts as a 'carmen rythmicum' or a 'carmen prosaicum'. Its most striking feature is alliteration carried to insane lengths:

Liquidum licebit non labar in lutum, lachrimis iam lotus libenter laboro in laude letari ac liquescere in lumen letificans levatos.[63]

Opinions vary as to the origins of Rolle's style. Certainly a number of stylists advocated various rhetorical devices, including alliteration, to heighten a Latin prose style.[64] It is, however, clear enough that in his English works at least, Rolle was following the English tradition of rhythmical alliterative prose that we have examined previously. Rolle's English compositions, both in rhymed verse and also in prose, are frequently characterised by the use of alliteration.

An English work generally regarded as Rolle's is *The Meditations on the Passion*.[65] This lyrical account of Christ's Passion makes subtle use of alliteration combined at times with a rhythmic patterning. At more impassioned moments, such as in this description of the Crucifixion, the rhythm falls into a predominantly four-stress pattern, not unlike that of the verse of the Alliterative Revival, though the movement is less regular:

> I se in my soule how reufully þou gost: þi body is so blody, so rowed and so bleddderyd; þi crowne is so kene, þat sytteth on þi hed; þi heere mevyth with þe wynde, clemyd with þe blood; þi lovely face so wan and so bolnyd with bofetynge and with betynge, with spyttynge, with spowtynge; þe blood ran þerewith, þat grysyth in my syʒt; so lothly and so wlatsome þe Jues han þe mad, þat a mysel art þou lyckere þan a clene man. Þe cros is so hevy, so hye and so stark, þat þei hangyd on þi bare bac trossyd so harde. (59–69)
>
> [reufully – *pitiably*; rowed – *made raw*; bledderyd – *swollen*; clemyd – *matted*; bolnyd – *puffed*; grysyth in my syʒt – *horrifies me to see it*; wlatsome – *loathsome*; mysel – *diseased person*; stark – *cruel*; trossyd – *fastened*.]

Later in the *Meditations* Rolle inserts passages of rhymed verse, both alliterative and non-alliterative.

Rolle's epistle on the text *Ego Dormio*[66] shows an even more interesting development, where the prose is interrupted for a few lines of rough alliterative verse on the transience of worldly things:

> Alle perisches and passes þat we with eghe see,
> It wanes into wrechednes, þe welth of þis worlde.
> Robes and ritches rotes in dike,
> Prowde payntyng slakes into sorow,
> Delites and drewryse stynk sal ful sone,
> Þair golde and þaire tresoure drawes þam til dede. (104–9)
>
> [dike – *ditch*; slakes – *dwindles*; drewryse – *loved ones*.]

These lines are not necessarily composed by Rolle himself, since he was in the habit of quoting pieces of verse in his treatises.[67] They are interesting, though, in that they show what might be regarded as a transitional form standing between Rolle's rhythmic prose and alliterative verse proper. Neither the vocabulary nor the alliterative patterns are characteristic of the verse of the Alliterative Revival, and yet the alliteration and rhythm are more regularly ordered than in Rolle's prose passage quoted earlier. *Ego Dormio* was most probably written in the early years of the 1340's, perhaps ten years before *Wynnere and Wastoure*, and so chronologically it stands on the threshold of the Alliterative Revival.

Joseph of Arimathie

The evidence assembled so far shows that alliteration was used in one way or another right up to the time of the Alliterative Revival, though for over one hundred years it was used only in rhymed verse and in rhythmic prose, and not in an unrhymed verse-line. In an important respect, therefore, the continuity of the alliterative tradition is not open to dispute. What may be questioned is Chambers' assumption of a hidden corpus of oral poetry faithfully preserving the expressions and style of Old English poetry, a venerable tradition that was inherited by alliterative poets in the mid-fourteenth century. There is no evidence for this assumption, and the Revival can be accounted for without it.

It is more likely that alliterative poetry was developed from the various types of alliterative writing current at the time, or at least still remembered, that is (possibly) from unrhymed verse of the Laʒamonic type, from rhymed alliterative poetry such as the *Harley Lyrics*, and from rhythmic prose such as that used for prophetic utterances as well as for the devotions of the mystics.

These are the sort of models on which the early poets of the Revival could have based their first attempts at what was for them an essentially new creation – an unrhymed alliterative line. It was a new creation and yet, because it was based on earlier alliterative writings, the poets themselves may have thought of it as a development, a modernisation perhaps, of an ancient and respected English tradition, so that they could, quite accurately, speak of its antiquity. It is reasonable to assume that perfection in this new style did not come all at once, and that the earliest poets must have fumbled and faltered their way to the forms of expression and the rhythms which were to be developed and standardised by their successors. Many of these earliest attempts would have been lost, abandoned by later readers and scribes as too unpolished and out-moded to bother with, but it looks as though at least one such work has survived.

Joseph of Arimathie is preserved in the huge Vernon manuscript, together with *A Talkyng of the Love of God* and a number of poems of the Revival including *Piers Plowman*. The manuscript was assembled in the last twenty years of the fourteenth century, but *Joseph of Arimathie* is always regarded as a very early alliterative work. It is a retelling in alliterative verse of an episode in the *Estoire del Saint Graal*, a French prose work of the thirteenth century that forms part of the enormous Vulgate cycle of Arthurian romance. The source is handled with skill, so as to place the emphasis on Joseph's conversion of Evalak, King of Sarras. The verse-form, by contrast, is crude. The metrical patterns are highly irregular by the standards of later poems; some lines are heavily alliterative, but many have no alliteration at all; some lines are so long that they burst at the seams, others are unusually short. The character of the poem may be illustrated by this delightful passage in which Evalak's wife describes how, as a young girl, she was converted to Christianity by a hermit, though she had first to overcome her repugnance of his ugly grey beard! Her mother had previously been cured by the hermit of a terrible disease, and here she asks her young daughter if she too cannot bring herself to believe:

Þenne heo seide to me, 'Douȝter ful deore,
Woltou beo as I am and on þis mon leue?'
And I wepte water warm, and wette my wonges,
And seide his bert was so hor I bad not on him leeue.
And he seide to me, 'Douȝter, he is feirore,
Þat þi moder has i-helet nou in þis tyme,
Þen I or þou or out þat is formed.'
And I tolde him aȝeyn, 'And he so feir weore
As my broþer is at home, I wolde on him leeue.'
'Sikerly, douȝter,' he seis, 'so may grace sende
Þat þou miȝt seo him þiself ar þow henne seche.'
Þenne com Ihesu Crist, so cler in himseluen,
Aftur þe furste blusch we ne miȝte him biholden,
And a wynt and a sauor whappede us vmbe,
We weore so wel of vrself we nuste what we duden.   (645–59)

[Woltou – *will you*; leue – *believe*; wonges – *cheeks*; his bert....leeue – *his beard was so hoary I asked not to believe in him*; he is...tyme – *he who has now healed your mother is fairer*; out – *aught*; formed – *created*; And I tolde...weore – *I replied if he (Christ) were as fair*; Sikerly – *certainly*; so may...seche – *may you be given the grace to see him yourself before you go*; cler – *bright*; blusch – *glance*; a wynt... duden – *a wind and a scent enveloped us, so that we felt so happy we didn't know what we were doing.*]

Metrical analysis reveals how very different this work is from the other poems of the Revival. Of the fifteen lines quoted, five have no alliteration at all (in the poem as a whole the proportion is 16%), and only one of them follows the standard alliterative pattern with two alliterating syllables in the first half-line and one in the second – aa/ax (9% in the poem as a whole).[68] In four of these lines the alliteration falls on the last stress, which once again is not common practice in verse of the Revival.

The vocabulary of this passage illustrates another distinguishing feature of *Joseph of Arimathie*. The specialised vocabulary of the poetry of the Revival is hardly used here, although there are two phrases worth commenting on. The expression 'wette my wonges' was something of a favourite with the alliterative poets, but it was already well established before this time, and its use was not restricted to alliterative poetry. I have quoted it earlier from the *Harley Lyrics*, and it is found several times there. On the other hand, the phrase 'þe furste blusch' is the first recorded instance of the noun. In early use, in the senses 'glance' and 'gleam' the word is recorded only in alliterative poetry, and even the verb from which it is formed, *bluschen* (from OE. *blyscan*, 'to shine'), is not common in the fourteenth century except in alliterative poetry. From the fifteenth century, however, the noun was in more general currency, particularly in the phrase 'at first blush' still in use today, and this suggests that the word in this sense may have been more widespread than early records indicate.

Joseph of Arimathie gives every appearance of being a transitional work, standing apart from the other works of the Revival, but looking forward to them. Most of the features typical of alliterative poetry are present in embryo. It is recognisably alliterative verse, as the prose of Rolle's *Meditations* is not, but it is verse that is still unsure of its footing. In style and technique it resembles more than anything else the few lines of alliterative verse in Rolle's *Ego Dormio*. On these stylistic grounds, therefore, it would be reasonable to date *Joseph of Arimathie* some years before Rolle's death in 1349. There is no evidence other than stylistic for dating the poem within narrow limits.[69]

The postulation that *Joseph of Arimathie* was composed early in the 1340's gives the alliterative movement some years after that in which to gather adherents, to build up a distinctive vocabulary and to establish its metrical norms. Two poems which are also generally regarded as early works, *Alisaunder of Macedoine* and *Alexander and Dindimus*, show a much greater regularisation of metrical and alliterative patterns, but their vocabulary is still not fully developed, and does not extend beyond the most common alliterative words such as those for 'man' or 'warrior' – *bern, freke, gome, lud, rink, segge, weie* and (in *Alexander and Dindimus* alone) *haþel* and *schalk*. (*Joseph of Arimathie* uses *bern, gome* and *schalk* only.) By the time *Wynnere and Wastoure* was composed, in the 1350's, the style had apparently become well defined, even if there were new developments to come later, and new techniques still to be exploited.

An early work that is fairly closely datable is *William of Palerne*. Like *Joseph of Arimathie* this is an adaptation of a French romance, and it was made for Humphrey de Bohun, Earl of Hereford, who died in 1361. It would have been written, therefore, about the same time as *Wynnere and Wastoure*. The author, who, like his hero, is called William, ends his work with a humble apology for his lack of craftsmanship and his choice of metre:

In þise wise haþ William al his werke ended,
As fully as þe Frensch fully wold aske,
And as his witte him wold serue, þouȝh it were febul.
But þouȝh þe metur be nouȝt mad at eche mannes paye,
Wite him nouȝt þat it wrouȝt; he wold haue do beter
ȝif is witte in eny weiȝes wold him haue serued. (5521–6)

[wold aske – *demands*; mad...paye – *made to suit everyone*; Wite...wrouȝt – *don't blame the one who composed it*.]

Is William afraid that his audience, schooled by generations of bards in the art of the poetry of their forefathers, will censure his less skilful attempt? Or rather are his feelings of insecurity inspired by doubt about the reception his audience will give to this new form of verse? Either interpretation is possible. I have argued in this chapter that the theory of an uninterrupted tradition of oral verse is without secure foundation, and it is therefore more likely that the poet William is nervously apologising for offending the more conservative among his audience by his piece of newfangledness. Had he been able to forsee the magnificent achievements that were to be made by poets writing only a couple of decades later he would not have apologised for composing in alliterative verse.

Chapter 2

THE REVIVAL

A School of Poets

The range and variety of alliterative poems written between the mid-fourteenth century and the early years of the fifteenth century are very wide. There are solid historical chronicles, romances involving incredible adventures, poems illustrating some moral or doctrinal point, biographies of saints, and poems deploring social and political conditions. Later on there are even parodies of alliterative verse. The poems range in quality from recognised masterpieces such as *Sir Gawain and the Green Knight*, *Pearl* and *Piers Plowman* to dull works such as *Alexander and Dindimus* or *St. John the Baptist*. In between these extremes of quality are a large number of works which, had they been written in a poetic style and in a language that required less effort to appreciate, would today have been well known and widely admired. Some of the more interesting of these will be discussed in later chapters. Though there are one or two short poems, such as the evocative description of *The Blacksmiths* which is a mere 22 lines, alliterative poems are characteristically narratives of considerable length. No other alliterative work now extant can match the 14,000 lines of *The Destruction of Troy*, but there are ten unrhymed alliterative poems of between 1000 and 7000 lines long. Later on in the period there was a vogue for alliterative poems composed in intricate rhyming stanzas, which, not surprisingly, tend to be rather shorter, although even so there are several of about 1000 lines. Both the bulk and the high quality of alliterative poetry written in this period of less than a hundred years are remarkable.

It is natural to seek for some explanation for this extraordinary burst of activity in alliterative poetry, but an answer can be given only in the most general terms. It is probably significant that most of the earliest poems were translations from French (*Joseph of Arimathie* and *William of Palerne*) and Latin (*Alisaunder of Macedoine* and *Alexander and Dindimus*), and it is logical to associate the Revival with the decline of French as a literary language in England in the mid-fourteenth century as well as the growth of a prosperous, literate and fairly sophisticated audience who for the first time wanted, perhaps in many cases needed, literature presented in English rather than in French or Latin.[1] The alliterative line, so eminently suitable in view of its adaptability and variations of pace for long narrative poems, seems to have been forged to fill the gap created by this new demand. Certainly it must have come as a godsend to a translator labouring to turn a lengthy original – often in prose – into English verse, for in England verse was still the natural medium for narrative. Perhaps, too, there was satisfaction in the knowledge that the alliterative line was a uniquely English form, without parallel in French or Latin literature, so that the author of a poem such as *William of Palerne*, though obtaining his *matière* from France, could claim to have fashioned it into an entirely English composition.

It is at once apparent that we are here dealing with a 'school' of poets, though one that embraces a huge variety of styles and subjects. All the poems are written in varieties of the same basic metrical form. They show many similarities in diction which distinguish them from poems of other traditions, and they have many parallels of phraseology and syntax. There are a number of favourite topics, suggesting that the poets knew the subjects at which alliterative poetry excelled and how they should be handled; topics such as the battle scene, the violent storm at sea, the precise descriptions of dress, of feasts and the like. The poems share, too, a sense of their own value that is far from universal in fourteenth-century poetry; a conviction sometimes openly expressed by the poet that what he communicates is important and is being treated with dignity and seriousness.[2] Alliterative poetry is not merely for entertainment, like the fables of that spinner of yarns, Homer:

> Homer was holden haithill of dedis,
> Qwiles his dayes enduret derrist of other
> Þat with the Grekys was gret and of Grice comyn.
> He feynet myche fals was neuer before wroght,
> And traiet þe truth, trust ye non other.
> Of his trifuls to telle I haue no tome nowe,
> Ne of his feynit fare þat he fore with:
> How goddes foght in the filde, folke as þai were!   (*Destruction of Troy*, 38–45)

[holden – *regarded*; haithill – *worthy*; derrist of other – *best of all*; gret – *esteemed*; He...wroght – *he invented many falsehoods that had never been heard of before*; traiet – *betrayed*; tome – *opportunity*; feynit...with – *falsehoods he perpetrated*; folke...were – *as if they were mortals*.]

Poets are God's instrument, and it is only God who can give them the grace to write in his honour and to the edification of the people:

> And wysse me to werpe owte some worde at this tyme
> That nothyre voyde be ne vayne, bot wyrchip tille hymeselvyne,
> Plesande and profitabille to the popule that them heres.   (*Morte Arthure*, 9–11)

[wysse...owte – (*may God*) *guide me in uttering*; wyrchip – *honour*; Plesande – *pleasing*.]

These similarities of technique, of style and of approach justify the description of the poets of the Revival as a 'school'. Nevertheless, we must not over-emphasise the closeness of the alliterative school and forget the very wide range of poetic styles that are included within it. We are not to visualise a sort of fourteenth-century Pre-Raphaelite Brotherhood, with members united by friendship and a common artistic programme and purpose. It is impossible to gauge how close the ties were between individual works and authors, though it is a reasonable assumption that at least some of the poets of the Revival, coming from the same parts of the country, were known to one another. But, unlike the Pre-Raphaelites, the authors of alliterative poems left no information about themselves, not even their names in most cases, and the only documents they left are their poems. These, although they display certain shared attitudes, do not present a common statement of artistic aims. This is sometimes implicitly denied by critics who claim to find in alliterative poetry some echoes of the 'heroic spirit of Anglo-Saxon verse', as though, like the Pre-Raphaelites, the alliterative poets were rebelling against contemporary literary styles, seeking in the attitudes of the past an escape from the degeneracy of the present. But there is no suggestion in alliterative poetry that the writers thought of themselves as anything but up to date and following contemporary fashions. *Wynnere and Wastoure's* nostalgia for the days of old is as conventional a pose as Chaucer's poem on *The Former Age* (or, indeed, as our own frequent sighs for the glories of the past); it is not a plea for a return to the verse-forms, the social organisation or the sentiments of the Anglo-Saxon age.

The striking similarities of vocabulary and style that are displayed in almost all of the alliterative poems have misled some critics into making unjustifiable claims about the links between the works. In particular, it was long believed that the parallels of phrase that so obviously exist were evidence of a complex chain of dependence and interrelationships. Thus a line such as 'With hard hattis on þaire hedis hied to þaire horsis' from *The Wars of Alexander* (2981) was taken to be a reminiscence of 'Hard hattes þay hent and on hors lepes' in *Purity* (1209), which also seemed to echo 'Harde hattes appon hedes and helmys with crestys' (*Wynnere and Wastoure*, 51). With patience and industry vast numbers of such parallel phrases were assembled, though in a rather haphazard manner and without any clear principles of selection. Sometimes the results were used to support theories of identity of authorship, and at other times to suggest borrowing. In the early years of this century these parallels were used to bolster one of the most absurd literary hypotheses of all time, in which it was argued that the author of the majority of alliterative poems was a certain 'Huchown of the Awle Ryale'. The name of this poet who was apparently so prodigiously prolific would have sunk without trace if he had not had the good fortune to be mentioned in the early fifteenth century by Andrew Wyntoun in his *Orygynale Cronykil of Scotland* as the author of three works – the 'gret Gest of Arthure, and the Awntyr of Gawane, þe Pistil als of suet Susane'. The last of these poems was identified, perhaps correctly, as the alliterative poem in rhyming stanzas, *The Pistill of Susan*, and so the other two titles were quickly attached to alliterative poems also. Apparent stylistic similarities led to the addition of other alliterative poems to the list of Huchown's works. Huchown himself proved somewhat elusive, but several identifications, a number of them Scottish, were proposed. This elaborate construction, lacking all scholarly foundation, tumbled to the ground when subjected to gentle probing.[3] It was pointed out that none of the proofs adduced in favour of the hypothesis had any substance, and that the poems, being written in a variety of styles, with different metrical patterns and in different dialects, could hardly be the work of one man.

Since it could no longer be argued that the verbal parallels were all attributable to identity of authorship, it was then assumed that they were the result of borrowing within a school of poets. J. P. Oakden, in his important book on alliterative verse,[4] listed the parallels that he regarded as indicating interdependence, and the conclusions to be drawn from his comparisons were that the majority of alliterative poems were linked to one another by borrowing. This would presuppose an extremely tight-knit school of writers, each writer knowing and drawing upon the works of his fellow poets.

However, like his predecessors, Oakden overlooked the fact that drawing upon well-established collocations is in the very nature of a poetic technique that works by associating groups of words that have the same initial sound. Alliterative poets made a virtue of necessity by creating a poetic style that exploited the use of such collocations. With a technique of this sort, parallel phrases are bound to occur frequently in unrelated poems, and it is therefore wrong to conclude from such parallels that one poem is indebted to another. Further investigation often reveals that the use of an apparently significant phrase is quite widespread. This point is self-evident with simple collocations such as 'king with crown' and the like, but it applies also to more complex constructions. It has been argued, for example, that the two descriptions of David's slaying of Goliath, in the *Morte Arthure* and in *The Parlement of the Thre Ages*, are dependent upon one another. At first sight this dependence seems certain. The former says 'For he slewe with a slynge be sleyghte of his handis' (3418), the latter 'And sloughe hym with his slynge and with no sleghte ells' (445). Wider enquiry, however, puts this conclusion in doubt. The combination 'slay...sleight' turns out to be common enough in alliterative poetry (cf. *Morte Arthure*, 4045; *Destruction of Troy*, 1251; *Piers Plowman*, C. vii, 107; *Wars of Alexander*, 2566; etc.), and *The Awntyrs off Arthure* provides a very close parallel in describing an attack on Gawain: 'He atteled withe a slenke haf slayne him in sliȝte' (616).[5]

What this illustrates is that verbal parallels are a very uncertain guide to establishing relationships between alliterative poems. The author of *Morte Arthure* might, in this case, have borrowed, and at times we may feel that the collocation is so unusual as to make it probable that one writer was indebted to another, but far from facilitating the tracing of relationships between the poems, the collocational style more often obscures the evidence and makes the process of investigation almost impossible.

There are two further difficulties which hinder the process of uncovering the details of these relationships. The first is that most of the poems are not closely datable. *Wynnere and Wastoure* and *William of Palerne* are exceptions in this, and the majority of poems can be dated only on the evidence of such imprecise clues as the styles of dress or architecture they describe, and the dates of the manuscripts in which they are preserved. This means that even when the inter-dependence of two poems seems likely, it is rarely possible to be confident about which was the borrower and which the lender. A second difficulty, often ignored, is that many alliterative poems have undoubtedly been lost. It is the merest chance that has preserved the most brilliant of them, *Sir Gawain and the Green Knight*, in the unique manuscript in which it shares a place with three other outstanding poems, *Pearl*, *Purity* and *Patience*. Indeed the majority of alliterative poems have survived damp, fire, rats, indifferent owners and all the other dangers to which manuscripts are subject, in only one copy. This suggests that many more were not so fortunate. Several of those that have been preserved are in an incomplete state, and an extreme example is the scrap now entitled *The Conflict of Wit and Will*. A few bits and pieces of 'þis long geste', as the poet describes it, were used to patch up the margins of an early six-teenth-century missal, and apart from these sad remnants nothing else of it now exists.[6] Many more poems must have vanished without leaving any trace. With such gaps in the records, no more than a partial picture of the alliterative school can ever be drawn.

The Poems and their Provenance

Although the detailed relationships between the poems cannot often be de-termined, it is still possible to trace certain developments within the alliterative school. Poems may be grouped broadly according to the areas in which they were composed, and then within this geographical grouping the connections between various poems may be studied on the basis of similarities of style and theme.

Chaucer's Parson indicates the geographical distribution of alliterative poetry negatively and dismissively when he says:

I am a Southren man,
I kan nat geeste 'rum, ram, ruf' by lettre.   (*Parson's Prologue*, 42–3)[7]

There can be little doubt that this is a reference to alliterative verse, and the Parson's implication that at this date this did not flourish in the south of England is supported by an analysis of the dialects in which the poems are preserved. However, there are several problems in working out the dialect of a poem, and it is as well to understand first of all the limitations of the evidence that such an analysis can hope to produce.

A major source of difficulty is that the dialect of the scribe will often differ from that of the poet, and the language in which the poem is preserved will generally be the scribe's, who will often have 'translated' his copy of the poem into his own dialect of English.[8] With rhymed verse there are usually clear traces of this process shown in spoilt rhymes, and so it is often possible to work back tentatively to the poet's own dialect. With unrhymed verse, however, the evidence is as a rule much less decisive, and consists of features that the scribe forgot to 'translate'. But these features may present problems of their own. A manuscript may contain, for example, a mixture of forms for 'them' – at times perhaps *thaym*, at other times *hem*. The former will suggest a writer from the north, the latter one from further south – but which was the scribe, and which the author? Further complications arise if, as is usually the case, more than one scribe was involved in the transmission of the text at different stages.

If the dialect of the manuscript is consistent enough or can be satisfactorily disentangled, it is possible to draw conclusions about the dialect of the scribe. But knowing the dialect of the scribe is one thing, and knowing the area in which he was working may be another, for men of education were not necessarily rooted in one part of the country. More important still, the dialect of the scribe does not necessarily reveal anything about the place in which the author himself was working.

A case where the language of the author is recorded apparently without much scribal alteration is the manuscript containing *Sir Gawain and the Green Knight* and associated poems. In such a case the language of the manuscript may be used to localise the author's dialect in a general area of the country. Some scholars hope that the more meticulous collection of dialect evidence now in progress will permit a very much greater accuracy in placing manuscripts and poems. On the basis of this evidence, it is maintained, the *Gawain* manuscript can be localised 'in a very small area either in SE Cheshire or just over the border in NE Staffordshire'.[9] The publication of this dialect material will undoubtedly be a great step forward, but helpful as it may be in establishing the dialects of the scribes, it is doubtful whether it will permit much greater precision in pinning down the areas of composition of the poems themselves. Even where we possess a manuscript which we are confident represents the poet's own dialect, allowance must be made for the possible influence of a literary standard associated with a poetic tradition and differing in some respects from the local dialect,[10] and also for the possibility that the author himself may have migrated from another district, merging his native dialect with that of his new neighbours.

Any statement about the provenance of individual alliterative poems should therefore be treated with circumspection, but it is safe enough to say that the

Revival was first and foremost a movement established in the west midlands. It is likely that alliterative poetry developed earliest in the south of that area, in Gloucestershire and the adjoining counties. It may be observed that this is the region where most of the Early Middle English alliterative works came from: the *Worcester Fragments* and Laȝamon's *Brut* from Worcestershire, the 'Katherine Group' of homilies and the *Harley Lyrics* from Herefordshire. *Joseph of Arimathie*, which on stylistic grounds I have argued is the earliest poem of the Revival now extant, was written in Gloucestershire or nearby, and there is good evidence that another early poem, *William of Palerne*, written before 1361, was composed for an audience near Gloucester, a town which is mentioned by the poet. Two fragmentary accounts of the life of Alexander (which may be extracts from one long chronicle), *Alisaunder of Macedoine* and *Alexander and Dindimus*, are generally regarded as early works composed rather further north, in Shropshire.

The only outstanding work to have emerged from the south-west midlands is *Piers Plowman*. Exceptionally, we know the name of the author of the poem, William Langland, but there are few other facts about him that are known with certainty. He may have come from the Worcestershire–Herefordshire area, near the Malvern Hills where Will the dreamer falls asleep at the beginning of the poem. He wrote the three versions of *Piers Plowman* between about 1365 and 1390. A passage in the last revision of the poem (C text, vi. 1–52) strikes a strongly personal note, and from it we may conclude that Langland spent some years in and around London, earning his bread by saying prayers for the living and the dead. There is much in the poem that reflects a deep involvement in the bustle of life in the metropolis.

In several ways *Piers Plowman* represents a departure from the practices of the alliterative tradition. Langland makes only sparing use of the specialised alliterative vocabulary that had become established by his time, and he writes in a less formal style. These modifications of the alliterative line were made partly with the aim of attracting a wider readership, and the large number of manuscripts of the poem demonstrates that *Piers Plowman* did indeed become a really popular poem, unlike any other alliterative work, and was read in most parts of the country.

Because it was such a highly esteemed poem, *Piers Plowman* greatly influenced the direction taken by later writers from the south-west midlands. Langland had shown that alliterative poetry could appeal to a wider audience by avoiding the ornateness and verbal complexity that characterised the works of the northern poets. This lead was followed by the Wycliffite author of *Pierce the Ploughman's Crede*, who rigorously excluded all traces of the characteristic alliterative diction. The poem takes as its starting point the prologue to the third of Will's dreams (*Piers Plowman*, viii), where Will questions two friars on how to find Dowel. The narrator of *Pierce the Ploughman's Crede* describes how, since he is ignorant of his Creed, he goes for information to the four orders of friars one after another. He gets no satisfactory answer from them, and eventually turns to Pierce the Ploughman. The poem is a clever and interesting attack on the friars, and it derives much of its inspiration, its satiric method and its handling of the metre and vocabulary of alliterative verse from Langland's poem. It was written towards the end of the fourteenth century, and its author probably came from the same general region as Langland.

Langland may have discovered for himself the power of the alliterative line as a vehicle for political and moral satire, but it is equally possible that he knew something of the tradition of satire and complaint that went back, by way of *Wynnere and Wastoure*, to the *Harley Lyrics* such as *The Song of the Husbandman* and *The Satire on the Consistory Courts* as well as other early fourteenth-century complaints.[11] *Richard the Redeless* and *Mum and the Sothsegger* are two poems, possibly by one author, that continued this tradition of political satire in alliterative verse after Langland. Both poems are incomplete and are now extant in different manuscripts, though a sixteenth-century reference suggests that both may have been included at one time in a single codex.[12] They are concerned with two distinct sets of political events. *Richard the Redeless*, once thought to have been composed by Langland himself, purports to be an address to Richard II after his downfall, offering him advice on what went wrong. The poem was therefore written after Richard's imprisonment in August 1399, but presumably before his death the following February. The later work, *Mum and the Sothsegger*, is an attack on Henry IV's household, and it tells of the frustrating search for someone who will not remain mum about the true state of affairs. The protracted quest for a 'sothsegger' (truthteller) through the bustle of town and court life is as tiring for the reader as for the narrator, but the poem suddenly springs to life with a delightful vision that comes to the exhausted narrator, who dreams of a countryside bursting with vigour and fertility, the cows and rabbits in the meadows, the gardens full of beans and 'pesecoddes', and in the midst of all this life a wise and ancient beekeeper, who knows the truth and is not afraid to speak out about it. Since events of 1402 are mentioned, *Mum and the Sothsegger* was composed soon after that date. In the opening lines of *Richard the Redeless* the author speaks of himself at Bristol, and the dialect of both poems is consistent with an author from that part of the country.

A shorter poem, *The Crowned King*, appears to comment on events leading up to Henry V's invasion of France in 1415. The author, much influenced by Langland, describes his own dream vision:

> Me thought that y houed an high on an hill,
> And loked doun on a dale deppest of othre.   (31–2)

> [houed – *stood*; deppest of othre – *deeper than any other*.]

Here he sees the King asking his commons for a subsidy to pay for his wars. The commons exact their price for the grant, in the form of a homily on the conduct befitting a king. This ranges widely, admonishing the King on his duty to the poor, on the need for him to avoid flatterers and promote men of talent, and on the dangers of avarice. It is the sort of appeal that was frequently made, and its application is not restricted to the particular set of circumstances to which it is ostensibly linked.

All these late fourteenth and early fifteenth-century poems from the southern half of the country show the influence of *Piers Plowman* in their preoccupation with contemporary political, social and religious conditions, in their unadorned alliterative style and, on a few occasions, in obvious reminiscences of, or references to, that famous poem.

I have suggested that the earliest poems of the Revival were composed in the south-west midlands, but if it was later that alliterative verse became popular in the north-west midlands (that is to say the counties from north Shropshire to Lancashire) it was certainly not much later. *Wynnere and Wastoure*, probably composed in 1352–3, is apparently the earliest work from the north-west midlands to have survived today. We have already examined its close relationship with two later poems probably from the same area, *The Parlement of the Thre Ages* and *Death and Liffe*, and we have considered its possible influence on Langland. Even though there is no certain evidence of direct relationship between *Wynnere and Wastoure* and *Piers Plowman*, the employment in both of the dream-vision frame for a satire of contemporary abuses is an interesting link and a valuable reminder that the two groups of poems from rather different parts of the country are not to be regarded as mutually exclusive.

The finest poems from this north-western area are found together in one manuscript, MS. Cotton Nero A.x., copied towards the end of the fourteenth century. This contains four alliterative poems which cover a wide range of styles and subjects: *Pearl*, composed in a complex pattern of interlocking twelve-line stanzas, *Purity* and *Patience* written in the unrhymed alliterative line, and *Sir Gawain and the Green Knight*, in which a stanzaic arrangement is maintained by rounding off a varying number of unrhymed lines with a group of five rhymed lines. *Pearl*, a poem as rich and ornate as its name suggests, is an elegy set in a dream-vision frame, and it describes the narrator's struggle to come to terms with the death of his baby daughter. *Purity* is an extraordinary poem, full of magnificent narrative detail: the wicked angels falling from heaven in such numbers that they resembled flour smoking beneath a fine sieve, Lot's embarrassment at having to shield two angels from a crowd of appreciative Sodomites, Belshazzar madly using the holy vessels from Jerusalem – chalices and platters intricately decorated with the shapes of parrots, castles and butterflies – for a drunken orgy. *Patience*, much the shortest of the four poems, is similar in approach, but structurally much simpler. The story of Jonah and the whale is used as an amusing and instructive lesson in the folly of not bowing patiently to God's will. Alone of the four poems, *Sir Gawain and the Green Knight* does not propound any explicit theological message, though its tale of Gawain's attempt to prove himself a perfect Christian knight shows an involvement in moral issues unusual in English romances. It is pre-eminent among romances in English, richer in human interest, more coherent in narrative structure and sophisticated in verbal texture, and (not least) more exciting and full of suspense than any other.

At first sight these four poems make rather a heterogeneous collection, but they reveal on closer inspection certain similarities of approach, imagery and verbal art.[13] Since, furthermore, they all occur in the same manuscript and were apparently composed in the same dialect, it is reasonable to assume that all four are the work of one man. Attempts to provide a name for the author have been numerous, but until more convincing evidence is produced the poet (if there was no more than one involved) must remain anonymous.

The highly polished style, which is a characteristic of the poems of this north-west midland area, is shown at its most perfect in the four poems in the Cotton Nero manuscript. They have a richness of poetic vocabulary that is unparalleled elsewhere, and this is combined in *Pearl* with a very intricate system of rhyming stanzas.

A poem that is sometimes attributed to the author of the poems in the Cotton Nero manuscript is *St. Erkenwald*, which in 352 lines relates how Bishop Erkenwald baptised a just pagan whose body had been discovered uncorrupted in the foundations of St. Paul's. The poem is a neat and pleasing piece of work, but it has none of the imaginative power of the Cotton Nero poems and indeed there seems no good reason to suppose that it is the work of the same man, even though it may have come from the same part of the country. Another work that is with more justification associated with the Cotton Nero poems is *The Wars of Alexander*, though there is no question of identical authorship. This is the longest and best of the three alliterative Alexander poems, and it gives a vivid and detailed account of the hero's life taken from a Latin chronicle, the *Historia de Preliis*. Between *The Wars of Alexander* and the Cotton Nero poems there are many similarities in vocabulary and phraseology which suggest that there may be some question of borrowing, but, as usual, it is impossible to feel sure that this was the case. Even assuming there was borrowing, it would be difficult to prove which was the borrower, because, as with most of the poems of this north-west midlands area, these works are impossible to date within narrow limits. The poems in the Cotton Nero manuscript can be dated not later than 1400, because this is the date of that manuscript, but to go further and suggest, as is often done, that *Purity* is a more youthful work than *Gawain*, is an argument based on the often demonstrably false belief that a poet's development is towards greater perfection and tighter control of his material. *The Wars of Alexander* is generally felt to be a later work. The two manuscripts in which it is preserved are later (*c.* 1450–1500), but this established only a *terminus ad quem*. *St. Erkenwald* has been dated *c.* 1386, in which year the two festivals of that saint were re-established at St. Paul's, but there is nothing in the poem to connect it specifically with that event. Unlike the political poems of the *Piers Plowman* group, the poems of the north-west midlands cannot be dated accurately, which means that it is not possible to chart the chronological development of poetry in this area.

By far the longest of all alliterative poems is *The Destruction of Troy*, which was probably written in Lancashire. This, like *The Wars of Alexander*, is a translation of a Latin chronicle, but it lacks the vitality and interest of the *Wars*. The author follows his source, the *Historia Destructionis Troiae* by Guido de Columnis, giving a full history of the rise and fall of Troy, an account that was of particular importance to medieval readers, who regarded the Trojans as founders of Britain, and Homer as no better than a propagandist for the Greeks. There are no firm grounds for dating the English translation, although there are suggestions (which fall far short of proof) that the author may have known Chaucer's *Troilus and Criseyde*, which would place *The Destruction of Troy* at some date after 1385.[14] Unfortunately, the date of the manuscript is of no help in dating the poem. It used to be thought that the scribe copied the text in the mid-fifteenth century, but it has since been shown that he was working about a century later than this.[15]

The destruction of another ancient city is recounted in *The Siege of Jerusalem*, the earliest manuscript of which dates from the early fifteenth century. The author of this spiteful poem, drawing on both French and Latin sources,[16] rejoices in the pain and misery suffered by the Jews during the siege, at the end of which the Jews are sold at thirty for a penny. Both the date and also the dialect of this poem are uncertain. It is extant in seven fifteenth-century manuscripts, which is more than any other major alliterative poem apart from *Piers Plowman*. Of these seven manuscripts, five are certainly associated with the east of the country: one is from east Yorkshire,[17] three from the east midlands,[18] and one apparently from the south-east.[19] In view of this, it is quite possible that the poem was itself composed in the east. At any rate, this illustrates that wherever the poems were composed, several works of the Revival attracted a readership outside the west midlands, at least during the fifteenth century, so that even if the Revival was a localised movement in its early stages, by the fifteenth century its readership had become more widespread.

Morte Arthure is another poem which, at least in its present state, shows more traces of the east than of the west midlands. This work gives a lively and often original account of Arthur's tragic fall from power. It is freely adapted from the chronicle tradition of Arthur represented by Geoffrey of Monmouth's *Historia Regum Britanniae* and the *Roman de Brut* by Wace. The poem shows many of the best qualities of alliterative histories: swift narrative pace, vivid descriptive detail, and a brilliant evocation of the heroism of a golden age of chivalry. There is evidence to suggest that *Morte Arthure* was circulating in Lincolnshire in the early fifteenth century,[20] and the extant manuscript was copied in east Yorkshire in the mid-fifteenth century.

The vogue of alliterative poetry, therefore, became much more widespread from the end of the fourteenth century. It extended also northwards into Scotland, where the alliterative line was most frequently incorporated into a rhyming stanza of thirteen lines. This stanza-form originated south of the Border, in both alliterative and non-alliterative poetry. Alliterative examples from the late fourteenth century are *Summer Sunday*, probably from the west midlands, and *The Pistill of Susan* and *The Quatrefoil of Love*, both from south Yorkshire or thereabouts.[21] The stanza-form in these three poems is characterised by a ninth line of one stress. Written at about the same time was *The Awntyrs off Arthure*, a strange and interesting poem that describes two encounters that Gawain has, the first with the ghost of Queen Guenevere's mother, and the second with a Scottish knight who claims to have been dispossessed by Gawain. The poem is a northern work, and its action takes place at Carlisle and in the surrounding countryside. It has valuable points of contact both with the school of north-west midland poets and with later Scottish poets. There are strong suggestions that its author was influenced by *Morte Arthure* and also possibly by *Gawain*,[22] and it has metrical links with the Scottish poems in that the stanzaic pattern that it uses, which has a ninth line of full length, is the one adopted by poets writing in Scotland throughout the fifteenth century and indeed until late in the sixteenth century.

To judge from the rather limited evidence available, it would seem, therefore, that the development of the Alliterative Revival was as follows. Probably during the 1340's the Revival established itself in the south-west midlands, that part of the country where alliteration had previously flourished in both poetry and prose. By the 1350's alliterative poetry was also being composed in the more northerly parts of the west midlands, and from there it spread further north and east during the last years of the century, thriving in Scotland during the fifteenth century. In England the creative force of the movement was spent by the mid-fifteenth century if not before, but in Scotland the alliterative line became incorporated into rhyming stanzas, in which form it prospered until the later sixteenth century.

In many ways the Revival appears to have been a rather self-contained movement. Its influence is sometimes traceable in other writers from the northern half of the country, such as the author of *Sir Degrevant* who makes noticeable use of the characteristic alliterative vocabulary; and later on the playwrights of York and elsewhere used many of the techniques of alliterative verse. However, its contacts with the poetry of the metropolitan, Chaucerian tradition seem to have been very slight. Apart from Chaucer's 'rum, ram, ruf', and the possible mention in *The Destruction of Troy* of *Troilus and Criseyde*, the two schools seem to have ignored one another. There is no evidence that alliterative poets ever drew material from the Chaucerian school, and even though Chaucer could hardly have failed to know of *Piers Plowman*, he makes no overt reference to the poem, and if he owes any debts to it they are hard to discover.[23] While Chaucer certainly understood and exploited the power of heavy alliteration for scenes of violent action, it is difficult to be sure that this was a technique he learnt from alliterative poets, and quite impossible to demonstrate that he borrowed from any particular alliterative poem.[24] It is only a slight oversimplification to say that the two schools of poetry co-existed without contact. Yet it would be quite wrong to give the impression that the Alliterative Revival looked only inwards. Alliterative poetry shares the same preoccupations as verse of the Chaucerian tradition; both choose the same objects of satire and use the same descriptive techniques, both look constantly to France for models for their themes and motifs and for structural devices such as the dream-vision.[25] In short, the poetry of the west is as firmly rooted in fourteenth-century literary culture as that of the south, and the separateness of the two traditions is a mystery which not even the difficulties of comprehension between the two dialects can fully explain.

Listeners and Readers

The Wars of Alexander opens with a delightful description of a medieval audience listening after a meal to a tale about glorious events of the past:

When folk ere festid and fed, fayn wald þai here
Sum farand þing efter fode to fayn þare hert,
Or þai ware fourmed on fold or þaire fadirs oþer. (1–3)

[ere festid – *have been feasted*; farand – *fine*; to fayn – *to gladden*; Or…oþer – *(that took place) before they or their fathers were born*.]

The reciter lists the wide range of subjects that different audiences appreciate – saints' lives, love stories, tales of knights and conquerors, noble tales for the wise, foolish tales for the frivolous:

Sum is leue to lythe þe lesing of sayntis
Þat lete þer lifis be lorne for oure lordis sake,
And sum has langing of lufe lays to herken,
How ledis for þaire lemmans has langor endured.
Sum couettis and has comforth to carpe and to lestyn
Of curtaissy of kynȝthode, of craftis of armys,
Of kyngis at has conquirid and ouercomyn landis.
Sum of wirschip, iwis, slike as þam wyse lattis,
And sum of wanton werkis, þa þat ere wild-hedid;
Bot if þai wald on many wyse a wondire ware it els,
For as þaire wittis ere within so þer will folowis. (4–14)

[Sum…sayntis – *some take pleasure in listening to legends of saints*; lorne – *lost*; langing…herken – *a desire to hear lays of love*; ledis – *men*; lemmans – *sweethearts*; couettis – *desire*; carpe – *talk*; at – *that*; slike…lattis – *those who regard themselves as wise*; þa…wild-hedid – *those who are frivolous*; Bot…folowis – *it would be strange if they didn't have various preferences, because their inclinations follow their mental dispositions*.]

The speaker then announces his own subject to be Alexander the Great, and promises his audience a part of the tale if they will only remain quiet:

And I, forwith ȝow all, ettillis to schewe
Of ane emperoure þe aȝefullest þat euer armys hauntid,
Þat was þe athill Alexsandire, as þe buke tellis,
Þat aȝte euyn as his awyn all the werd ouire.
For he recouerd quills he regnyd þe regions all clene,
And all rialme and þe riches into þe rede est;
I sall rehers, and ȝe will, renkis, rekyn ȝour tongis,
A remnant of his rialte, and rist quen vs likis. (15–22)

[forwith – *before*; ettillis – *intend*; aȝefullest – *most formidable*; hauntid – *practised*; athill – *noble*; aȝte – *possessed*; werd – *world*; recouerd – *won*; quills – *while*; clene – *entirely*; rialme – *realm*; rehers – *relate*; and – *if*; renkis – *men*; rekyn – *control*; remnant – *part*; rist – *we shall pause*.]

This idealised setting is a commonplace of most romances and romantic chronicles.[26] By launching his poem with an address to the aristocratic audience sitting in a noble hall, with a request for silence for his story of 'old time', the author creates a romantic environment for his poem and an atmosphere of intimacy in which he himself is present among his listeners.

Because this type of opening is a convention which has a *literary* function, we should not place too much trust in it as a factual account of a performance of an alliterative poem. There is nothing to prevent us believing that authors themselves sometimes recited their poems to their audience, in the way that a manuscript illustration depicts Chaucer reading aloud *Troilus and Criseyde* to the court.[27] However, it would be unwarranted to regard the opening lines of *The Wars of Alexander* as firm evidence that the poem was composed to be read aloud by its author. The writer would in any case have been strongly tempted to begin with what had become a conventional way of introducing a poem of this sort, even if he had conceived his poem as a text for private reading rather than a tale for communal entertainment.

The convention is taken a stage further by the poet who wrote *Sir Gawain and the Green Knight*, that most intricately patterned of the romances. The author of *The Wars of Alexander* at least refers to a written source for his account ('as þe buke tellis'), but *Gawain* is set in an entirely oral context. The narrator is portrayed as an entertainer who has heard the story and, even though (as he goes on to say, ll. 33–6) the story exists in written form also, he is merely transmitting it as he heard it:

If ȝe wyl lysten þis laye bot on littel quile,
I schal telle hit as-tit, as I in toun herde,
    With tonge.

    (30–2)

[as-tit – *at once*; in toun – *in company*.]

In this case we can see more clearly the distinction that has to be drawn between the author and the 'narrator'. The author of the poem – the man who moulded the basic plot-elements into his brilliantly organised structure, and who wrote it down so that scribes could make copies of it – is obviously not giving a portrait of himself. What he is doing is creating a fictional *persona* of the 'narrator', of the court-entertainer who is so characteristic an inhabitant of the world of romance. Another alliterative romance, *William of Palerne*, stresses repeatedly the importance of the court-entertainers within this idealised world:

No tonge miȝt telle þe twentiþe parte
Of the mede to menstrales þat mene time was ȝeue
Of robes wiþ riche pane and oþer richesse grete.

    (5354–6)

[mede – *reward*; ȝeue – *given*; pane – *fur*.]

The 'narrator' in *Gawain* is therefore part of the fiction created by the poet. This device tells us something about the conventions of romance, but it cannot give us reliable information about the status of the author himself. Furthermore, if the 'narrator' is fictitious, then the nature of the 'audience' he is addressing may be equally so. For example, the 'narrator' of *Alisaunder of Macedoine* begins with this misleadingly precise description of his 'audience':

Yee þat lengen in londe, lordes and ooþer,
Beurnes or bachelers þat boldely thinken
Wheþer in werre or in wo wightly to dwell,
For to lachen hem loose in hur lifetime,
Or dere thinken to doo deedes of armes,
To be proued for pris, and prest of hemselue,
Tend yee tytely to mee and take goode heede. (1–7)

[lengen – *live*; Beurnes – *warriors*; bachelers – *young knights*; thinken – *intend*; wightly – *bravely*; lachen hem loose – *gain fame*; dere – *worthily*; proued for pris – *recognised as noble*; prest of hemselue – *well-prepared*; Tend yee tytely – *listen closely*.]

Whatever their *actual* social and physical positions, however decrepit or preoccupied with mundane affairs they may be, the listeners and readers (whether in the fourteenth century or the twentieth) are invited to imagine themselves for the occasion as a noble company sitting in some baronial hall, attending gravely to the reciter as he tells them of the martial deeds of the great conqueror. It stands to reason that the 'narrator' of such a poem addresses an 'audience' bent on martial prowess; if in reality they are gouty bailiffs – or even students of Middle English – it is not the duty of the poet to remind them of it. The 'audience' is created to match the poem, and this audience may be as fictional as the action of the poem itself.[28] A chronicle of war calls for an audience of warriors, whereas a political satire demands a less courtly setting. It is for this reason that the setting of *Wynnere and Wastoure* smacks more of the ale-house than the baronial court, as the narrator twice pauses for drinks. This is not because the author foresaw that when reciting his poem he would need to wet his whistle at these points and be unable to find the words to ask for refreshment, but it is because the convivial atmosphere is part of the world of the poem. And so there are actually two levels of fiction in this poem. One is the action of the dream-vision, and the second is the 'narrator' telling his 'audience' about it. There is not a rigid distinction between the two, since the narrator is active within his own dream, and moves easily from a position as participant to a position as storyteller. A drink in the dream-world spills over into the narrator-world:

The kynge waytted one wyde, and the wyne askes;
Beryns broghte it anone in bolles of siluere.
Me thoghte I sowpped so sadly it sowede bothe myn eghne.
And he þat wilnes of this werke to wete any forthire,
Full freschely and faste, for here a fitt endes. (213–17)

[waytted one wyde – *looked about him*; Beryns – *men*; bolles – *cups*; sadly – *heavily*; sowede – *bleared*; eghne – *eyes*; wilnes – *wishes*; wete – *know*; Full – *fill*.]

The conclusion we must draw is that the conventional author-to-audience opening provides no trustworthy evidence about either author or audience. Nor, since it may be an entirely fictional account, does it provide foundation for the popular assumption that poetry was always listened to rather than read in private. This is a widespread belief, particularly where alliterative poetry is concerned. It is probable enough that recitation, whether by a professional 'disour' or a member of the family, was one method of dissemination, although much of the evidence used to show that this was standard practice may be suspected of being idealisation of the same sort as I have been discussing.[29] The belief in the oral presentation of alliterative verse has been strengthened by the assumption that this poetry owes its continued existence to a long oral tradition. If the theory of oral tradition is rejected, there is no longer any reason to regard alliterative verse as especially fitted for oral presentation. Its inherent onomatopoeic qualities do not imply that it was intended for the ear alone. After all, rhyme is also a device that makes its appeal through the ear, but it is a very unsophisticated reader who needs to chant rhymed verse aloud to perceive its effects. It is probable that the ways in which the alliterative poems reached their public varied as widely as the types of poems themselves. If many were composed with the listener in mind, some of them openly address themselves to a reading public. Indeed, the author of *Richard the Redeless* goes so far as to hope the King himself will turn over the pages of his book:

> And if it happe to ȝoure honde, beholde þe book onys,
> And redeth on him redely rewis an hundrid,
> And if ȝe sauere sum-dell, se it forth ouere.

(Prologue, 53–5)

[happe to – *falls into*; rewis – *lines*; sauere … ouere – *enjoy some of it, read it through*.]

He hopes, too, that both young and old will pore over it:

> And þouȝ þat elde opyn it oþer while amonge,
> And poure on it preuyly, and preue it well after,
> And constrewe ich clause with þe culorum,
> It shulde not apeire hem a peere.

(Prologue, 70–3)

[þouȝ … amonge – *if the old man should open it now and then*; preue – *test*; culorum – *conclusion*; apeire … peere – *hurt them a bit*.]

On the whole, authors seem to have left the choice of recitation or private reading open to their public. It is apparent that many poems are organised in such a way that they *could* be read aloud if the opportunity arose, in several instalments if necessary.[30] The poems in the Cotton Nero manuscript are an example of this. *Patience* is a little over 500 lines long, and would not demand much of the virtue it commends from its listeners. *Gawain*, at 2530 lines, falls naturally into the four divisions marked by the scribe with especially large coloured capitals at lines 491, 1126 and 1998. A recitation extending over four evenings would pause at these moments of intense curiosity and expectation. *Pearl* has 1212 lines, though the lines are shorter than in the other poems. Since the stanzas are so closely interlocked by repetition of word and phrase, there seems no obvious place for a pause, except that, by design or accident, this linking fails approximately half-way through the poem, at line 721, after twelve groups of twelve-line stanzas. Large capitals divide the 1812 lines of *Purity* at line 557 and line 1157, and each section contains one of the 'three ways' in which the author shows the merits of purity. The author himself indicates the second of these pauses by turning to his audience to give them a foretaste of the lessons that are to come if he is only given the chance to relate them (ll. 1149–56). *Gawain* and *Purity*, and possibly *Pearl* as well, thus fall naturally into sections of roughly 600 lines, and each such section might take little more than half an hour to recite. Similar divisions occur in most other alliterative poems, and these would be for the ease of the reciter and the private reader alike. *The Wars of Alexander*, for example, is divided into *passus* averaging 200 lines, and at line 3467 the author marks a more substantial pause:

> Al be þe metire bot mene, þus mekill haue I ioyned,
> Forthi, lordis, be ȝour leue, list ȝow to suffire;
> Now will I tary for a time, and tempire my wittis;
> And he þat stiȝe to þe sternes stiȝtill vs in heuen!

(3464–7)

[Al – *although*; mene – *weak*; ioyned – *composed*; Forthi – *therefore*; list … suffire – *please put up with me*; stiȝe – *ascended*; sternes – *stars*; stiȝtill – *(may he) establish*.]

The 14,000 lines of *The Destruction of Troy* are conveniently divided into thirty-six books. If the massive work was ever read from cover to cover, it must have required a great many instalments, but it is more probable that it was intended principally as a work of reference. In its surviving manuscript the poem is provided with a list of contents, which would enable the reader to pick his way about, and although its chapters open and close with conventional addresses to the listeners, the nature and length of the poem suggest that it was not written for the ear at all.

The Nature of the Audience

We have seen that it would be unwise to place too much credence in the romanticised audience whom alliterative poets ostensibly address, and so we have to call on other evidence in order to establish the sort of person for whom the poems were intended. There is one early alliterative poem, *William of Palerne*, that is explicit about the milieu for which it was written, but we must hesitate to draw from this one, perhaps exceptional, example sweeping conclusions about alliterative poetry in general, for we must be prepared to find that the nature of the audience varied as widely as the themes, interests and styles of the poems themselves. Nevertheless, in that *William of Palerne* is the only poem to give us firm evidence about its audience, it is important to examine its position closely, and to avoid oversimplifying, and thereby misrepresenting the situation.

William of Palerne was translated from French at the request of Humphrey de Bohun, Earl of Hereford and Essex from 1336 to 1361.[31] The author of the poem, who announces that his own name is William, asks for prayers for his patron:

> Preiȝes for þat gode lord þat gart þis do make,
> Þe hende erl of Hereford, Humfray de Boune –
> Þe gode King Edwardes douȝter was his dere moder –
> He let make þis mater in þis maner speche
> For hem þat knowe no Frensche, ne neuer vnderston. (5529–33)

> [gart...make – *had this made*; hende – *worthy*; let make – *had made*; vnderston – *understand it.*]

In respect of his wealth, Humphrey was one of the greatest lords of his time, though he took no part in political life, and delegated his hereditary office of Constable of England to his younger brother on the grounds of infirmity. His estates, castles and manors extended right across the country, from the family residence at the castle of Pleshey in Essex, to a group of castles and marcher lordships in Wales. It is clear that all Humphrey's sympathies lay in the east rather than the west, for his life was centred on Pleshey (where he died) and London (where he was buried).[32] Nevertheless, the great Bohun lordships situated somewhat precariously in the Welsh marches, at Caldecot, Brecon, Hay and Huntingdon, needed some supervision, and Humphrey must have maintained a retinue of considerable size on his western estates, to which, together with his chief officials, he may have paid periodic visits.

Two adjoining manors a few miles to the south of Gloucester were maintained in some style, and may have been staging posts on the journey to Wales. At one of them, Wheatenhurst (now Whitminster), Humphrey had obtained licence to crenellate the manor-house, and at the other, Haresfield, there was a private chapel built in 1318, and there was probably also a deer-park, where the lord and his guests could hunt.

There is, therefore, a strong likelihood that *William of Palerne*, which seems to have been composed in the dialect of Gloucestershire, and which mentions the town of Gloucester, was intended for the entertainment of those established at Wheatenhurst and Haresfield. It was not, and this the poet makes clear, intended for the ears of the Earl himself, but 'for hem þat knowe no Frensche, ne neuer vnderston'. Humphrey, residing far from the centres in which alliterative poetry was at that time being composed, and brought up (almost certainly) on verse in French, would have made little of this Gloucestershire poem. He may have had a number of motives for commanding William the poet to translate the French *Guillaume de Palerne* for a western audience. Perhaps one purpose was simply to assure them of the benevolent interest of their absent overlord. Perhaps, also, Humphrey was prompted by educational motives, and regarded the poem as an instructive guide to the virtues of 'gentilesse' and 'cortaysie', virtues which he may have found sadly lacking among his Gloucestershire dependents. On one level, certainly, the poem is a text-book of 'cortaysie'. Even a cowherd can offer his foster-son – the hero – good advice on courtly behaviour:

> Whanne þou komest to kourt, among þe kete lordes,
> And knowest alle þe kuþþes þat to kourt langes,
> Bere þe boxumly and bonure, þat ich burn þe loue.
> Be meke and mesurabul, nouȝt of many wordes,
> Be no tellere of talis, but trewe to þi lord,
> And prestely for pore men profer þe euer.

(330–5)

[kete – *distinguished*; kuþþes – *manners*; langes – *pertain*; Bere…bonure – *behave courteously and affably*; burn – *man*; mesurabul – *moderate*; prestely – *quickly*.]

The poem gives a detailed, though romanticised, impression of court life, and much of the last section is taken up with elaborate ceremonial, weddings and coronations. Humphrey could not have chosen a better work to polish the rough diamonds of Gloucestershire.

That this was in fact Humphrey's purpose in commissioning the translation can be no more than speculation. The more important point is that *William of Palerne* was not composed for the instruction and delight of the Earl himself, and in this respect Humphrey's patronage of the alliterative poem is not strictly comparable to the commissioning by later members of the Bohun family of the exquisite Bohun psalters, so delicately illuminated, which were obviously for the personal use of the family.[33] It may be concluded, therefore, that the example of *William of Palerne* does *not*, as is usually assumed, show that the audience for alliterative poetry was in general an aristocratic one; on the contrary, it shows that this early alliterative poem was addressed to an audience humbler and less sophisticated than the higher nobility. Humphrey's personal interest, we must suppose, was in the French original and not in the English translation. And so to argue from the case of *William of Palerne* that 'our picture of this fourteenth-century literary "revival" cannot be completed without more intensive study of the households of the great magnates whose estates lay in the west and north of England'[34] is to direct the search on altogether the wrong scent.

The conviction of critics that the poems of the Revival were composed to entertain the higher nobility at their courts in the west midlands fitted comfortably with the belief in the continuous oral tradition of alliterative poetry, since it could be maintained that it was only the patronage of the nobility in remote western castles that preserved the ancient tradition over so many generations of court *scops*. But a glance at the lives and tastes of some of Humphrey's contemporaries, the Duke of Lancaster, the Earl of Warwick, the Earl of March, all powerful magnates of the west in the middle of the fourteenth century, and all mentioned by critics as possible patrons of the early Revival, confirms that it is not to them, or to men like them, that we should go for information about alliterative verse. First of all, even though the spoken language of the nobility may by this time have been English, their interests still lay in literature written in French. Henry, Duke of Lancaster was born at Grosmont Castle Monmouthshire, and he possessed vast estates in the west and north, which at his death in Leicester in 1361 were to pass to John of Gaunt. Henry tells us that his first language was English, and he felt his French was a little rusty;[35] nevertheless, in 1354, at the same time as *Wynnere and Wastoure* and *William of Palerne* were composed, Henry wrote his *Livre de Seyntz Medicines* for his own circle of friends in French. A magnificent manuscript of it was given by Lord Carew to Humphrey Duke of Gloucester, the great-grandson of the author of the work. In their literary interests the great lords were conservative, and as late as the end of the fourteenth century their wills and the inventories of their books reveal that they maintained their adherence to literature in French. It is significant that the books bequeathed in 1399 by Eleanor de Bohun, the great-niece of the patron of *William of Palerne*, are all in French or Latin. The list begins with 'a Chronicle of France, in French, with two silver clasps, enamelled with the arms of the Duke of Bourgogne', and continues with a verse 'History of the Swan Knight'.[36] Eleanor's sister Mary possessed an early fourteenth-century manuscript of *Lancelot du Lac* with handsome illuminations. The manuscript is preserved in the British Museum.[37]

Even if they had not confined their interests to French verse, it is unlikely that the great lords would have shown much appreciation for English verse written in regions dialectically and geographically remote from the metropolis, for their preoccupations were national rather than local. At this date their attention was directed towards the centre of government. Furthermore, their western estates, like those of the Bohuns, were only a part of their possessions,[38] and even though their ancestors had sometimes identified themselves with the west, under Edward III most of the nobles were totally taken up with the King's chivalric wars and with the court in London. The Beauchamps, Earls of Warwick, are a classic example of this. During the thirteenth and earlier fourteenth centuries they had been much involved with Warwickshire and Worcestershire, where they maintained the base of their power, even though they held land in six other counties. Guy Beauchamp lived and died at his castle in Warwick, where in 1312 he imprisoned Edward II's hated favourite, Gaveston; he founded a college of priests at Elmley in Worcestershire, gave his collection of books in French and Latin (but none, of course, in English) to Bordesley Abbey, Worcestershire, in 1305, and was buried there in 1315.[39] But the life of his son, Thomas Beauchamp, was devoted to the wars against the Scots and the French, and almost every year sees him campaigning in the north or in France. In 1348 he was one of the founder Knights of the Garter, and he died in 1369 in Calais, from where his body was brought home to be buried in Warwick with his ancestors.[40] Roger Mortimer, Earl of March, one of the wealthiest nobles under Edward III, also spent a great deal of his time fighting in France, and he too died there. He was knighted at Crécy, and was with the King in Picardy in 1355 and again in 1359. His obsequies were performed, fittingly, in the royal chapel at Windsor in 1360, and his body was buried at Wigmore where his family had their castle.[41] These are not the men to have inspired the Alliterative Revival, to have enjoyed poetry written in obscure western dialects, and to have delighted in translations of works which they would have understood rather better in the original language.[42]

Nor do the manuscripts in which alliterative poetry is preserved give support to the belief that the poems ever found a home in aristocratic households. A good picture of the sort of manuscripts owned by the very rich is given by the inventory of the eighty-four 'livres de diverses rymances et estories' in the library of Thomas Duke of Gloucester at his death in 1397.[43] The only English volumes are a Bible, a book of the Gospels, and a 'new book of the Gospels glossed in English'. Among the more expensive items are 'un large livre en Fraunceis, tresbien esluminez, de la Rymance de Alexandre', priced at sixteen shillings and eight pence, 'un large livre en fraunceis appellez le Romance de Launcelot, pris xiii s iiii d', and a large volume of Godefroy of Bouillon with enamelled clasps of silver at thirteen shillings and four-pence.

English works began to find their way into de-luxe manuscripts at the very end of the fourteenth century, and then increasingly during the fifteenth century, when Chaucer and Gower became popular in aristocratic and courtly circles. When John of Trevisa, towards the end of the fourteenth century, translated works from Latin into English at the request of Lord Berkeley, he (or was it, in reality, his patron?) felt it necessary to justify such translations for educated men, and the *Dialogue between a Lord and a Clerk*, where the subject is discussed, makes amusing and instructive reading.[44] In the early fifteenth century Trevisa's translations were copied out in two de-luxe manuscripts, one of which was made for Richard Earl of Warwick, son-in-law of the last Lord Berkeley.[45] By contrast, alliterative poetry was always copied into unpretentious, workmanlike and unadorned manuscripts, and this is true even in the fifteenth century (to which period most of the texts of alliterative verse belong) at a time when some other styles of English composition were finding favour with an aristocratic audience.

In fact the only alliterative poem to have been preserved in a de-luxe manuscript found its way there as a result of a curious misunderstanding. It is a sad irony that, of all the magnificent poems of the Revival, it was the incompetent and tedious *Alexander and Dindimus* alone on which both scribe and illuminator lavished their professional attention. It came about in this way. In 1338 a scribe working probably in an *atelier* in northern France finished copying the *Romans d'Alixandre*, and passed it on to the illuminators, one of whom, Jehan de Gris, finished his beautiful work in 1344. However, there remained one or two blank spaces which had been left in the manuscript by the scribe. The manuscript later came to England, where a fifteenth-century scribe noticed one of the gaps, at the bottom of the second column on folio 67, and mistakenly concluded that here was an omission in the text which, by good fortune, he could remedy. He therefore transcribed with great elegance 1139 lines of an alliterative poem based on an entirely different version of the Alexander story. This he had handsomely illuminated with nine miniatures, and appended it to the French romance. In the gap on folio 67 he wrote: 'Here fayleth a prossesse of þis rommance of Alixander, þe wheche prossesse þat fayleth ȝe schulle fynde at þe ende of þis bok y-wrete in Engelyche ryme; and whanne ȝe han radde it to þe ende, turneþ hedur aȝen'. This manuscript, now MS. Bodley 264, was in 1466 in the possession of Lord Rivers in London.[46] Was he, by this strange chance, the only nobleman to own an alliterative poem?

More typical manuscripts of the mid-fifteenth century containing alliterative poetry are the two that were compiled in 1430–40 by Robert Thornton, a country gentleman of East Newton near Pickering in Yorkshire. These two manuscripts (B.M. Additional MS. 31042, and Lincoln Cathedral Library MS. 91) are large miscellanies, assembling works of diverse origins for the instruction and amusement of the Thornton household. As well as much else, they preserve a large number of alliterative poems: *Morte Arthure, The Awntyrs off Arthure, St. John the Evangelist, The Siege of Jerusalem, The Quatrefoil of Love, The Parlement of the Thre Ages* and *Wynnere and Wastoure*. There is no discernible order in the contents of these two large volumes; romances jostle with works of religious instruction, with verses by Lydgate and with texts of more practical application such as the *Liber de Diversis Medicinis*, which gives remedies for every conceivable malady, including one 'for to do away frekles' and another 'to mak maydyns pappis harde'. It seems that Robert Thornton took out his pen whenever he came across anything that interested him, and in this sense the manuscripts may be described as anthologies for the use of the family.[47]

The Thornton manuscripts show that one sort of reader who was interested in alliterative poetry in the mid-fifteenth century was the educated, well-to-do country gentleman, in particular (but not exclusively) those living in the northern half of the country. These two anthologies are pretty typical in character and scope of the manuscripts in which alliterative poems appear at this date. We may test this by taking one of the poems in a Thornton manuscript and examining the other copies of it. There are six more fifteenth-century copies of *The Siege of Jerusalem*. Apart from that in the Thornton manuscript, three others are also included in household anthologies: one of these (Cotton Caligula A.ii) is a collection of romances, several of which are rather moralistic in tone, while two (Huntington HM 128 and Lambeth Palace 491) are more varied collections, which include texts such as *How the Good Wife Taught her Daughter* and a manual of hunting. Two manuscripts are certainly for church use: Laud Misc. 656, which also contains *Piers Plowman*, a sermon and maxims from the Bible, and Cotton Vespasian E. xvi, which includes ecclesiastical charters and a chronicle. Another manuscript (Camb. Univ. Mm. v.14) consists entirely of historical chronicles – Guido's *Historia Destructionis Troiae* and the Alexander legend *Historia de Preliis*. This too was probably a reference work for church use, though an educated household might have treasured it equally. The conclusion to be drawn from the character of these various manuscripts is that, in the fifteenth century at least, the readership of *The Siege of Jerusalem* consisted of affluent land-owners and also the clergy.

The few fourteenth-century manuscripts of alliterative poetry still in existence give no grounds for believing that alliterative verse had descended the social scale by the fifteenth century. During the fourteenth century, also, the owners of the manuscripts were not the super-rich, but those who had the education and leisure to assemble the manuscripts themselves, or alternatively could afford to pay for a text to be copied out very simply and without ornamentation. The earliest of them all, MS. Kings College, Cambridge, 13, which dates from about 1360–75, is a good example of this. It is in two parts, the first containing *William of Palerne* and the second, which is copied by a different hand, a number of saints' lives.

The stanzaic-alliterative poem *The Pistill of Susan*, which retells the story of Susannah and the Elders, appears towards the end of the fourteenth century in two huge religious miscellanies which are closely related to one another.[48] These are the Vernon and Simeon manuscripts, both produced before 1400 in the same scriptorium. There is evidence to suggest that this scriptorium was at the Cistercian abbey situated in northern Worcestershire, at Bordesley, which I have already mentioned as the repository of the Earl of Warwick's books in 1305. It is likely enough that these two texts of *The Pistill of Susan* were intended for the entertainment and instruction of Cistercian monks at Bordesley and elsewhere.

There is one fourteenth-century manuscript, however, which stands apart from all the other manuscripts of alliterative poetry. This is MS. Cotton Nero A.x., containing *Pearl*, *Purity*, *Patience* and *Gawain*. These four poems are its only contents. It is unusual among manuscripts of English poetry of this date in that it is illuminated. Each poem is accompanied by a number of illustrations, all except one occupying a full page. The quality of these is dreadful, and they have been described – with pardonable exaggeration – as 'infantile daubs'.[49] In all there are twelve of these paintings, representing, sometimes inaccurately, the events of the poems. The script is fairly clear and careful, but it is not the formal hand reserved for expensive manuscripts. An interesting hypothesis that has been put forward to account for this strange manuscript is that it is a copy of an original de-luxe manuscript from a nobleman's household.[50] This theory is used to explain the painter's apparent awareness (however imperfectly realised) of some of the contemporary developments in representing scenery and architecture. However, it is difficult to believe that even an incompetent artist would reveal such an imperfect grasp of the principles of composition and arrangement if he was actually copying pictures from a de-luxe manuscript. The dim recollections of contemporary styles, as well as the failure at times to match the illuminations to the descriptions in the poems (the picture of the New Jerusalem bears no resemblance to the detailed account in *Pearl*, and the Green Knight is not even green) may be more satisfactorily explained by supposing that the artist had seen richly decorated psalters, Books of Hours and other fine manuscripts, perhaps in an abbey library, and was doing his humble – very humble – best to imitate the style.

The question remains of who would have caused such a volume to be produced. Certainly no nobleman would have given it house-room beside his professionally illuminated de-luxe manuscripts. Once again, therefore, we are forced to look lower down the social scale, and once again the country gentleman, interested in the writings of this English poet, with leisure to read, able to afford a manuscript but unable to afford a very good one, suggests himself. Perhaps, for it is a common failing, he wished to be thought rather better than he was, and envied the rich with their finely illuminated volumes. The illustrations, apparently painted after the manuscript was sewn together,[51] display such amateurishness that it is not unlikely that the artist was a member of the family playing with paints.

There are many features that distinguish *Piers Plowman* from the other works I have been dealing with, and these raise the possibility that Langland's readership was radically different. It seems clear that Langland set out to attract a *wider* readership than that enjoyed by other alliterative poets. To this end he modified the alliterative line, writing in a less tightly controlled style and avoiding the vocabulary restricted to alliterative poetry. He was certainly successful in his attempt, since *Piers Plowman* survives in over fifty manuscripts.

One class of readers of *Piers Plowman* attested in the fourteenth century is the clergy.[52] In his will in 1396, Walter de Bruge, who was a canon of York Minster, bequeathed a copy of the poem, and earlier still John Ball, the priest who led the Peasants' Revolt in 1381, had at least some knowledge of the poem (though this is not to suggest that he expected his peasant followers to know it). I have already described one of the earliest manuscripts containing the poem, the Vernon manuscript, which is of clerical origin, and many of the fifteenth-century manuscripts of *Piers Plowman* were evidently owned by the clergy, such as the manuscript in the Library of the Society of Antiquaries (no. 687) which contains religious treatises and instructions to the clergy. However, it was not only the clergy who took an interest in Langland's poem, at any rate by the fifteenth century. For example, a copy was owned by a member of Lincoln's Inn, as is shown by an inventory of his books taken in 1459, another belonged to Sir Thomas Charleton, Speaker of the House of Commons, who died in 1465,[53] and the accompanying contents of several other manuscripts suggest a secular readership.

It will be seen, therefore, that the difference between the audience of *Piers Plowman* and that of other alliterative poems is not the clear-cut distinction that has often been posited. By the fifteenth century, in fact, the same man might be reading *Piers Plowman* as well as other alliterative poems. Indeed, in several manuscripts Langland's poem appears in company with other alliterative works: twice with *The Siege of Jerusalem*, twice with *The Pistill of Susan*, once with *The Wars of Alexander*. However, *Piers Plowman* seems always to have had a greater preponderance of clerical readers.

The difference in the readership of *Piers Plowman* is less one of social class than of geographical distribution, at least in the fourteenth century. Langland's poem was designed to be understood by a far-flung audience, centred particularly on London and the midlands. Most other alliterative poems are composed with a more localised audience in mind, though later manuscripts often show that their readership had expanded far outside the west midlands.

We have therefore seen that the evidence of the manuscripts of alliterative poems suggests that the poems were owned and read not by the higher nobility, but rather by those below them. We must be prepared to include here a wide range of social classes with different interests. *Piers Plowman* had a particular interest for the thoughtful cleric. *Pierce the Ploughman's Crede* praises Wycliffe and one of his more eccentric followers, the Welshman Walter Brute, and the poem would only have appealed to those with strong Lollard sympathies, from the gentry downwards. Fifty years earlier *Wynnere and Wastoure* addressed those concerned about the political and social welfare of the country, and *Morte Arthure* may also have appealed to those with enough interest in national affairs to draw general comparisons between the campaigns of Arthur and the wars of Edward III.[54] *Sir Gawain and the Green Knight* and *The Parlement of the Thre Ages* presume in their audience a knowledge of and a fascination for the details of courtly life: the rituals of feasting and hunting, the armour and the architecture, and the scale of courtly values. It is likely that the wide-ranging audience for alliterative verse included the gentry (such as Robert Thornton), knights, franklins and the clergy, the educated men often with positions of local authority. Many of them might have served the great lords in their retinues, and attended upon them in their castles and on their estates, and thus have had a good understanding of the practices of courtly life. We have to go outside the alliterative tradition, to Chaucer's Franklin, for the most intimate portrait of the kind of man we may imagine would have enjoyed many of the poems of the Revival: a country gentleman with a substantial estate, an Epicurean, and a man who also carried out duties of local, and even national, administration (*General Prologue*, 339–60), a man with a high regard for 'gentilesse' and an admiration for the truly refined (*Franklin's Words to the Squire*).[55] All the evidence goes to show that it is men such as Chaucer's Franklin rather than members of the higher nobility whom we should envisage as the audience of alliterative poetry.

Chapter 3

METRE

Varieties of the Alliterative Style

The most strikingly distinctive features of alliterative verse will be the subjects of this and the following chapter: metre and diction. So characteristic are the metrical form of alliterative poetry and the vocabulary it employs that a reader of today, attempting to understand a poetic tradition so different from any other that he knows, may be forgiven for thinking that the alliterative style is a more or less homogeneous one. It is easy to fall into the error of believing that the style is suitable for descriptions of storms, battles and violent activity, but not fitted for much else. It is true, of course, that the vigour of the alliterative line as used in *Patience* splendidly conveys the violence of the storm at sea that tosses Jonah in the boat as he tries in vain to flee from the face of God:

> Þe bur ber to hit baft, þat braste alle her gere,
> Þen hurled on a hepe þe helme and þe sterne,
> Furst to-murte mony rop and þe mast after,
> Þe sayl sweyed on þe see, þenne suppe bihoued
> Þe coge of þe colde water, and þenne þe cry ryses.
> Ʒet coruen þay þe cordes and kest al þer-oute,
> Mony ladde þer forth lep to laue and to kest,
> Scopen out þe scaþel water þat fayn scape wolde.   (148–55)

> [Þe bur...baft – *the storm struck the ship's stern*; braste–*broke*; to-murte – *snapped*; sweyed – *fell*; suppe – *drink*; coge – *boat*; coruen – *cut*; laue – *bale out*; to kest – *to unload*; Scopen...wolde – *all who dearly wanted to escape scooped out the dangerous water*.]

In this breathtaking *tour-de-force* all the rhythmical and auditory resources are directed towards the description of the boat buffeted and reeling in the waves and wind.

However, the belief that alliterative poetry is all noise and bombast is very far from the truth. Today, because we are more used to types of verse that employ alliteration only as an occasional device for special effects, we are apt to overemphasise its auditory qualities in alliterative verse. It takes some adjustment in our approach for us to appreciate alliteration as a regular metrical feature. To an ear attuned to the alliterative style, however, alliteration need be no more obtrusive than end-rhyme in rhyming couplets. Once we have accepted this principle, we may more easily grasp why the alliterative line is such an excellent medium for narrative, and why it became so popular in an age when the demand for verse-narrative in English was greater than ever before. The most remarkable quality of the alliterative line is its capacity to accommodate a vast range of expression. At one extreme it can convey the turbulence of the storm at sea, at the other it captures the atmosphere of stealth as the poacher waits, silent and unobtrusive, for the chance to shoot down the stag:

> I waitted wiesly the wynde by waggynge of leues,
> Stalkede full stilly no stikkes to breke,
> And crepite to a crabtre and couerede me ther-vndere.
> Then I bende vp my bowe and bownede me to schote,
> Tighte vp my tylere and taysede at the hert.
> Bot the sowre þat hym sewet sett vp the nese,
> And wayttede wittyly abowte and wyndide full ʒerne.
> Then I moste stonde als I stode and stirre no fote ferrere,
> For had I myntid or mouede or made any synys,
> Alle my layke hade bene loste þat I hade longe wayttede;
> Bot gnattes gretely me greuede and gnewen myn eghne.
> And he stotayde and stelkett and starede full brode,
> Bot at the laste he loutted doun and laughte till his mete;
> And I hallede to the hokes and the hert smote.

(Parlement of the Thre Ages, 40–53)

[waitted – *watched*; wiesly – *carefully*; bownede me – *prepared myself*; Tighte – *tightened*; tylere – *crossbow*; taysede – *aimed*; the sowre...nese – *the young deer that accompanied him took scent*; wayttede – *looked*; wittyly – *cautiously*; wyndide – *sniffed*; ʒerne – *carefully*; myntid – *aimed*; layke – *sport*; gnewen – *chewed*; eghne – *eyes*; stotayde – *stopped*; stelkett – *moved forward*; full brode – *all around*; loutted – *bent*; laughte...mete – *took his food*; hallede to – *released*; hokes – *catches (of the crossbow).*]

The poacher's frozen immobility is most tellingly depicted. The deer look round uneasily, while the gnats mercilessly pester the man as he waits silently under the crabtree.

Alliterative poetry, then, excels at narrative description, but it is capable also of encompassing the syntax, the colloquialisms and the pace of conversation. Its power to do this lies in its flexibility. Of all the metrical forms available to fourteenth-century poets, the alliterative line is, from the point of view of its rhythm, the least constricting, in that it allows more freedom than any other to the natural movement of the language. Many passages of discussion and argument from *Piers Plowman* might illustrate this, because the dream-characters, even though they may be allegorical personifications, speak with the passion and vigour of everyday life. Dame Study, though she may be more at home in the world of books, condemns her husband in a most forthright manner for casting the pearls of his wisdom before the Dreamer:

> And seyde, '*noli mittere*, man, margerye-perlis
> Amanges hogges that han hawes at wille.
> Thei don but dryuele ther-on, draffe were hem leuere
> Than al the precious perre that in paradys wexeth.
> I sey it bi suche', quod she, 'that sheweth bi her werkes
> That hem were leuer londe and lordship on erthe,
> Or ricchesse or rentis, and reste at her wille,
> Than alle the sothe sawes that Salamon seyde euere.
> Wisdome and witte now is nouʒt worth a carse,
> But if it be carded with coueytise as clotheres kemben here wolle.'

(x. 9–18)

[noli mittere – *don't cast*; hawes at wille – *plenty of haws*; Thei...leuere – *they merely slobber over them, and would rather have swill*; perre – *jewels*; carse – *cress (i.e. anything)*; But...coueytise – *unless it is enhanced with avarice*; kemben – *comb*.]

In the scathing speech of Dame Study, the swine of biblical parable take on new life as dribbling farmyard hogs. Langland is rightly praised for his closeness to the everyday world, but it is not so often recognised that this is in part a *metrical* achievement.

It is little wonder that writers of the middle of the fourteenth century were quick to seize upon the potential of the alliterative line for extended narrative. Other popular verse-forms, such as the tail-rhyme stanza which was much used for certain types of romance, had their own strengths which could be brought out by the rare poet who was in full command of his metre. But even at its best the tail-rhyme stanza lacks the suppleness of the alliterative line and, however capably handled, always has a dreadful tendency towards triteness, which Chaucer mercilessly parodies in *Sir Thopas*. The difficulty is that the form is too constricting in length, rhythm and rhyme-scheme to be used effectively over hundreds of lines, and the range of expression it can convey is woefully limited. It is sometimes maintained that a stanza-form of this sort is best suited to the expression of emotion.[1] Yet the emotion of Dame Study comes across far more powerfully than the perfunctory expressions of love between the fairy Triamour and Sir Launfal in a typical example of the tail-rhyme stanza:

> Sche seyde, 'Launfal, my lemman swete,
> Al my joye for þe y lete,
>   Swetyng paramour!
> Þer nys noman yn Cristenté
> Þat y loue so moche as þe,
>   Kyng neyþer emperour!'
> Launfal beheld þat swete wyȝth
> (All hys loue yn her was lyȝth)
>   And keste þat swete flour,
> And sat adoun her bysyde,
> And seyde, 'Swetyng, whatso betyde
>   I am to þyn honour!'[2]

It is the flexibility of the alliterative line that makes it so valuable to a writer of a long and diverse narrative poem full of action, description, argument, reflection and any number of topics demanding variations of pace and emphasis. In *Morte Arthure* and *The Wars of Alexander* the form proves suitable for the excitement and turmoil of the careers of those two great heroes; in *Piers Plowman* and *Wynnere and Wastoure* it can accommodate the niceties of theological discussion and political debate; in *Patience* and *Purity* it can revivify Old Testament history. Nothing is more mistaken than the belief that the alliterative style is a homogeneous one.

I have so far discussed the varieties of style as a matter that depends upon the poet's aims and his topics. The techniques of a writer describing a storm at sea will inevitably be different from one giving an account of an angry woman's tirade. However, there are other factors which may account for stylistic differences from poet to poet. An early and influential critic postulated that the alliterative line was progressively regularised as the Revival developed.[3] However, if indeed it is possible to make any such generalisations, the following chronological progression might tentatively be proposed. The very earliest poems were marked by great metrical irregularity, because the techniques of the new style had not yet become established. In works written a few years later, the authors went to the other extreme, maintaining a rigid conformity to a few metrical patterns. Once again this was an indication of the writers' uncertainty about how to handle their metre. Only with the growth to maturity of the alliterative line did poets write with a due regard both to the potential flexibility of the form and to the limits beyond which it could not be stretched. These three stages would be represented by *Joseph of Arimathie*, which I have suggested was composed before the rhythms of alliterative verse had been regularised, *Alexander and Dindimus*, which is monotonously regular, and in the third stage *Gawain* and *Piers Plowman*.[4] If metrical patterns were used in this way for dating alliterative poems (which would, in the absence of other evidence, be a hazardous process, since allowance must be made for the preferences and abilities of individual poets), the chronology I have outlined would mark *The Destruction of Troy*, with its extreme regularity, as a work from the second stage of development. This would conflict with the general view that it is a late work, possibly even as late as the mid-fifteenth century. But there are other tenuous indications that it may be early,[5] and it is a possibility worth considering.

There are also striking dissimilarities in style between the poetry of the north midlands and that of the south midlands, which are illustrated by the quotations from *Patience* and *Piers Plowman* above. The southern poets are more prone to compose lines that do not fully accord with the stricter metrical practices of the northern poets. Also they make much less use of the rich alliterative vocabulary so characteristic of the writers of the north. The differences between the poems of the two dialect groups are already present in the 1350's and a comparison of the metre of *Wynnere and Wastoure* which is very regular, and *William of Palerne* which is comparatively irregular, would reveal something of these variations. However, it is later in the century that the two groups diverge more markedly. In the north the *Gawain*-poet exhibits a richness of vocabulary and an emphasis upon metrical skill which, although unequalled anywhere else, is characteristic of other northern poets, such as the author of *The Wars of Alexander*. In the south Langland had a decisive influence on other poets of that area in his modifications of the alliterative style. Langland shuns the verbal exuberance of the northern poets, composing verse that in both language and rhythm tends towards conversation and argument. It is perhaps helpful to talk of the 'high style' of the north and the 'plain style' of Langland and his disciples, though it has to be emphasised that this is a question of a different *sort* of poetry, and not a register of comparative literary excellence.

These differences that exist between the styles of various alliterative poets, differences to be explored in more detail presently, should not disguise the fact that the same underlying principles characterise the work of every alliterative poet. The stylistic differences are variations upon a basic metrical pattern, and it is this pattern that must first be analysed if we are to understand how the poets can achieve such powerful and diverse effects. Beginning with a study of the underlying metrical principles, I shall examine the techniques of the un-rhymed alliterative line as used by the author of *Sir Gawain and the Green Knight*, who develops the potentialities of this line further and more successfully than any other poet, and who best illustrates the effects that could be created within this highly flexible verse-form. How his techniques differ from those of Langland will be discussed subsequently, and finally the use in *Gawain* of a rhymed section, the 'bob and wheel', will be related to the practices of poets writing in rhymed alliterative stanzas.

The Metre of Gawain

The basic principles of the alliterative line as used in *Sir Gawain and the Green Knight* are as follows. Each line may be analysed as two half-lines, which are generally separated by a syntactic pause. Each half-line contains two syllables that bear stress and a variable number of unaccented syllables. The term 'lift' is sometimes used of the former, while 'dip' denotes a group of unaccented syllables. The two halves of the line are bound together by alliteration, which most commonly falls on both stressed syllables of the first half-line and on the first stress in the second half-line:

Bi a moúnte on þe mórne   méryly he rýdes   (740)

Such an alliterative pattern may conveniently be designated as aa/ax. The alliteration, it must be remembered, is not primarily decorative but structural. It has two metrical functions: it links the two halves of the line and it gives prominence to the stressed syllables. Since it lacks alliteration, the last of the four stresses of the line is the least prominent.

The alliteration may be of initial consonants, of consonant groups such as *sk*, *sp*, *st*, or of vowels. Any initial vowel may alliterate with any other, or with *h*:

Hit watz Énnias þe áthel,   and his híghe kýnde   (5)

Despite many variations, these principles underlie the metre of every unrhymed alliterative poem.[6]

The flexibility of the half-line is principally a result of the many possible arrangements of the two accented syllables among a variable number of unstressed syllables. However, in order to analyse the rhythms of the alliterative line it is first necessary to dispose of a question which also affects an understanding of Chaucer's rhythms, the question of whether -e at the end of a word was pronounced as a separate syllable or not.[7] The gradual reduction of what was in most cases originally an inflectional ending took place at different speeds in different parts of the country. In the north final -e was no longer pronounced by the end of the thirteenth century, in the midlands by the mid-fourteenth century, and in the south by the end of that century.[8] However, poetic language tends to be more conservative than the spoken language, and it is generally accepted that the metrical considerations of the Chaucerian line might demand the retention of final -e in certain positions. In the more northerly language of the alliterative poems there seem to be no overriding metrical considerations that would demand the retention of final -e in verse when it had long disappeared from the spoken language. Some readers, while accepting that it was not pronounced within the line, argue that the *Gawain* poet's preference for 'feminine' endings suggests that it was pronounced at the end of the line, but since it is clear that the poet was ready to accept lines ending on a stressed syllable, this argument does not hold. Actually this last point is not a matter of much metrical importance, since it does not affect the rhythmic patterns within the line.

On the assumption that final -e was not pronounced within the line, we may say that the most characteristic rhythm in *Gawain* consists of a disyllabic interval between the stresses.[9] Thus, 'bi a mounte on þe morne' has the stress-pattern XX′XX′. The interval may be longer than that: 'meryly he rydes' (′XXX′X); or longer still: 'Bot styʒtel þe vpon on strok' (X′XXXXX′). On the other hand there need be no interval at all between stresses: 'þat on þat self nyʒt' (XXX′′). This is often referred to as 'clashing' stress. More often than not the regular alternation of stressed and unstressed syllables is avoided, for fear of setting up an alien rhythmic pattern, but it certainly occurs sporadically (e.g. 'for grem þat fallez').[10] There are differences in the distribution of the stress-patterns between first and second half-lines. The first half-line is normally longer than the second, and so it tends to favour the fuller rhythmic patterns.

Because the fourteenth-century alliterative line has been regarded as the direct descendant of the Old English line, it has been customary to analyse the rhythms of *Gawain* in terms developed to describe *Beowulf*. This has obscured a fact as remarkable as it is obvious, which is that the rhythmic structure of the two types of alliterative verse is entirely dissimilar. The essential factor that they have in common is that they both use alliteration rather than rhyme as their organising principle.

The way in which the author of *Gawain* handles the rhythm and alliteration, and to what effects, may be illustrated by a straightforward passage of narrative description.[11] Gawain is riding on his horse Gringolet through the forest in search of the Green Knight. The weather is miserably cold, and it is Christmas Eve:

> Bi a mounte on þe morne meryly he rydes
> Into a forest ful dep, þat ferly watz wylde,
> Hiȝe hillez on vche a halue, and holtwodez vnder
> Of hore okez ful hoge a hundreth togeder;
> Þe hasel and þe haȝþorne were harled al samen,
> With roȝe raged mosse rayled aywhere,
> With mony bryddez vnblyþe vpon bare twyges,
> Þat pitosly þer piped for pyne of þe colde.
> Þe gome vpon Gryngolet glydez hem vnder,
> Þurȝ mony misy and myre, mon al hym one,
> Carande for his costes, lest he ne keuer schulde
> To se þe seruyse of þat syre, þat on þat self nyȝt
> Of a burde watz borne oure baret to quelle.   (740–52)

[mounte – *hill*; ferly – *very much*; halue – *side*; holtwodez – *woods*; hoge – *huge*; haȝþorne – *hawthorn*; harled al samen – *tangled together*; roȝe...aywhere – *rough shaggy moss growing everywhere*; vnblyþe – *unhappy*; pyne – *torment*; gome – *man*; misy – *swamp*; myre – *bog*; al hym one – *all alone*; Carande...costes – *anxious about his plight*; keuer – *manage*; To se...quelle – *to attend the Mass of the Lord who on that very night was born of a maiden to end our strife*.]

In these lines we follow Gawain's solitary progress through the forest, past the oaks, through the tangled hazel and hawthorn trees on whose branches sit birds tormented by the cold. Gawain's predicament is intensified by his worry that he will find nowhere to attend Christmas Mass. As always in this poem, the account is vivid and lively. Gawain moves steadily through the trees on Gringolet, and the movement of the verse carries the reader with him. From a metrical point of view this is a regular and characteristic passage. Gringolet does not stumble.

Most often the statement opens in the first half-line ('Þe hasel and þe haȝþorne') and is completed in the second ('were harled al samen'). Unlike the Old English line, therefore, where the syntactic break comes usually in the middle of the line, the typical arrangement in Middle English is for the line to be a syntactic unit, more or less complete in itself. In some poems this tendency is even more marked, but in *Gawain* the author often composes his sentences in units of several lines, so that they run over from one line to the next: 'lest he ne keuer schulde/To se...'.[12] Even in *Gawain* the major pause completing a sentence nearly always comes at the end of the line. From the point of view of the syntax, therefore, the second half-line is usually complementary to the first, although there is no necessary rhythmic relationship between the two.

Because the second half-line rounds off the statement, it shows less rhythmic variation than the first. In nine of the second half-lines in the above passage the stress pattern is $(X)'XX'(X)$ (e.g. 'þat ferly watz wylde'). The greater rhythmic variation of the first half-line is in this way resolved in the second.

As a general rule the first half-line has an unstressed 'prelude' before the initial stress. This remains unstressed, even though, as will be seen later, it may sometimes consist of a number of syllables and contain words of great semantic weight in the sentence. Without this 'prelude' the line gives the impression of starting rather abruptly, as the only example in this passage shows: 'Carande for his costes'. The break in the flow of the lines parallels the switch of the poet's concern from Gawain's physical surroundings to his personal anxieties.

Further metrical variation is achieved by adjustments to the alliterative pattern in relation to the stress pattern. The only essential principle that this poet seems to insist upon is that the alliteration of each line must span the medial pause, thus binding the two halves together.[13] The second line of the above passage illustrates one possible alliterative variant, ax/ax:

> Into a forest ful dep,   þat ferly watz wylde.

The effect of the alliterative pattern of this line is to pick out only two of the four stresses, and correspondingly to reduce the prominence of the stressed word 'dep'.

Another common variant in the alliterative pattern is xa/ax, which has the same effect of reducing the emphasis on one of the stresses. Less commonly used is the pattern that reverses the alliteration of the second half-line, aa/xa. This has a rather startling effect of throwing the weight from the sensitive third stress onto the last stress, as in:

> And set hir ful softly   on þe bed-syde.   (1193)

So marked is the disruption of the rhythm caused by this arrangement that it is altogether avoided in some poems, notably in *Patience* and *Purity*. A further pattern used with more frequency has all four stresses alliterating, aa/aa. The poet uses this to powerful effect, as I will illustrate later.

Quite a large proportion of first half-lines contain three syllables that alliterate together. In the passage quoted above there are several such lines, as for example:

> Þurȝ mony misy and myre,   mon al hym one.

There has been much debate about how these so-called 'extended' half-lines should be analysed. They are of many types, and it may be the case that some should be read as half-lines of two metrical accents and others of three. However, a metrical pattern once established is not easily broken, and the context of the two-stress half-lines imposes its rhythm upon lines which might, out of that context, be interpreted in another way. It is logical, for this reason, to start out from the assumption that all 'extended' half-lines will conform to the standard pattern of the line, that is to say that only two of the three alliterating syllables will bear metrical stress. If it is at all possible to interpret the lines in this way it seems more satisfactory to do so. A thorough analysis of 'extended' half-lines in *Gawain* seems to show that it is always possible to subordinate one of the alliterating syllables without distorting the rhythms inherent in the language.[14] To begin with the half-line 'Þurȝ mony misy and myre', it would seem discordant with both meaning and natural accentuation to make the adjective 'mony' bear stress equal to that on the nouns 'misy' and 'myre'. As it happens, the passage provides another line which demonstrates this well. 'With mony bryddez vnblyþe' has the same rhythmic pattern ($XXX'XX'$). In both lines 'mony' occupies the same accentual position and has the same grammatical function. In the case where it does not share in the alliteration there is no temptation to give it any prominence. Where it does alliterate it calls a certain amount of attention to itself, but there is still no need to give it metrical stress. In other words, when it alliterates it contributes to the total effect of the line, making the line fuller, but it does not alter the pattern of metrical stresses.

In cases like this, misunderstandings arise from expressions such as 'minor chief syllable' or 'secondary stress'. In strict prosodic terms there are only two grades of syllable, stressed and unstressed. This is a conceptual pattern of relationship, perceived in the mind rather than heard by the ear. Naturally enough, *in performance* the syllables of a line of verse will receive innumerable gradations of emphasis, but the *metrical structure* remains unaffected.[15] So, in alliterative verse, each line contains four accents, and upon this underlying structure a whole range of patterns may be built.

The impact of the extra alliterating word in the 'extended' half-line depends entirely upon its semantic importance. 'Mony' in the lines just analysed is of less semantic interest than 'hiȝe' in the line:

> Hiȝe hillez on vche a halue,   and holtwodez vnder.

Even though 'hiȝe' is subordinate to the two stressed words of the half-line, the alliteration combines with the semantic weight of the word to give it some prominence.

In both these cases the unstressed alliterating word has been an adjective which was subordinated to its noun. In other lines an alliterating verb may be subordinated to its object:

> To se þe seruyse of þat syre,   þat on þat self nyȝt.

In this case the verb is part of the unstressed 'prelude' of the line, preceding the first metrical accent on 'seruyse'. The alliteration draws attention to the syntactic and semantic weight of the verb 'se'. A line of similar grammatical structure in which, however, the verb does not alliterate, gives an interesting comparison:

> To sech þe gome of þe grene,   as God wyl me wysse.   (549)

In this case where the verb is not marked out by alliteration it is easier to see how it is tucked away in the 'prelude'.

The conventional formulation for lines with extra alliteration is aaa/ax.[16] This is accurate in so far as it is taken to represent the *alliterative* pattern alone. However, the alliterative pattern is only significant in its relation to the stress-pattern. The formulation aaa/ax is misleading in that it suggests that all the alliterating syllables bear metrical stress. To show that the first alliterating word, while possessing some weight and contributing to the sound and pace of the line, is not one of the four accents, the designation (a)aa/ax might be used. The bracketed element alliterates but is not equivalent to the stressed syllables.

Where an unstressed word alliterates, it may be said that alliteration is used decoratively and not (in the strict sense) structurally. We have also seen that there need be no more than one alliterating syllable in the first half-line. It is possible, therefore, that a half-line may include one stressed syllable that does not alliterate and at the same time an alliterating syllable that is not stressed.

That such lines occur, in which an alliterating syllable is metrically subordinated to a non-alliterating syllable, is demonstrated by a line that we have already analysed:

> Into a forest ful dep,   þat ferly watz wylde.

It is evident that 'ful', although alliterating, cannot be stressed in preference to 'dep'.

Another line from this same passage takes the process a stage further:

> With roȝe raged mosse   rayled aywhere.

There is alliteration on both elements of what is in fact a compound adjective, 'roȝe-raged', but the metrical accents fall on 'roȝe' and 'mosse'.[17] It is a case of two registers, the stress-register and the alliteration-register, which most commonly work in conjunction to point the scansion, but which in this instance are pulling in different directions. A decided tautness in the line is thus produced, as the alliterating word sets up a tension with the non-alliterating stress. It may be noticed in passing that the conventional designation of this line, aa/ax, would give an entirely false picture of the complex relationship between stress and alliteration. More precisely it could be described as a(a)x/ax.

This cannot pretend to be an exhaustive survey of the alliterative and rhythmic resources of the *Gawain* poet, but enough have been examined from this one passage to show the ways in which the great range and flexibility of the alliterative line is maintained. The relationship between the stress and the alliteration of the line is often a tense one, and their competing claims are a prime source of what has been called the 'muscularity' of the verse.

The passage I have been examining was chosen because it illustrated the principles of the alliterative line and the standard ways in which the poet achieved narrative variety. Now and again, in order to achieve a particular rhetorical effect, the poet groups together lines of a certain type. A remarkable example is the description of Gawain's departure with the guide from the castle in search of the Green Chapel. Gawain's circumstances change abruptly from one extreme to the other. When he leaves the castle he moves from the warmth of the fireside to the bitter cold of a midwinter morning, from the security of companionship to the loneliness of a quest which, it seems, can only end in his death. The poet focuses attention on Gawain's altered circumstances by a highly-wrought descriptive passage in which all the stressed syllables except one alliterate:

> Þay boȝen bi bonkkez þer boȝez ar bare,
> Þay clomben bi clyffez þer clengez þe colde.
> Þe heuen watz vphalt, bot vgly þer-vnder;
> Mist muged on þe mor, malt on þe mountez,
> Vch hille hade a hatte, a myst-hakel huge.
> Brokez byled and breke bi bonkkez aboute,
> Schyre schaterande on schorez, þer þay doun schowued.   (2077–83)

[boȝen – *pass*; bonkkez – *hills*; boȝez – *branches*; Þe heuen...þer-vnder – *the clouds were high but beneath them it looked threatening*; muged – *drizzled*; malt – *drenched*; mountez – *hills*; myst-hakel – *cloak of mist*; Brokez...aboute – *brooks boiled and foamed on the hills around*; Schyre...schowued – *crashing white onto the slopes as they rushed down*.]

The alliteration on all four accents maintains equal emphasis throughout the line. The first two lines parallel one another closely. Both contain this grammatical structure: þay – *verb* – bi – *plural noun* – þer.... Words of two syllables alternate with words of one. The rhythm of the two lines is identical, and each first half-line matches each second half-line. The rhythmic and syntactic repetition combines with the unusual heaviness of the alliteration to produce lines of regular and powerful emphasis, lines which echo the stubborn effort involved in climbing through the hostile wintry landscape. The last four lines of the passage have three alliterating syllables to each first half-line. In two of these (2080 and 2082) it is a subject noun that occupies the unaccented 'prelude', and which must therefore be subordinated. The resulting tension is extreme. Only in the final line is there a non-alliterating stressed syllable, and this is the third of the four stresses, which is as a rule always alliterated. The effect of this unusual pattern is to throw vast weight onto the final alliterating word 'schowued', echoing the tumbling and crashing of the streams rushing down the hillside.

It is principally through rhythmic variation of this sort that the poet creates echoic and onomatopoeic effects. That this is an achievement of the total movement of the line rather than of the alliteration in itself may come as a surprise to the modern reader who, accustomed to the use of alliteration as a decorative device, is apt to look first and foremost to the alliteration for onomatopoeic effects. This is not to deny the onomatopoeic effects of alliteration altogether, particularly since it has already been observed that in *Gawain* alliteration is at times used decoratively and not strictly structurally. By and large, however, alliteration is a structural feature which need not – which indeed most often does not – attempt to imitate the sound or represent the quality of what is described. The search for onomatopoeic effects in the alliteration seems generally to direct the wrong kind of attention onto the alliterating syllables and to lead to statements of mere subjectivity. Now and again the poet uses a word that is by its nature and origin echoic, and in this way releases the onomatopoeic potential of the alliteration of a line, but this is a rare device. The echoic word 'wharred' has this effect in the line describing the Green Knight grinding his axe:

What! hit wharred and whette, as water at a mulne.   (2203)

As a contrast to vivid and rhetorical passages with heavy alliteration we may look at one in which the alliteration is unusually light. Here the poet is explaining how the pentangle, and in particular the Five Joys of the Virgin, apply to his hero:

And quere-so-euer þys mon in melly watz stad,
His þro þoȝt watz in þat, þurȝ alle oþer þyngez,
Þat alle his forsnes he feng at þe fyue joyez
Þat þe hende heuen-quene had of hir chylde;
At þis cause þe knyȝt comlyche hade
In þe inore half of his schelde hir ymage depaynted,
Þat quen he blusched þerto his belde neuer payred.   (644–50)

[in...stad – *was present in battle*; þro – *steadfast*; þurȝ – *above*; forsnes – *strength*; feng at – *received from*; hende – *gracious*; At þis cause – *for this reason*; comlyche – *appropriately*; inore half – *inside*; Þat quen...payred – *so that when he looked at it his boldness never wavered.*]

These lines exhibit the tendency of explanatory and discursive passages to be lightly alliterated. In three of the lines there are only two alliterating stresses (644, 649–50). Many of the stresses fall on unimportant words, which may or may not alliterate: 'euer' (644), 'þat', 'þurȝ' (or 'alle'?) and 'þyngez' (645), 'had' (647 and 648), and 'þerto' (650). One second half-line (648) is of only three syllables. The lack of emphasis in these lines may be contrasted to the powerful effects of the descriptive passage quoted previously. This lightness of touch is not common in the 'high style' of alliterative poetry, but it is more characteristic of the 'plain style' of *Piers Plowman*.

The Destruction of Troy and Piers Plowman

Gawain shows the art of the alliterative poet at its highest. It shows how the flexibility of the lines can be exploited for the sake of variety or to express particular moods and emotions. This, we have seen, is a matter of controlling the alliterative pattern and the rhythmic pattern of the line, so that the two systems work – sometimes in conjunction, sometimes in counterpoint – to support and enhance the narrative context. Such metrical skills were not granted to every poet. To enable us to grasp the consummate artistry of a writer, particularly one working in a tradition far removed from our own, it is often helpful to compare the practices of a writer from the same stylistic tradition who is competent but no more than that. The author of *The Destruction of Troy* was a poet of this calibre. He was apparently commanded by some unknown patron to translate Guido's *Historia Destructionis Troiae*.[18] He brought to his task the skills of a highly competent and rather attractive versifier. He was a writer who knew the standard patterns of alliterative verse, and for fourteen thousand lines he applied them rigidly and without much variation to his faithful translation. The resulting poem moves at a regular and stately pace through the long account of the Fall of Troy, never hesitating or fumbling, and rarely struggling against its metrical shackles. Its qualities as well as its shortcomings may be observed in this passage, which describes the coming of winter as the Greeks prepare to sail home from Troy:

> Hyt fell thus by fortune, þe fairest of þe yere
> Was past to the point of the pale wintur;
> Heruest, with the heite and the high sun,
> Was comyn into colde with a course low;
> Trees, thurgh tempestes, tynde hade þere leues,
> And briddes abatid of hor brem songe;
> The wynde of the west wackenet aboue,
> Blowyng full bremly o the brode ythes;
> The clere aire ouercast with cloudys full thicke,
> With mystes full merke mynget with showres;
> Flodes were felle thurgh fallyng of rayne,
> And winter vp wacknet with his wete aire.   (12463–74)

[fairest – *best season*; Heruest – *autumn*; Was comyn into – *had turned to*; course – *path of the sun*; tynde – *dropped*; brem – *loud*; wackenet – *was aroused*; bremly – *violently*; ythes – *waves*; merke – *dark*; mynget – *mixed*; felle – *terrible*.]

As we have seen, this was the kind of topic that was seized upon by the *Gawain*-poet for a display of alliterative pyrotechnics. But despite the winter tempests and floods, no storms ruffle the even pace of the verse of *The Destruction of Troy*. The description progresses through a series of parallel two-line units. The rhythmic movement admits little variation; a half-line with a disyllabic interval between the stresses, $(X)'XX'(X)$, is regularly used, often balanced in the second half-line by clashing stress, XX''. 'With mystes full merke' is an entirely typical half-line. It has two stresses that are alliterated, and a regular number of quite unprominent unstressed syllables. Only in the half-line 'The clere aire ouercast' is there any feeling of tension, for in this case the noun is not stressed or alliterated. The alliterative pattern throughout this passage, as indeed throughout the fourteen thousand lines of the poem, is aa/ax. The result is pleasing enough, fittingly solemn, and eventually soporific.

To move from *The Destruction of Troy* to *Piers Plowman* is to face once again the wide range of the alliterative line. The author of *The Destruction of Troy* works closely within the standard metrical and rhythmic patterns, whereas Langland, writing in the 'plain style', fully exploits the rhythmic variety of the line, but keeps the machinery of his metrical and rhetorical resources carefully concealed. It is Will the Dreamer who speaks in *Piers Plowman*, and Langland pushes the flexibility of the verse to its limits in an effort to capture the restlessness and passion of his narrator, his anger as well as his delight, his frustration, bewilderment or contempt. Will harangues, berates and lectures us. The stately flow of *The Destruction of Troy* and the rhetorical exuberance of *Gawain* are both far removed from the style of *Piers Plowman*.[19]

In the 'plain style' as seen in Langland and his followers, all the inherent tendencies of the line towards grandeur and sonority are deliberately undercut and dissipated. The formal devices of the line are much less prominent than in the 'high style' of *Gawain*. The alliteration itself is reduced, and the half-line with three alliterating syllables is less common.[20] In a few lines there is no alliteration at all (though some of these may be corruptions due to scribal error); in rather more the alliteration does not span the medial pause (aa/bb or aa/xx). The emphasis of the line is still further reduced by the practice of making words of minor prominence – verb-forms such as 'be' or 'was', or even prepositions – bear metrical stress, and the effect of this is particularly noticeable when it is the sensitive third stress of the line that falls on such words.

These effects are achieved only at some risk to the cohesion of the line. It is with some justification that Gerard Manley Hopkins complained that in *Piers Plowman* the rhythm 'is so loose that not only the syllables are not counted but not even the number of beats in a line which is commonly two in each half-line but sometimes three or four. It almost seems as if the rhythm were disappearing'.[21] Even though this is an exaggeration, it is true that there is at times doubt about the stress-pattern of the line, so that the reader has to hesitate and go back over the line to discover its structure. The difficulties are increased by the variations in line-length. Lines may be loose with a long interval between the accents:

'Now be þe peril of my soule' quaþ Peris, 'I shal appeire ȝow alle'.

(A. vii. 156)[22]

Or they may be so light that the reader cannot find enough prominent syllables for the stresses:

Tauerners to hem tolde þe same.

(A. Prol. 106)

Therefore, although the basic structure of the alliterative line remains the same in *Piers Plowman* as in *Gawain*, the impression conveyed by each poem is very different. A characteristic passage of Langland's verse will show this. It is the satiric description of the pilgrim who has travelled the world to visit shrines, but yet does not know the route to find St. Truth:

An hundrit of ampollis on his hat seten,
Signes of Synay, and shilles of Galis,
And many crouch on his cloke, and keiȝes of Rome,
And þe vernicle beforn for men shulde knowe
And sen be his signes whom he souȝt hadde.
Þis folk fraynide hym faire fro whenis þat he come.
'Fro Synay,' he seide, 'and fro þe sepulcre.

At Bedlem, at Babiloyne, I haue ben in boþe,
In Armonye, in Alisaundre, in manye oþere places.
Ӡe mowe se be my signes þat sitten on myn hat
Þat I haue walkid wel wide in wet and in driӡe,
And souӡt goode seintes for my soule hele.'

(A. vi. 8–19)

[ampollis – *phials*; Signes – *souvenirs*; Synay – *Sinai*; shilles – *shells*; Galis – *Galicia*; crouch – *cross*; fraynide – *asked*; Bedlem – *Bethlehem*; Armonye – *Armenia*; Alisaundre – *Alexandria*; mowe – *may*; soule hele – *good of my soul*.]

The stress-pattern of the alliterative line in its standard form builds up to a peak on the third stress, after which it tails away with a non-alliterating final stress. In this passage, however, and not infrequently elsewhere in the poem, Langland's line operates like a wave which never quite builds up to a crest. The third stress several times falls on a word of little semantic weight, and the lines run into the sands without ever reaching their resounding culmination. The way this is done is illustrated in the passage above. In line 11 the alliteration falls on the conjunction 'for',[23] in line 13 on the preposition 'fro'. In neither case can the word bear the stress, which must therefore fall on the following non-alliterating word.[24] In line 14 the last stress falls on an alliterating word 'sepulcre'. This time there is no choice for the third stress but to fall on the humble and non-alliterating 'fro'. In line 15 all the four stresses alliterate, and the third is the weakest of them all, falling on the participle 'ben'.

The result of this practice is to distort the basic rhythm of the alliterative line much more radically, and much more daringly, than anything attempted by the author of *Gawain*. Langland, writing in the 'plain style', brings his verse much closer to prose. It still works as verse, for the most part at least, because the standard pattern of the alliterative line emerges often enough to act as a model from which other lines diverge. It is frequently asserted that Langland pays little attention to his metrical structure. Paradoxically, in his flouting of prosodic norms, Langland is more consciously moulding his verse-form than the author of *The Destruction of Troy*, who is always content with the most regular metrical patterns.

Line-Groups and Stanzas in Alliterative Verse

In both *The Destruction of Troy* and *Piers Plowman* the largest regular pattern is the line. Beyond that there is the *passus* or chapter, but the length of this is quite variable. As a result the writers are able to maintain complete flexibility over the pace of their narrative. They avoid the difficulty that sometimes cripples the writers of more restricting narrative forms, such as the tail-rhyme stanza, of having to extend a short statement over a long stanza. However, just as there is nothing to impede the flow of the narrative, so also there are no formal bounds to give it symmetry. As a result both poems suffer at times from a rambling shapelessness, from a lack of direction that a stanzaic arrangement would have helped to correct.

Some other poets who used the alliterative line felt the need for formal restrictions over their narrative, and dealt with the problem in a variety of ways. One method is illustrated by *The Wars of Alexander*. This poem, which lacks its final part, now consists of twenty-six completed *passus* and a fragment of a twenty-seventh. The number of lines in each *passus* varies, but the number is usually a multiple of twenty-four (a fact sometimes obscured by eccentricities of line-numbering in the edition).[25] The poet's intention was that this arrangement should be kept up from beginning to end, and this may be confirmed by comparing the texts of the two fragmentary manuscripts of the poem where these run side by side. Both scribes are careless about following their exemplar and they miss out a line every now and again, but the text can be reconstructed satisfactorily by a comparison between the two manuscripts. This inspection reveals that this part of the poem (and, by implication, the poem as a whole) is composed consistently in 24-line units. The nearest modern equivalent to these units is the paragraph, and indeed most of the sporadic paragraph-marks in the Ashmole manuscript correspond to these divisions and presumably descend from the archetype manuscript. Within the 24-line paragraph the 'sentences' or sense-units fall with noticeable (though not invariable) regularity into groups of four lines. Thus the whole poem is organised in paragraphs, each subdivided regularly into six four-line sentences. To call this a stanzaic arrangement is misleading, because a stanza involves some form of linking (usually by rhyme) between the lines to preserve at least a formal break between one stanza and the next.[26] The purpose of the arrangement into 'paragraphs' and 'sentences' in *The Wars of Alexander* is to impose a regular *external* pattern upon a long and episodic narrative of events that leaves little impression of thematic patterning. The author may also have had in mind considerations which we, with the benefit of our carefully punctuated modern editions, are apt to overlook. An alliterative poem in a manuscript is not provided with syntactical punctuation, and unless the poem has formal divisions to act as guidelines its sense is difficult to follow where the syntax is at all ambiguous or convoluted. Furthermore, a regular pattern maintains – or might be expected to maintain – some check on the scribe, who was all too prone to skip lines or even to supply lines of his own. If the author of *The Wars of Alexander* hoped that his numerical arrangement would impose controls over his scribes, he was to be disappointed in the two scribes whose fragmentary work remains, and who undoubtedly did not recognise the formal divisions within the poem. In fact it is a rather startling oversight and a sad comment on scribal proficiency, since the author took some pains to emphasise his arrangement at the beginning of the poem. The introduction, which I have already quoted in chapter 2, was originally composed as a 24-line unit of six four-line 'sentences', with alliteration running on the same letter through each group of four lines to make the point absolutely clear. Carelessly the scribe of the unique copy of this passage dropped one line from the first group and another from the third, thus obscuring the author's intentions from all future readers.

The four-line grouping is also a feature of some other alliterative poems. It is used most regularly in *Patience*, and less regularly in *Purity*, *St. Erkenwald* and *The Siege of Jerusalem*. In the manuscript of *Patience* and *Purity* the scribe marks off the four-line units with strict and mechanical regularity, and is not troubled when, particularly in the latter poem, the syntax contradicts his ticks in the margin. The curious fact is that whenever the marks in the manuscript get out of step as a result of an exceptional group of *five* lines, the author eventually brings them back into step by composing a unit (or units) amounting to seven lines.[27] As a result of this, each major section of these poems contains a multiple of four lines. In this sense the scribe is justified in continuing his ticks unperturbed, and it is possible that the reader of the manuscript is encouraged by them to admire the panache with which the poet breaks away from his formal pattern for a short passage before bowing to it once again.

Of course the modern editor of these poems is faced with an insoluble problem. If he splits the lines up into stanzas (as is most often done) he will find that he is imposing excessive rigidity upon his text and giving a false impression of the movement of the narrative.[28] Probably the best he can do is to number the lines in fours (as an equivalent to the marginal mark) and to punctuate in such a way as to highlight this grouping where it occurs.

In *Sir Gawain and the Green Knight* the author felt the same need to organise his unrhymed lines. The way he chose to do this was to add a five-line rhyming section at the end of a number of unrhymed lines varying from twelve to thirty-seven lines. The rhyming section consists of a one-syllable 'bob', followed by a 'wheel' of four lines of three syllables, the whole section rhyming *ababa*. This device is very effective in signalling a break by changing the pace of the rhythm, and because the stanzas are of variable length the poet has no need to spin out or cut short his narrative to fit the stanzaic pattern. Although the 'bob and wheel' can occasionally be used with striking effect, as when the remarkable colour of the Green Knight and then the identical colour of his horse are revealed in successive 'wheels', it is more often used simply to round off a particular stage in the narrative by summing up or by generalising upon what has been described in the preceding unrhymed lines, or alternatively to point forward to the subject of the next stanza.

This combination of unrhymed alliterative lines and a rhymed section – a combination which is unique to *Gawain* – brings together two separate developments within the alliterative tradition. The 'bob and wheel' was a device used in a number of alliterative poems written in rhyming stanzas. There are early examples from the *Harley Lyrics*,[29] and the device was taken up by several later poets working within the traditions of the Alliterative Revival. These poets used the full range of alliterative vocabulary to create rhyming alliterative stanzas of amazing intricacy and ornateness. The commonest pattern is a stanza of thirteen lines, consisting of eight four-stress lines rhyming alternately, followed up by a 'bob and wheel'.[30] The patterns of alliteration are less regular than in the unrhymed poems. There is a strong tendency for the stanzaic poets to alliterate all four of the stressed syllables in the line, and even to have ornamental alliteration in addition to this, but other lines have less alliteration, or alliterative patterns which do not span the half-line (e.g. aa/bb). In rhymed verse there is no feeling that the last syllable should not bear alliteration, which indicates how end-rhyme changes the stress-pattern of the alliterative line. An occasional device in these poems is to link the lines in pairs by running the same alliterative letter through two lines.

Two attractive poems in the thirteen-line stanza are *The Quatrefoil of Love* and *The Pistill of Susan*. The former is a paean to the Virgin Mary, describing her as the fourth leaf of a truelove flower, in which the other three leaves represent the Trinity. The poet emphasises the importance of the Virgin throughout the life of Christ, and advises us all to beseech her to intercede on our behalf:

> Blyssede be þat trewlufe so meke and so mylde,
> Sekir and stedfaste and stabill at assaye;
> When we hafe wrethede þer thre leues with our werkes wilde,
> Þe ferthe es gracious and gude for to helpe aye.
> Þan kneles þat lady down bifore hir dere childe,
> And sare wepys for our sake with hir eghne graye;
> Scho es euer full of grace, ells were we bygylede,

Scho wynnes with hir wepynge many faire praye
<blockquote>To kepe.</blockquote>
<blockquote>Sen scho es welle of oure wele,
And alle oure cares will scho kele,
Allas, whi gare we hir knele
And for oure werkes wepe?</blockquote>

(339–51)

[Sekir – *reliable*; assaye – *trial*; wrethede – *angered*; þer – *these*; eghne – *eyes*; praye – *booty*; welle – *source*; wele – *happiness*; kele – *assuage*; gare – *make*.]

The Pistill of Susan is a pleasing adaptation of the story of Susanna and the Elders (in the Vulgate, Daniel, xiii). The poet, despite the demands of the verse-form, follows the biblical account closely, but he pauses for an extended list of the trees and flowers in the orchard where the lecherous Elders spy on Susanna as she washes herself, and adds again to his source by recounting with pathos a touching scene in which Susanna, falsely accused by the Elders of fornication in the garden, and about to be put to death, says farewell to her husband Joakim:

Heo fel doun flat in þe flore, hir feere whon heo fond,
Carped to him kyndeli, as heo ful wel couþe:
'Iwis I wraþþed þe neuere, at my witand,
Neiþer in word ne in werk, in elde ne in ʒouþe.'
Heo keuered vp on hir kneos, and cussed his hand:
'For I am dampned, I ne dar disparage þi mouþ.'
Was neuer more serwful segge bi se nor bi sande,
Ne neuer a soriore siht bi norþ ne bi souþ;
<blockquote>Þo þare
Þei toke the feteres of hire feete,
And euere he cussed þat swete:
'In oþer world schul we mete.'
Seid he no mare.</blockquote>

(248–60, Vernon text)

[hir...fond – *when she met her husband*; Carped – *spoke*; couþe – *knew how*; wraþþed – *angered*; at my witand – *to my knowledge*; keuered – *rose*; cussed – *kissed*; disparage – *dishonour*; serwful – *sorrowful*; segge – *man*; bi se...sande – *anywhere*; Þo – *then*.]

The quotations from both poems illustrate that the tight scheme of the stanza, with its complex patterns of rhyme and alliteration and its abrupt changes in rhythm, has great potential for the expression of emotion and pathos. The forward movement of the narrative is kept up by the alternating rhymes of the long lines; the 'bob' line introduces a new rhyme and a very noticeable pause in the rhythm; the three monorhymed lines in the wheel hold the narrative flow at that point; the last line reverts to the rhyme of the 'bob' and encloses the whole of the 'bob and wheel' section, neatly rounding it off.

Surely the most delightful poem in this stanza-form is *Summer Sunday*, in which the narrator describes how he goes out one Sunday with the hunters. While searching for a boat to cross the river he loses track of the hunting party, and eventually, tired of chasing after them, he rests under a tree. There he has a vision of Lady Fortune and her Wheel:

So passede I þe pas, priuely to pleye,
And ferde forþ in þat frith, folk for to fynde.
Lawly longe I lustnede and vnder lowe lay,
Þat I ne herde hond, horn, hunte, hert ne hynde.
So wyde I walkede þat I wax wery of þe wey,
Þanne les I my layk and lenede vnder lynde;
And als I sat beside I say, soþ for to sey,
A wifman wiþ a wonder whel weue with þe wynde,
<blockquote>And wond.
Opon þe whel were, I wene,
Merye men and madde i-mene;
To hire I gan gon in grene,
And fortune y fond.</blockquote>

(27–39)

[pas – *crossing (of the river)*; ferde – *went*; frith – *wood*; Lawly – *quietly*; lustnede – *listened*; lowe – *hill*; les – *lost*; layk – *game*; lenede – *rested*; lynde – (*linden*) *tree*; say – *saw*; A wifman...wond – *a woman with a marvellous wheel moving in the wind, and it revolved*; I wene – *indeed*; madde – *maddened by grief*; i-mene – *together*; gan gon – *went*; in grene – *over the meadow* (or *wearing green*).]

On the wheel he sees in turn the four stages of human life: the ambitious youth, the rich King, the disappointed old man, and finally:

A bare body in a bed, a bere i-brouth him by,
A duk drawe to þe deþ wiþ drouping and dare.   (132–3)

[bere – *bier*; i-brouth – *brought*; drawe – *carried*; drouping – *sorrow*; dare – *dismay*.]

So the youthful gaiety of the hunt gives way to the bitterness of defeated hopes and the humiliation of death. The poem's rich symbolism and its stylisation of the pattern of human life find full reflection in the formal complexity of the stanza-form.

There are several varieties of the thirteen-line stanza. All have in common the first eight four-stress lines in an alternating rhyme-scheme, but different patterns are used in the last five lines of the stanza. In a poem of extraordinary virtuosity, *De Tribus Regibus Mortuis*, the last five lines are all of three stresses, rhyming *cdccd*. This must be the most highly patterned and technically complex poem in the language. The difficulties already inherent in an alliterative poem written in an intricate rhyme-scheme are hugely increased by two further complicating factors: the lines alliterate together in pairs or even fours, and the choice of rhyme is cripplingly restricted by maintaining the same final consonant throughout the eight long lines and another throughout the 'wheel'.[31] The first stanza of this poem which describes, as in *Summer Sunday*, the narrator's day out with the hunters shows the result:

An a byrchyn bonke þer bous arne bryȝt
I saw a brymlyche bore to a bay broȝt.
Ronke rachis with rerde þai ronnon a-ryȝt,
Of al hore row and hore rest lytil hom roȝt.
Me þoȝt hit ful semele to se soche a siȝt
How in a syde of a salȝe a sete him he soȝt.
Fro þe noyse þat hit was new til hit was ne nyȝt,
Fro þe non bot a napwile, me þoȝt hit bot noȝt.
    Me þoȝt hit noȝt bot a þrow
    To se how he þrobyt and þrew.
    Honters with hornes þai kowþ blow,
    Þai halowyd here howndys with 'how!'
    In holtis herde I neuer soche hew.   (1–13)[32]

[*On a birchwood hill where the boughs gleam I saw a fierce boar brought to bay. Strong hounds ran barking, they cared little about peace and rest. I thought it very pleasant to see such a sight, how the boar tried to find cover at the side of a willow. It seemed to me no time at all from when the noise began until nearly night-time – and from midday only an instant (lit. nap-time). It seemed to me only a short while, watching how the boar quivered and twisted about. Huntsmen blew their horns, they urged on their hounds with 'how!' Never did I hear such a din in the woods.*]

The poem goes on to tell an *exemplum* that is found elsewhere in German and French literature and also widely in art. Three Kings on the hunt get lost in the forest, where they come face to face with three dreadful apparitions – their dead fathers. The fathers point to their own putrefaction as a warning to the pleasure-loving kings of the horrors of death. The theme is another version of that in *Summer Sunday*; it is the parable of man's confrontation with his own mortality. The similarity between the two poems is emphasised by the opening scene in both of a carefree hunt to introduce the sombre theme and to typefy the life of thoughtless gaiety that may end at any moment.[33]

Another variation on the same theme in a similar stanza-form is *The Awntyrs off Arthure*. This is a much longer poem which falls into two distinct episodes.[34] Here there are *nine* four-stress lines and four shorter lines that round off the stanza. The story of the first episode is as macabre as that in *De Tribus Regibus Mortuis*. Arthur and his knights ride out hunting, while Gawain and Guenevere remain together in a leafy bower in the forest, where they are confronted by Guenevere's dead mother. The physical corruption of the ghost is described with ghastly clarity:

> Bare was þe body and blak to þe bone,
> All biclagged in clay, vncomly cladde.
> Hit wariet, hit waymented as a woman,
> But nauthyr on hide ne on huwe no heling hit hadde.
> Hit stemered, hit stonayde, hit stode as a stone,
> Hit marred, hit memered, hit mused for madde.
> Agayn þe grisly goost Sir Gawayn is gone;
> He rayked to it on a res, for he was neuer rad.
> Rad was he neuer, ho so right redes.
> On þe chef of þe cholle
> A pade pikes on þe polle,
> With eighen holked ful holle
> That gloed as þe gledes. (105–17)

[biclagged – *bedaubed*; vncomly – *unattractively*; waried – *cursed*; waymented – *lamented*; hide – *skin*; huwe – *figure*; heling – *covering*; stemered – *staggered*; stonayde – *was dazed*; marred – *wandered confusedly*; memered – *muttered*; mused for madde – *stared madly*; Agayn – *towards*; rayked – *went*; on a res – *at a rush*; rad – *afraid*; redes – *understands*; chef – *top*; cholle – *jaw*; pade – *toad*; polle – *head*; With...holle – *with hollow sunken eyes*; gledes – *embers*.]

The ghost contrasts her former beauty and power, and warns Guenevere to take heed; Guenevere is to avoid pride and adultery and is asked to say prayers for her mother's soul. In particular she must have pity on the poor who starve outside the castle gates. From what we learn from other accounts of the character of Arthur's queen and her subsequent involvement in the downfall of the Round Table, this message acquires particular poignancy, and to underline this the destruction of Arthur's court is foretold by the ghost. After giving this explicit warning she glides away, and her daughter and Gawain return to the court. The episode which then follows comes as a surprise because it seems to have nothing to do with the terrible apparition just witnessed. The theme returns to the conventional activities of the romance world so rudely interrupted by the visitor from the dead. Gawain undergoes a trial by combat with a stranger to Arthur's court called Galeron, who claims that his lands have wrongfully been given away to Gawain. The prolonged and inconclusive struggle is called off at Guenevere's request, and Galeron's lands are returned to him, while Gawain is granted vast possessions elsewhere. In the final stanza we are told that Guenevere arranges for masses to be said for her mother's soul. Perhaps the poet's message lies in the very lack of connection between the two episodes: the ghost's warning has made no impression on the life of Arthur's court as, absorbed in their own world, the proud knights and exquisite ladies continue with their struggles and extravagance as if death and the dissolution of the Round Table were never to be. Though Guenevere arranges for 'a mylion of masses' to be sung, this is in reality a perfunctory reaction to her mother's revelation of what lies beyond the walls that enclose the garden of romance. The gate has been opened, but Arthur's courtiers will not look outside.

The stanzaic pattern used for *The Awntyrs off Arthure* (i.e. without a 'bob' line) became the form used for a number of fifteenth-century Scottish poems. In England, fifteenth-century dramatists used a wide variety of thirteen-line 'bob and wheel' stanzas, with and without alliteration. It appears that during the fifteenth century the composition of alliterative verse was most often in one form or another of the thirteen-line stanza.

There are also a few poems written in a fourteen-line stanza. This begins like the stanzas of thirteen lines with a four-stress octave of alternating rhymes, but the stanza concludes with six two-stress lines rhyming either *ccdccd* or *bbcddc*. Following the first scheme are two poems, *St. Katherine* and *St. John the Evangelist*, and following the second is *St. John the Baptist*. Only *St. Katherine* is a poem of much merit. It relates with vigour the grisly torturing and martyr-dom of the saint whose instrument of torture gave rise to the term 'Catherine wheel'. The author conveniently leaves his name in an acrostic in the final stanzas – Richard Spalding. Perhaps he was a monk at the Cistercian house at Pipewell in Northamptonshire.[35] That Spalding also wrote *St. John the Evangelist* is suggested by the technical and verbal similarities between the two poems. Both have an identical rhyme-scheme with fairly consistent grouping of pairs of lines throughout the octave and verbal linking of the octave to the sestet. Both poems are written in the form of an address to the saint, whose tortures at the hands of a wicked Emperor – in both cases described as 'the Devil's limb' – are gruesomely recounted.

If Spalding also wrote the third poem, *St. John the Baptist*, his poetic powers were in sad decline. Although it too is in fourteen-line stanzas and addresses the saint as the other poems do, it does not share the technical com-plexities of the other two works. It might be an imitation by another writer.[36]

The Form of Pearl

The finest of all the poems in rhyming alliterative stanzas, *Pearl*, stands apart from the others we have been examining, not only because of the supreme technical skill displayed by the poet, but also because of the perfect match of external form with subject-matter. The poem is written in stanzas of twelve lines, each line of four stresses. As in the other rhyming alliterative poems, the first eight lines rhyme alternately, but the last four lines are bound to the octave by rhyme, so that the result is a tight and unified stanza with the rhyme-pattern *ababababbcbc*. As in the sonnet of later tradition, pauses often come at every fourth line, to mark a new stage in the argument or narrative, or to pre-pare for a summary of what has previously been stated. Alliteration is used with great sensitivity; just as in *Gawain*, the poet knows the value of emphatic alliteration for passages of rich description and for moments of great emotional tension, but recognises that for speeches of rational argument and exposition (of which there are many in *Pearl*) less obtrusive alliteration is more suitable. In the ornate descriptions of the other-world of the narrator's dream, heavy alliteration, often on all four stresses, is particularly appropriate since it emphasises the 'otherness' of the Heavenly Kingdom:

> Dubbed wern alle þo downeȝ sydeȝ
> Wyth crystal klyffeȝ so cler of kynde.
> Holtewodeȝ bryȝt aboute hem bydeȝ
> Of bolleȝ as blwe as ble of Yndе;
> As bornyst syluer þe lef on slydeȝ,
> Þat þike con trylle on vch a tynde.

Quen glem of glodeʒ agaynʒ hem glydeʒ,
Wyth schymeryng schene ful schrylle þay schynde.
Þe grauayl þat on grounde con grynde
Wern precious perleʒ of oryente:
Þe sunnebemeʒ bot blo and blynde
In respecte of þat adubbement.   (73–84)

[Dubbed – *adorned*; downeʒ sydeʒ – *hillsides*; cler of kynde – *naturally radiant*;
Holtewodeʒ – *woods*; bydeʒ – *are placed*; bolleʒ – *trunks*; ble of Ynde – *indigo*;
bornyst – *burnished*; on slydeʒ – *slides over (another leaf)*; þike – *thickly growing*; con
trylle – *quivered*; tynde – *branch*; Quen…glydeʒ – *when the gleam of the clear sky
falls on them*; schene – *brilliance*; schrylle – *dazzlingly*; con grynde – *crunched*; blo
and blynde – *pale and dim*; In…adubbement – *in comparison with that splendour*.]

The rhythm of the line in *Pearl* is much more regularly syllabic than the unrhymed line of *Gawain*, but on the other hand the alliterative patterns are much
less regular, with the alliteration frequently falling on the last (and rhyming)
stress, as can be seen in the passage above.

It is again the *Harley Lyrics* which show the earliest use of a similar stanzaic
pattern. The lines quoted in chapter 1 from *The Poet's Repentance* illustrate a
twelve-line stanza (though of a slightly different rhyme-scheme) with heavy
alliteration and stanza-linking as in *Pearl*. Later in the fourteenth century the
rhyme-scheme used in *Pearl* became quite a favourite among poets of the west
midlands. There are a number of examples in the Vernon manuscript.[37]
They are not alliterative poems in the sense that alliteration is a *structural*
feature of the line, since the rhythmic pattern of them all is regularly iambic,
but several of them use ornamental alliteration heavily though sporadically.
Many of them, like *Pearl*, link stanza to stanza, and end every stanza with a
refrain.

The medieval reader, with his awareness of the symbolism of numbers,
would have regarded the use of a twelve-line stanza as particularly appropriate
to the subject-matter of *Pearl*.[38] The number twelve is associated especially
with the New Jerusalem of the Apocalypse, where the objects of St. John's
vision are consistently grouped in twelves. In the paraphrase of the Apocalypse
which forms the climax of the narrator's dream in *Pearl*, the poet describes
the twelve foundations of the Heavenly Jerusalem made of twelve jewels, the
twelve furlongs in height, breadth and length of the city, the twelve gates of
pearl bearing the names of the twelve tribes of Israel, and his subsequent
vision of the procession of the 144,000 virgins. To reinforce the numerical
symbolism, the total number of lines in the poem is 1212.

The meaningfulness of the number of lines in the stanza and in the poem are
only relatively trivial aspects of the way in which the formal organisation of the
poem reflects and controls the patterns of the poet's vision. The stanzas
are grouped together by a common refrain into twenty groups, each group
containing five stanzas, except the fifteenth group which has six. Furthermore
each stanza is linked to the next by repetition or echoing of the rhyme-word of
the refrain in the first line of the following stanza. This results in certain words
and certain phrases acquiring great prominence, since the refrain and the
link-word have each to be repeated five times in the stanza-group. The refrain,
as is naturally the case in refrain-poems, centres the argument of each stanza-
group on a particular theme. The skill of the *Pearl* poet lies in the sophistication
with which he develops the various aspects of each group-theme, so that the
poem consists not of twenty static reflections, but of a logical progression of
thought mapped out around twenty key ideas.[39] The movement is maintained
sometimes by exploring different aspects of the same concept, as in the eighth

group where the idea of 'cortaysye' as it applies to the Kingdom of Heaven is contrasted to the 'cortaysye' of earthly kingdoms, sometimes by introducing new concepts with a play on words, as in the first group where the two senses of *spot* – 'place' and 'stain' – are involved. One sense of the word concentrates our attention on the physical spot where the narrator lost his 'pearl' and where he has his vision, the other focuses on the spotlessness of the pearl-maiden which is to become so important for the discussion later in the poem.

The last refrain, containing variations on the theme of 'Prynceȝ paye' ('what is pleasing to the Prince, i.e. God') echoes the very first line of the poem: 'Perle, plesaunte to prynces paye'. But it is much more than an echo – it is a development, a transformation even, of the original statement, for the worldly prince who sets such store on precious jewels has become the Prince of Heaven, whose jewel, the Pearl, has revealed herself as a symbol of spiritual values that the earthbound narrator had not previously dreamt of. The reader, like the dreamer, now approaches these concepts with new insights. The dreamer returns to the waking world, but with a deeper understanding of the ways of God, and armed with this knowledge he can set out once again to reconcile himself to the 'doel-doungoun' (1187) of this world. The circularity of the poem's verbal and thematic structure prompts us to compare the state of mind of the dreamer at the beginning and at the end of the poem. Furthermore, it imitates the structure of the pearl itself, which in its turn reflects the nature of the Heavenly Kingdom:

> This makelleȝ perle, þat boȝt is dere,
> Þe joueler gef fore alle hys god,
> Is lyke þe reme of heuenesse clere,
> So sayde þe Fader of folde and flode;
> For hit is wemleȝ, clene, and clere,
> And endeleȝ rounde, and blype of mode. (733–8)

[makelleȝ – *matchless*; þat...dere – *that is dearly bought*; Þe joueler...god – *for which the jeweller gave all his goods*; reme of heuenesse – *Heavenly Kingdom*; folde – *earth*; flode – *sea*; wemleȝ – *spotless*; And endeleȝ...mode – *and endlessly round and pleasing.*]

Heaven, the pearl and the poem are all constructed with the same flawless circularity, an idea which reflects the words at the beginning and the end of the Apocalypse: 'I am Alpha and Omega, the beginning and the end, saith the Lord God'.

The echoing of the first line in a line at the end of the poem is also a feature of *Gawain*, and there too its purpose is to highlight a superficial similarity in the situation at both points in the poem – Gawain is at Arthur's court again among his companions – so that the reader may compare the essential *dissimilarities* in the hero's perception of his situation. In both *Pearl* and *Gawain* there are 101 stanzas, which, like the 'twelvemonth and a day' in which Gawain must meet the Green Knight for the return blow, is a number suggesting the completion of one cycle and the start of another. For both Gawain and the dreamer in *Pearl* increased awareness is not an end in itself but the starting-point for a new journey.

Pearl is the finest of all the rhymed alliterative works, and the one that most clearly demonstrates the way in which external form is interwoven with theme and content. We have seen that several other poets use rhyming alliterative stanzas successfully as a way of organising and enriching a carefully patterned structure or of heightening a moment of great emotion, but only in *Pearl* are form and content indissolubly linked with such perfect fittingness.

Chapter 4

POETIC DICTION

The Alliterative Vocabulary

From the very opening lines of *The Parlement of the Thre Ages* the reader learns much about the style of the poem:

In the monethe of Maye when mirthes bene fele,
And the sesone of somere when softe bene the wedres,
Als I went to the wodde my werdes to dreghe,
Into þe schawes myselfe a schotte me to gete...   (1–4)

[fele – *many*; my werdes to dreghe – *to try my luck*; schawes – *copses*.]

The poet is in no hurry to move his story along. The pace is measured and stately, and each concept is assimilated before a new one is presented. The opening phrase 'the monethe of Maye' is restated as 'the sesone of somere', and the idea of the joyousness of the time is expressed first as 'when mirthes bene fele' and again as 'when softe bene the wedres'. The locality ('the wodde') and the purpose ('my werdes to dreghe') of the narrator's activity are respectively repeated and more closely defined by 'schawes' and 'a schotte me to gete'.

This pattern of detailed and repeated statement is a feature of the high style of alliterative poetry. If it is more obvious, even at times obtrusive, in the *Parlement* than in *Gawain*, this is perhaps a mark of the *Gawain*-poet's greater subtlety. Only occasionally in *Gawain*, for example in the passage analysing the Pentangle, is the reader aware that the narrative pace has slackened, but much of the charm of the *Parlement* is the author's unconcealed delight in elaboration of detail and richness of ornamentation. This reaches a high point, and appropriately so, in the set-piece description of Youth, the first of the Three Ages, whose self-indulgence and love of luxury is fittingly expressed in the full panoply of the high alliterative style. Here is the first part of that description:

The firste was a ferse freke, fayrere than thies othire,
A bolde beryn one a blonke bownne for to ryde,
A hathelle on ane heghe horse with hauke appon hande.
He was balghe in the breste and brode in the scholdirs,
His axles and his armes were i-liche longe,
And in the medill als a mayden menskfully schapen;
Longe legges and large, and lele for to schewe.
He streghte hym in his sterapis and stode vprightes;
He ne hade no hode ne no hatte bot his here one –
A chaplet one his chefe-lere, chosen for the nones,
Raylede alle with rede rose, richeste of floures,
With trayfoyles and trewloues of full triede perles,
With a chefe charebocle chosen in the myddes.   (109–21)

[freke – *man*; beryn – *man*; blonke – *horse*; bownne – *fitted out*; hathelle – *man*; balghe – *rounded*; axles – *shoulders*; i-liche – *also*; medill – *waist*; menskfully – *gracefully*; lele – *lovely*; streghte hym – *stretched*; here one – *hair alone*; A chaplet... nones – *a beautiful garland on his head*; Raylede – *arrayed*; trayfoyles and trewloues – *three and four-leaved flowers*; triede – *fine*; chefe – *lovely*; charebocle – *carbuncle*; chosen – *exquisite*.]

The descriptive technique of the first three lines here is the same as that of the opening lines of the poem. Youth is called in one line a 'freke', in the next a 'beryn', and in the third a 'hathelle', and the three epithets have no distinction in meaning. In one line he rides a 'blonke', and in the next he is mounted on a 'heghe horse'. The account continues with minute detail of his figure, and then of his clothes and the decoration upon them. In the lines that follow the passage quoted, the poet names ten different precious stones that are embroidered on Youth's clothes.

It is obvious that this sort of style, with its repetitions or variations of a single concept, demands a very wide vocabulary. The reader new to alliterative poetry will be immediately struck by the large number of words for which his reading of Chaucer has not prepared him. In the description of Youth that I have just quoted, he will search in vain through Chaucer's works to find *freke*, *beryn*, *blonke*, *hathelle*, *balghe*, *axles*, *menskfully*, *lele*, *chefe-lere*, *raylede* (in the sense 'arrayed'), *trayfoyles* and *triede* ('choice'). This is a substantial list from a short passage. There may be a number of reasons for their absence from Chaucer's works. A few are words which Chaucer presumably would have used if the occasion had arisen, often words of a more or less technical nature such as *trayfoyles*, which in itself indicates a feature of the style of alliterative verse – that alliterative poets were fond of rich description full of technicalities. Other words such as *axles* are dialect words, which would sound natural to an audience in the northern half of the country, but unacceptable, even perhaps incomprehensible, in London. A third group, of which *hathelle* is an example, consists of words that are, by and large, restricted to alliterative verse in the fourteenth century, and are found rarely elsewhere, even in non-alliterative works from the same part of the country.

The evolution of a style that required a huge stock of synonyms was at least partly a matter of making a virtue of necessity. The technique of the alliterative line, usually involving three important words in the alliterative pattern, meant that it was very useful for the poet to have at his disposal a number of words covering each common concept to slot into his alliterative scheme. If, for instance, he is giving an account of a battle, a set-piece description which appears again and again in poems such as *The Destruction of Troy*, he needs the wide vocabulary to describe what is basically only a limited range of activities: rushing up to an opponent, running him through with a spear or dismembering him with a sword. If the only available word for the combatants is *knyʒtes*, the range of possible variation will be small indeed. And so the vocabulary for 'man' or 'warrior' in general use is extended by the use of synonyms such as *burne*, *freke*, *gome*, *hathel*, *lede*, *kempe*, *renk*, *schalk*, *segge*, *tulke* and *wyʒe*. When the warrior is to move, the poet has a huge choice of synonyms which have come to mean little more than 'go'. Apart from the everyday words for this, there are many more that are less common or have taken on unusual senses. A list of these would include the following:

Ayre, attle, bowe, bowne, cayre, cach, chese, do, dresse, drive, ferke, founde, glyde, hale, helde, kever, loute, mete, ricche, raike, schake, schowve, seche, skelte, strake, strike, swey, tourne, thring, trine, wade, win, wind.

Since in battle *rapid* movement is generally either brave or prudent, the concept 'quickly' may be expressed both by more common words such as *belyve*, *deliverly*, *faste*, *ȝerne*, *hastily*, *kene*, *radly* and *swiftly*, all of which are also found in Chaucer, and by a supplementary vocabulary which includes the following:

> *Cofly, graythely, ȝarely, ȝapely, ȝederly, naitely, prestly, rapely, rekenly, spackly, skete, taytely, titly, wyȝtly.*

The emphasis created by the alliteration focuses attention onto the words themselves, which encourages the use of a varied stock of synonyms. This characteristic also prompts the alliterative poet to concentrate on the details of what he sees, to observe a scene through powerful binoculars rather than to rest content with a distant and generalised view. This, in its turn, increases the need for a wide and all-embracing vocabulary.

However, the extent to which the individual alliterative poets make use of the characteristic alliterative diction varies considerably. It is markedly little used in *Joseph of Arimathie* and *Cheuelere Assigne*, both probably very early works, and it is not very extensive in *Alisaunder of Macedoine* and *William of Palerne*, the latter certainly being one of the earlier poems of the Revival. The probable explanation is that there was a gradual process of amassing and establishing the vocabulary. Certainly later on in the century, in the poems of the *Gawain* group and in *The Wars of Alexander*, the vocabulary is at its richest. Poems written in the south midlands make much less use of the vocabulary than their northern fellows. There may be two reasons for this. One is that many of the alliterative words are drawn from northern dialects, so that they would not be available to southern writers. The other factor in the later period is the influence of Langland, who deliberately avoided all but the commonest elements of the alliterative vocabulary, partly because he was looking for a readership that was not localised and not necessarily accustomed to alliterative verse, and partly because a vocabulary associated with works of a romantic and heroic cast was not suitable to the world of *Piers Plowman*.[1] Therefore the absence of much of the alliterative vocabulary from *Piers Plowman* is to a major extent a stylistic decision, and it underlies the differences of approach and outlook between Langland and the authors of poems such as *The Parlement of the Thre Ages*. A number of writers were influenced by Langland both in their subject-matter and in their avoidance of a specialised vocabulary. This is particularly true of the author of *Pierce the Ploughman's Crede*, who avoids words associated with the high style of alliterative verse even more rigorously than Langland himself.

Some Words and their Origins

In order to examine aspects of the diction of alliterative poetry, it is helpful to divide the words according to their derivation from French, Scandinavian or Old English. This is more than a mere convenience, because words carry their histories with them, and as a result their origins are reflected in their character, signification and distribution. We may begin with some words of French origin.

By the fourteenth century the influence of French upon the English vocabulary was all-pervasive. A fourteenth-century writer could no longer attempt, as Laȝamon had apparently attempted, to exclude words of French origin from his poems. As a result the French element in the vocabulary of alliterative works is large, but it consists for the most part of common words, and there are few French borrowings that may be described as 'characteristically alliterative', that is to say words that are used regularly in alliterative verse but rarely elsewhere. Nevertheless the more unusual French words illustrate an important feature of the alliterative style, that is to say the delight in technical detail that the educated Englishman would know or (perhaps equally frequently) would be ashamed to admit he did not know. As an example of this we may examine the description in *Morte Arthure* of the hero arming himself for battle, a topic with a long heroic tradition behind it. Despite the antiquity of the topic, the technical vocabulary is up to date. The chamberlain may be summoned to bring the *herewedis* or the *stelgere*, but when the time comes for the hero to don his armour piece by piece it can only be referred to by using a highly technical French vocabulary. Alliterative writers felt quite free to introduce technical expressions into poetry, as we see when Arthur arms himself for the combat with the giant of St. Michael's Mount:

Aftyre euesange, sir Arthure hymeselfene
Wente to hys wardrope and warpe of hys wedez,
Armede hym in a actone with orfraeez fulle ryche,
Abouen one that a jeryne of Acres owte ouer,
Abouen that a jesseraunt of jentylle maylez,
A jupone of Ierodyne jaggede in schredez;
He brayedez one a bacenett burneschte of syluer,
The beste that was in Basille, wyth bordurs ryche,
The creste and the coronalle enclosed so faire
Wyth clasppis of clere golde, couched wyth stones;
The vesare, the aventaile, enarmede so faire,
Voyde withowttyne vice, with wyndowes of syluer.   (900–11)

[warpe of – *took off*; actone – *quilted jacket*; orfraeez – *gold embroidery*; jeryne – *tunic*; jesseraunt...maylez – *fine coat of mail*; jupone – *surcoat*; jaggede in schredez – *slashed in long pendants*; brayedez – *puts*; bacenett – *helmet*; coronalle – *crown*; enclosed – *surrounded*;[2] couched – *set*; vesare – *visor*; aventaile – *neck armour*; Voyde...syluer – *plain without emblem, with silver plates* (?).]

Throughout *Morte Arthure* the poet's aim is to depict life in the heroic past in terms of fourteenth-century attitudes and manners, and as this passage shows, the words for fashionable items of armour were nearly all French.[3] The *actone* (with, in Arthur's case, its *orfraeez*) was a jerkin stuffed to protect the body from blows. Above this Arthur wears a tunic called a *jeryne*; the word is not recorded elsewhere in English, but it is the French *giron*. The *jesseraunt* is the coat of mail, though the word seems at this date to have been something of an innovation, replacing the more usual *bruny* (which was a Germanic word that had been borrowed by the French). Over his mail-coat Arthur puts on a *jupone*, slit in the most fashionable manner. This word also is not recorded in English before the late fourteenth century.

The account then turns to Arthur's helmet. By this period the unwieldy *helm* was unfashionable for combat (though it still continued in use in tournaments), and so Arthur puts on a *bacenett*, mounted with *creste* and *coronalle*, and fitted with the moveable *vesare* to protect his face, and the attached *aventaile* (probably of chain-mail) which hangs down over his neck.[4] Arthur is dressed as a chivalric knight of the late fourteenth century, and to achieve this effect the poet has to use the appropriate technical French vocabulary. Likewise the hero and his horse in *Gawain* are armed in a flurry of gallicisms before they set out for the Green Chapel (ll. 566–618).

A large number of areas of fashionable activity called for a French vocabulary if the subjects were to be described in detail. A man may take his *mete* and *drynk*, but if his *haute cuisine* is to be itemised then the words will be French (as in *Wynnere and Wastoure*, 332–55, and *Morte Arthure*, 176–205). Fashionable sports such as hunting and hawking have a very specialised vocabulary (see *Gawain*, 1319–71, and *Parlement*, 25–31, 67–91, 210–45), and no self-respecting nobleman would own a castle without the latest *abataylment*, *barbican* and many a *pynakle* (*Gawain*, 785–802).

This technical vocabulary is not confined to alliterative poetry, for many of the best parallels are to be found in the most prosaic sources, household accounts, wills and inventories. However, the fact that these technical gallicisms are much more prominent in alliterative than in non-alliterative poetry is a mark of the loving attention to detail that is so characteristic of alliterative verse, and it is also a measure of the ease with which the alliterative style accommodated words from 'unpoetic' contexts.

Only a very few words of French origin can be described as principally restricted to alliterative poetry. Two of them are verbs of motion, *aire* (OFr. *errer*) commonly used in the sense 'to go' in *The Wars of Alexander* and *Morte Arthure*, and *brusch* (perhaps OFr. *brosser*, 'to travel through woods') used in several alliterative poems in the sense 'to rush'. Also occurring here and there are the verbs *fylter*, 'to crowd together, become matted', and *frunt*, 'to kick, strike'. *Angard* is apparently derived from the French noun meaning 'vanguard', but its sense has developed in *The Destruction of Troy* to mean 'forwardness' or perhaps 'excess', and even as an adjective to mean 'arrogant'. All of these were unusual words in English which were picked up, perhaps in some cases directly from French works, to extend the alliterative vocabulary in areas where variety was necessary (as with the verbs expressing movement) or occasionally to provide a word with forceful onomatopoeic qualities, as with *frunt*. None of these words, with the possible exception of *aire*, is used often enough to be described as really characteristic of alliterative verse.

The total number of Scandinavian loan-words is much smaller than those derived from French, but nevertheless many of the words that strike the reader as unusual or characteristically alliterative are Scandinavian. They call attention to themselves because they were not in general literary use in the Middle Ages and have not descended into modern standard English. Most of them are northern dialect words, which would have sounded odd in a poem composed by a writer from the south. As dialect words they could be exploited by southern writers for comic effect, as when Chaucer's two northern students in *The Reeve's Tale* use a word such as *hethyng* (ON. *hǽðing*), 'contempt', in 'Now are we dryve til hethyng and til scorn' (*Reeve's Tale*, 4110). When used, however, by a northern writer the word is unremarkable, as when Darius contemptuously sends Alexander a present – 'for hething a hatt made of twyggis' (*Wars*, 1714). Not surprisingly these northernisms are more common in alliterative poems written in the north and north midlands than in those from the south midlands, though the need and desire for a wide vocabulary meant that northern expressions spread further south in alliterative verse than in prose and verse of other sorts.

To survey the character and distribution of words of Scandinavian origin that were in fairly general use in the northern half of the country and are found so frequently in alliterative verse as to become characteristic of alliterative diction, we may look at a group of verbs. A verb such as *carpe*, 'to speak', was in very general use in the north, and was even sometimes used by southern writers such as Gower and Chaucer. It is extremely common in alliterative poetry. *Busk*, 'to get ready, dress, hasten', is also common in alliterative poetry as well as in northern works such as *Cursor Mundi*. The verb *attle*, 'to intend', is almost exclusively restricted to northern poetry, and it is also found in modern dialect in the north, which suggests that the word may have been in earlier spoken currency there. Once again, it is widespread in alliterative verse, although, unlike *carpe* and *busk*, it is not used by Langland and his followers. Possibly it would not have been fully understood by the audience they were attempting to reach.

Caire, meaning 'to ride, travel' (ON. *keyra*) is a word of very restricted currency in non-alliterative works, but it is widely used in alliterative poems (though again not in the *Piers Plowman* group) as an addition to the stock of verbs of motion. Another such verb, *rayke*, 'to wander, leave' (ON. *reika*) is found in the more northerly alliterative works and also in Scottish poems. The form *raken*, found in *Pierce the Ploughman's Crede*, is derived from a different source, OE. *racian*, 'to move, hasten': 'ryʒt as Robertes men raken aboute/ At feires' (72–3).

A verb that is even more restricted geographically is *frayst*, 'to ask' or 'to test'. To judge from the quotations recorded in the dictionaries, its use extended no further south than Lincolnshire in the east (Robert Mannyng of Bourne) and Shropshire in the west (John Audelay). None of the more southerly alliterative writers uses the word in the fourteenth century, though it is found often enough in *Gawain* and the related poems, as well as in *Morte Arthure*, *The Destruction of Troy*, *The Wars of Alexander*, *The Awntyrs off Arthure* and Scottish alliterative poems. It is evident, therefore, that these Scandinavian verbs illustrate a wide range of regional and contextual patterns of use, which demonstrates the dangers of generalising about the effect of the Scandinavian element in alliterative poetic diction.

None of the Scandinavian words discussed so far is restricted absolutely to alliterative verse, though most are found there much more regularly than in other northern works. There are, however, a few words of Scandinavian origin that in this period are recorded only in alliterative poetry. One of these is the verb *donke*, 'to moisten', first found in one of the *Harley Lyrics*, and later only in a number of alliterative poems, usually (as in the *Harley Lyrics*) in conjunction with *dew*:

The dewe appon dayses donkede full faire.   (*Parlement*, 10)

Although the verb is not recorded outside alliterative verse in the fourteenth century, it is found in modern dialects of the north with the meaning 'to make damp, drizzle'. This suggests that it was always a colloquial word in northern dialects, one that would not normally have been in written use, but an element of the spoken language that was taken over by the alliterative poets to be incorporated into their poetic diction.

The commendatory adjective *wale*, 'excellent', is a great favourite of alliterative poets, and it is exclusive to them in the fourteenth century, although recorded in the thirteenth-century poem *Genesis and Exodus*. Its primary sense is 'chosen', and it was developed from the noun *wale* (ON. *val*), 'choice', and from the verb meaning 'to choose' (which was in later use as a dialect word in Scotland and the north). Its popularity in alliterative verse may be attributed to its usefulness as an adjective of lax application registering general approval. Gawain's behaviour can be described as *wale*, and so (in *Purity*) can wine. In *The Destruction of Troy* it is at times used almost without meaning, as a mere metrical convenience, as when Antenor pulls up anchor: 'Wound vp full wightly all his wale ancres' (1943).

A word of special interest is one of the group of alliterative words for 'man' – *tulke*. This has a different history from the other alliterative synonyms for 'man' which are ultimately inherited from the Old English poetic vocabulary. *Tulke*, however, is a loan-word from Scandinavia, where its meaning was 'spokesman, interpreter'. In English it is very rare outside alliterative poetry; indeed there seems to be only one occurrence and that is in the Anglo-Norman Chronicle of Peter Langtoft, composed early in the fourteenth century by a native of Bridlington in Yorkshire. Though the chronicle is in Anglo-Norman, the part of it that deals with Edward I's wars against the Scots contains rough alliterative tail-rhyme stanzas in English, which some earlier readers took to be faithful records of the songs of the opposing armies. One of the stanzas rounds off Langtoft's account of the rout of the Scots at the battle of Dunbar in 1296. It is a song abusing a defeated enemy and wryly commending the English footsoldier. In the process the Scotsman is referred to as a *tulke*:

Bi waye
Herd I never saye
Of prester pages,
To pyke
The robes of the rike
That in the felde felle.
They token ay tulke;
The roghe raggy sculke
Rug ham in helle![5]

[*Nowhere did I ever hear of lads swifter in robbing the robes of the rich who fell in the field. They seized any man – may the rough shaggy Skulker tear them apart in Hell!*]

It is highly unlikely that these verses were genuinely composed on the battlefield, but the important fact is that they are represented as such, and that *tulke* may therefore be regarded as the sort of word a northern soldier might have used, a colloquial word and, in this instance at least, a term of abuse.

However, the word was later elevated into better company. It is found in six alliterative poems, all from the northern half of the midlands, *The Parlement of the Thre Ages*, *Gawain*, *Purity*, *St. Erkenwald*, *The Wars of Alexander* and *The Destruction of Troy*. It is a neutral word implying neither commendation nor blame, for in the same poem it can be used both of God and of the thwarted Sodomites (*Purity*, 498 and 889). As the only synonym for 'man' alliterating on the letter *t*, its value to an alliterative poet in increasing the range of possible alliterative combinations is obvious. The fact that it is recorded only once outside alliterative poetry, and that it did not descend into modern dialect use, suggests that the word was not of general currency and may have been used only very locally.

It appears that quite a number of the Scandinavian loan-words that entered the alliterative poetic vocabulary were taken from the spoken language. They were northern dialect words. It is difficult at this distance to gauge the effect of introducing dialectal elements into alliterative verse that was itself, in the main, regionally based. Some words were presumably used so regularly in alliterative verse that they *became* poetic words, shaking off their former associations and taking on connotations that they had not earlier possessed. Their range of associations and their stylistic status would be quite different in speech from that in alliterative poetry. When asked about the rainfall, the nineteenth-century native of Cumberland is reported to have replied gloomily, 'It donks an' dozzles an' does, but niver cums iv any girt pell',[6] and perhaps his fourteenth-century ancestor would have used *donke* in much the same sense in that situation. But in the context of alliterative verse the word conjures up the sprinkling of dew in the forest glade before the warm sun had dried the leaves; it has become part of a romantic, heroic and poetic world. However, other words were valuable to the poet precisely because they retained their dialectal associations, signifying aspects of the everyday world in which the north-western audience lived and worked.

The clearest example of this is the topographical vocabulary used by several alliterative poets, in particular the authors of *Gawain* and *The Wars of Alexander*. These are dialect words that describe the rugged landscape of the north. Although most of them are of Scandinavian origin, one or two descend from Old English, such as *clogh*, 'cliff', and *knarre*, 'crag'. The evidence of the use of these two words as elements in place-names shows them to be northern terms, since names containing elements derived from OE. *clōh* are found north of Staffordshire and Derbyshire, and those with OE. *cnearr* are recorded in the West Riding of Yorkshire and in Northumberland.[7]

Many more of the distinctively northern topographical terms are Scandinavian loans, and this vocabulary is used strikingly in *Gawain* to evoke the harsh and hostile character of the northern countryside into which Gawain ventures.[8] There are in particular two episodes which bring out the ruggedness and peril of these northern hills: the boar hunt and the meeting at the Green Chapel. The boar hunt is one of the most dramatic scenes of the poem, because the setting for every stage of the struggle with this fierce beast is so graphically visualised. The boar is first tracked down 'in a knot bi a clyffe, at þe kerre syde' (1431). *Knot* (ON. *knǫttr*), 'hillock', is found in place-names in the north-west, but its only literary use as a topographical term is in *Gawain*. *Ker* (ON. *kjarr*), 'a marshy thicket', is a frequent place-name element in the Danelaw. The lord of the castle bravely follows the boar through *ronez* (ON. *runnr*), 'thickets', and finally corners the beast in the narrow opening of a *rasse* (1570), which is probably the Norse word *rás*, 'a water course'.[9] Both these terms are in topographical use in northern parts of England.

Towards the end of the poem Gawain faces his most perilous trial, and he stands alone, scanning the unfriendly, wintry landscape for any sign of the Green Chapel:

> And seȝe no syngne of resette bisydez nowhere,
> Bot hyȝe bonkkez and brent vpon boþe halue,
> And ruȝe knokled knarrez with knorned stonez;
> Þe skwez of þe scowtes skayned hym þoȝt.   (2164–7)

[resette – *shelter*; brent – *steep*; halue – *side*; ruȝe...stonez – *rough and rugged crags with gnarled stones*; Þe skwez...skayned – *the clouds were grazed by the jutting rocks*.]

The three alliterating words in the last line are all of Scandinavian origin. *Skwez*, like the modern 'sky', is from ON. *ský*, while *skayned* is from ON. *skeina*, 'to scratch'. *Scowtes* is particularly interesting. It represents ON. *skúti*, which means 'an overhanging rock'. The *O.E.D.* does not record the noun elsewhere in English literature, but it survives as a place-name element in Kinder Scout in the Peak District and Scout Moor in Lancashire. The implication must be that this was a dialect word used regularly by the poet and his audience to describe the craggy peaks in the regions they lived in and through which Gawain (no soft southerner, he) is travelling. For an audience in the north-west midlands this word and a number of others like it would have conjured up the bleak and desolate landscape of the Peaks and the Pennines that they knew so well.

There is, as we see, a particular aptness in the language used to describe the terrain through which Gawain must venture. The same Scandinavian topographical vocabulary is used quite noticeably in *The Wars of Alexander*, but in this case the poet is describing Alexander's expedition through Asia. Here, too, are the *fellis*, and beyond the Ganges lies an unscalable mountain, described in terms that a native of the north-west of England might have used of his local peaks:

> Cloȝes at was cloude-he, clynterand torres,
> Rochis and rogh stanes, rokkis vnfaire,
> Scutis to þe scharpe schew sckerres a hundreth. (4863–5)

[Cloȝes... torres – *cliffs high as the clouds, craggy peaks*; Rochis – *boulders*; Scutis... hundreth – *a hundred crags jut out to the jagged clouds*.]

Clynterand is formed on the noun *clynt* (Old Danish *klint*), 'cliff', and *sckerres* is ON. *sker*, 'rock', and both nouns are preserved especially in place-names of the north-west. *Scutis* is the verb related to the noun *scowte* in *Gawain*, discussed above. A word here which is not Scandinavian nevertheless merits attention. *Torres*, 'rocky peaks', is of Celtic origin (borrowed into OE.), and is a term in very restricted currency in place-names, confined almost entirely to the extreme south-western counties and also to Derbyshire and adjacent parts of Staffordshire.[10] It must have been a very expressive word to north-western audiences, for it is several times used in alliterative verse to portray vivid and dramatic scenes, as in *Pearl*, 875, in a description of the thunderous voice from Heaven coming 'as þunder þroweȝ in torreȝ blo' – 'as thunder crashes around dark peaks'.

In scenes like this in *The Wars of Alexander* the topographical vocabulary of the north lacks the special appropriateness that it has in *Gawain*, but the function of these words is to represent the distant Asian mountains in terms that were meaningful and striking to an audience in the north-west of England. The power of these words is such that the author can also use them as vivid images, as when the blood flows from the dying Darius 'in grete gill-stremes' (3231). *Gill*, meaning 'ravine', is a word of Norwegian origin, one not used by the Danes who established themselves in England in such numbers, but only by those Vikings who left Ireland and the Isle of Man to settle in the north-western counties of Cumberland and Lancashire.[11] It is a word found quite frequently in place-names in the north-west, as at Blagill (i.e. 'Dark Ravine') in Cumberland. The *gill-stremes* of blood must have been an image of unusual power for the original audience of the poem.

Generally speaking, then, the Scandinavian words used by the alliterative writers have the following characteristics. They are not by origin literary words but words of northern dialect, some in widespread use in the northern half of the country, but others apparently of more limited currency. A number of them, by frequent use, probably became distinctively alliterative and poetic words, but many more retain their associations as local words descriptive of everyday objects and activities: the hills, valleys and streams, talking and riding.

We have been examining a variety of words that were introduced into the English language at some time during the Middle Ages. The characteristic alliterative diction also includes quite a number of native words, some of which had been poetic words in *Beowulf*, although in general the changes in poetic diction, in line with the changes in the language itself, had been very sweeping between the Old English period and the fourteenth century. In both periods the poet felt the need for a wide vocabulary, but in each case he answered this need by drawing on very different verbal resources. For example, both Old English and fourteenth-century alliterative poetry needed a wide range of words to describe the business of fighting. In *The Battle of Maldon* the concept of 'battle' itself is expressed by the following nouns and compounds: *beadu(-ræs)*, *gecamp*, *fæhð*, *gefeoht*, *garræs*, *guð(-plega)*, *here*, *hild*, *gemot*, *getoht* and *wig(-plega)*. Of these, *gefeoht* is represented in the fourteenth century by *fyȝt* which is in general use, *kempe* is found twice in *Morte Arthure* but not elsewhere, *here* is used in alliterative verse but in the sense 'army'. Of the others no trace remains. They have been displaced by such synonyms as *batayl*, *stour*, *strif* and *werre*, all of which are French loan-words.

Despite these massive and inevitable changes in the poetic vocabulary, there is one remarkable group of words that survives in poetic use from the tenth to the fourteenth century. The synonyms for 'man, warrior' in *Beowulf* include *beorn*, *freca*, *guma*, *hæleð*, *leod*, *rinc*, *scealc*, *secg* and *wiga*. The corresponding words in *Gawain* are *burne*, *freke*, *gome*, *haþel*, *lede*, *renk*, *schalk*, *segge* and *wyȝe*.[12] Of these only *haþel* and *schalk* are absent from the vocabulary of *Piers Plowman*. None of these words is used by Chaucer, none has descended into modern standard English, and most of them are rarely recorded in the fourteenth century outside alliterative poetry. Since they are not words in general use, their presence in the poetry of the Revival is a distinctive feature of the alliterative style, and it raises questions about the relationship between the poetic vocabulary of Old English and Middle English alliterative verse. It is not easy to follow the routes these words took from the Old English to the late Middle English period, owing to the scarcity of records in early Middle English. Nevertheless, an examination of the history of the individual nouns, in so far as it can be recovered, does suggest that there were a number of different patterns of survival and regeneration, and it illuminates the methods and resources of fourteenth-century alliterative poets.

The evidence is most extensive for the three words *burne*, *gome* and *lede*. From the eighth to the fifteenth century these were words of heroic or romantic poetic diction. All are in Laȝamon's *Brut* at the beginning of the thirteenth century, in the *Harley Lyrics* at the beginning of the fourteenth, and in non-alliterative romances from the beginning to the end of the fourteenth century, from *Guy of Warwick* and *Kyng Alisaunder* (both *c.* 1300) to *Libeaus Desconus* and *Sir Degrevant*. Naturally alliterative poets took up these words as a welcome contribution to their stock of synonyms. *Cheuelere Assigne* is the only alliterative poem of àny length that uses none of them.

Another two of the synonyms may owe their survival at least partly to their use as colloquial and dialectal words. It is always difficult to be sure that a word was colloquial, since of necessity the only direct evidence is in written documents, but if a word is found as a personal name, or is later recorded in dialects, there is reason to suppose that it was used colloquially. Both pieces of evidence apply to *freke*;[13] there are records of names such as Hugo le Freke, and the word reappears in modern dialects of the north, where it has slipped

down the social scale and means 'fellow'. Whether, side by side with its colloquial use, the word was in continuous use throughout the early Middle Ages
as a poeticism is difficult to determine. It is not found in early Middle English
verse such as Laʒamon's *Brut*, but it is in *St. Katherine*, the alliterative prose
work contemporary with Laʒamon. In the fourteenth century it is found only
occasionally outside alliterative verse, in romances such as *Kyng Alisaunder*
and, later in the century, in *Firumbras*.

About *schalk* there is less evidence. The word is found in several early
Germanic languages in the sense 'servant',[14] and this is apparently its meaning
in Scottish dialects.[15] The implication is that it was used colloquially from Old
English times. Early Middle English records of the word are sparse. It is used by
Laʒamon, and then in *Joseph of Arimathie*. In the works of the Revival it is
mainly restricted to northern poems, which is again a possible indication that its
poetic use in the fourteenth century was borrowed from northern dialect.

Like *schalk*, the synonyms *renk* and *segge* are recorded in one of the two
texts of Laʒamon's *Brut*, the Cotton Caligula manuscript. The scribe of the
other text in the Cotton Otho manuscript, however, extensively revises
Laʒamon's work, reducing its length and modifying its vocabulary. In the
process of this revision, Caligula's *rink*, *segg* and *scalc* are replaced by *man* or
cniht. Of the many words that the Otho scribe consistently removes from his
version, several, including *blonk*, 'horse', and *douth*, 'troop', appear again in
the poetry of the Revival.[16] There could be a number of reasons for the Otho
scribe's prejudice against these words; that they were archaic, or too exclusively poetic, or that they were dialectal. Whatever his precise motives for
rejecting them, the basis for his dislike of them must have been that the words
had a stylistic flavour that he wished to exclude.

Though rejected by the Otho scribe, both *renk* and *segge* are used widely
in the poetry of the Revival, and continue in use by Scottish writers into the
sixteenth century. In what contexts they survived in the century separating
Laʒamon from the poets of the Revival remains unclear. It may be that more
complete records of the poetry during that century would show that the words
continued to be used as occasional poeticisms, and were then seized upon by
alliterative poets. It is also possible, however, that they were dialect words
of the north and west. In support of the latter hypothesis is the fact that the
change of vowel from Laʒamon's *rink* (OE. *rinc*) to the common fourteenth-
century *renk* suggests the influence of the Norse *rekkr* (earlier **renk-*). If
Scandinavian influence at some stage is granted, then it is likely that the word
was in use in northern dialects, and that it was at least partly by this route that it
reached the alliterative poets.

Haþel replaces in the alliterative scheme the Old English *hæleð*. The Middle
English word is probably a development of *æðele* by association with *hæleð*.
In Old English *æðele* is used only as an adjective meaning 'noble'. The last
recorded instance of *hæleð* and the first example of *aðel* as a noun meaning
'noble warrior' are both in Laʒamon's *Brut*. The form *haþel* is first found in
the *Harley Lyrics*. In the Revival it is a word favoured by the more northern
writers.

Lastly, *wyʒe* is something of a puzzle. It does not seem to have been recorded
at all in the early Middle English period, and first reappears in *Wynnere and
Wastoure* and *William of Palerne*. After that it is used by most alliterative poets,
though it is rarely found outside alliterative verse. However, it becomes quite
a favourite of sixteenth-century Scottish writers. Did they borrow it from the

alliterative tradition which was strong in Scotland during the fifteenth century? Or was it a dialect word of Scotland and the north? *Wiga* was not exclusively a poetic word in Old English, and its use may have continued unrecorded in speech for a very considerable time.

The history (or rather the lack of it) of a word such as *wyȝe* stresses how very tentative any conclusions about its stylistic status must be. When the author of *Wynnere and Wastoure* describes himself as a 'westren wy', is he using a colloquial, everyday word that poets writing in other traditions would shun, perhaps a word a bit like *bloke* today? Or is it a precious, literary word, as *wight* is now? Whatever the original connotations of the word, once it had become a part of the traditional alliterative diction it took on new connotations arising from that context.

The particular value to alliterative poets of *wyȝe* and its synonyms was that they were words of very general application. Unlike *knyȝt*, *lorde* and *prynce*, they were not elevated or idealising words denoting something specific such as 'heroic warrior', but words that could be used in any situation to mean 'man', or sometimes even more broadly still 'being'. God is a *wyȝe* in *Gawain* (2441), but on the other hand the guide warns Gawain not to venture towards the Green Chapel since 'Þer wonez a wyȝe in þat waste, þe worst vpon erþe' (2098). In *Morte Arthure* the giant of St. Michael's Mount, who roasts infants for his supper, is described as *bierne*, *lede*, *renke*, *schalke* and *segge*, while Arthur himself is usually referred to in that episode as *kyng* or *prynce*.[17] It is the latter words that are elevated in meaning. In such cases it is important to distinguish between the denotation and the associations of a word. The alliterative synonyms for 'man' are general in their denotation, but because they are used typically in heroic or romantic environments, they become inhabitants of that world, whether they be chivalric knights or evil giants.

It has often been maintained that the survival of these synonyms requires us to suppose the continuity of an oral alliterative tradition from Old English verse. However, we have seen that nearly all of them can be traced intermittently in written documents through the early Middle English period. The most that can be said is that they were not commonly used in writing, and that some of them at least, such as *burne* and *lede*, were poetic words mainly reserved for certain types of romantic and heroic (but not necessarily alliterative) verse. The synonyms for 'man' are indeed a remarkable group, enduring when so large a proportion of the Old English poetic diction had disappeared, but they perhaps demonstrate not the stability and purity of an unbroken alliterative tradition, but instead the resourcefulness of alliterative poets and their readiness to embrace words from every conceivable environment.

There are other ways, too, for a poet to add to the stock of alliterative synonyms. By a process which is common in language generally, and particularly so in poetry, words may be used in meanings that have been extended beyond their normal range, and there are numerous examples in alliterative verse. The verbs of motion are a fruitful group for studying this, since several words whose original meanings were more specialised have become generalised with the sense 'to go, travel'. Thus *chese*, 'to choose', was frequently used in the phrase *chese the way*, and by abbreviation the verb alone came to be used in alliterative verse in the sense 'to move'. The basic sense of *hale* is 'to haul, pull', but its meanings become diversified in alliterative verse. In *Gawain* alone its semantic range includes 'to go' ('Halled out at þe hal dor', 458), 'to come' ('hales in at þe halle dor', 136), 'to rise' ('hit haled vpon lofte', 788), 'to pass' ('þe halidayez holly were halet', 1049), 'to pull' ('Haled hem by a lyttel hole', 1338), and 'to let fly' ('Haled to hym of here arewez', 1455).

Another process common in language generally, and exploited to the full by alliterative poets, is the practice of using one part of speech for another, which in alliterative verse most often means using an adjective absolutely, as a noun. By taking advantage of this, the poet not only increases the scope of his vocabulary in areas where there are gaps, but more important, he is able to draw attention very economically to one particular aspect of the object that he wishes to emphasise. For example, although the *Gawain*-poet can hardly be said to have a technical need for extra alliterative synonyms for 'man', he also uses to denote his hero the absolute adjectives *gentyl*, *hende*, *noble*, *semly* and *wlonk*. Whereas the nouns, *gome*, *freke* and the others, are used with very broad signification, the meaning of the absolute adjectives is very sharply defined. Their function is to stress the aspect of the character that is relevant to the reader at that point in the poem.[18] Those applied to Gawain himself all stress his nobility of manner. On the other hand, the Green Knight entering the hall to the horrified amazement of the knights of the Round Table is described appropriately as *þe sturne*, i.e. 'the threatening one' (214), and this appellation occurs significantly during the description of his sharp and menacing axe. The advantages of being able to use an adjective as a noun are even clearer in the case of defining aspects of the concept 'woman'. For this the stock of Old English poetic words was relatively meagre, since women had been creatures of less significance in early heroic literature. The nouns of Old English derivation were *burde*, *lady*, *may*, *wif* and *woman*, and to these were added nouns from French such as *dame* and the terms of rank, *duches* and *prynces*. But women earn their place in medieval romance because they attract a man's attention with their beauty and grace, their kindness and their wiles, and so the use of the absolute adjective is an ideal method of emphasising these qualities. 'Comaundez me to þat *cortays*, your comlych fere' (2411) – 'commend me to that courteous lady, your lovely wife', Gawain says ruefully, and not without irony, after the Green Knight has unveiled to him the trick that the lady has played in her game of 'cortaysye'. Elsewhere in alliterative poetry women are defined by a range of absolute adjectives including *þe clere*, *comly*, *dere*, *fayr*, *fre*, *gay*, *hende*, *menskful*, *schene*, *swete*, *wlonke* and *worþy*. *Schene*, 'bright one', is used absolutely with three different applications. It emphasises a young girl's radiant beauty as contrasted with the grotesque ugliness of the hairy monster who is threatening to ravish her:

He wald haue schowid on þat schene had noȝt men halden.   (*Wars*, 4759)

[schowid – *used force*.]

It is used of the shining blade from which Gawain involuntarily flinches as he catches sight of it coming down on his neck (*Gawain*, 2268). Also it denotes the bright sun which casts its burning rays on Jonah, who is disgruntled at having been deprived of his shelter (*Patience*, 440).

We have been considering the principal ways in which alliterative poets built up their poetic diction and established an exceedingly rich and varied vocabulary. The impetus to do this sprang from the demands of the alliteration, although, of course, it was quite possible to write alliterative poetry without using this specialised vocabulary, as *Pierce the Ploughman's Crede* shows. The majority of alliterative poets, prompted by the needs of alliteration, quarried every conceivable source to provide themselves with a vocabulary that helped them to write alliterative verse more fluently and, more important, that gave to their poetry a distinctiveness and an exuberance equalled by no other school of writers. There are quite a number of words, and we have looked at some of them, which were not in general use and yet were used regularly in alliterative verse. Some, we have seen, are northernisms used now and then in other northern poems, some which are not found elsewhere in written records are arguably taken over from colloquial northern dialects, and a few words are derived, through one channel or another, from the poetic diction of Old English verse. It is difficult to judge what stylistic flavour these 'chiefly alliterative' words had for their audiences, and since they were taken from such a wide variety of stylistic contexts it is probably wrong to generalise. However, the 'chiefly alliterative' words undoubtedly had for alliterative poets a distinctive and special quality. *Blonk* was not simply an alternative for *stede* and *horse*,[19] and *schalk* was distinguished from *man* or *kny3t*, as was *wale* from *gode* or *noble*. It is not the meaning that distinguishes them, for *schalk* denotes the same thing as *man*. The outward sign of the special status of these words is their function and position in the alliterative line. The synonyms in general use – *stede* and *horse*, *man* and *kny3t*, *gode* and *noble* – may be used anywhere in the line, alliteratively or non-alliteratively, but those words restricted to alliterative verse and characteristic of it are used, in the majority of cases, only in alliterative positions.[20] This may be illustrated by quoting a passage from *Purity*, where the master of the wedding-feast is reproving the guest who arrived in foul clothes:

'Say me, frende', quod þe freke wyth a felle chere,
'Hou wan þou into þis won in wedez so fowle?
Þe abyt þat þou hatz upon, no halyday hit menskez;
Þou, burne, for no brydale art busked in wedez!
How watz þou hardy þis hous for þyn unhap to ne3e
In on so ratted a robe and rent at þe sydez?
Þow art a gome ungoderly in þat goun febele;
Þou praysed me and my place ful pover and ful gnede,
Þat watz so prest to aproche my presens hereinne.
Hopez þou I be a harlot þi erigaut to prayse?'
Þat oþer burne watz abayst of his broþe wordez,
And hurkelez doun with his hede, þe urþe he biholdez.   (139–50)

[felle – *fierce*; wan – *arrived*; won – *house*; abyt – *clothing*; menskez – *honours*; brydale – *wedding-feast*; busked – *dressed*; hardy – *bold*; unhap – *misfortune*; ne3e – *approach*; ratted – *ragged*; ungoderly – *vile*; febele – *mean*; gnede – *ungenerously*; prest – *ready*; Hopez þou – *do you think*; harlot – *beggar*; erigaut – *cloak*; abayst – *abashed*; broþe – *fierce*; hurkelez – *cowers*.]

In these lines the words that are characteristic of alliterative poetry but not used by Chaucer – the nouns *burne*, *freke* and *gome*, the verbs *busked* and *hurkelez*, and the adjective *broþe* – are all used in alliterative positions. On the other hand, the words used for the non-alliterating fourth stress are found in Chaucer and generally elsewhere: *chere*, *sydez*, *wedez* and *wordez*, *biholdez*, *ne3e* and *prayse*, *febele*, *fowle* and *gnede*,[21] and the adverb *hereinne*. Yet there is one exception. Usually in alliterative poetry the verb *menske* and its related noun, adjective and adverb are used in alliterative positions, and the words, which are of Scandinavian derivation, are part of the northern vocabulary, common enough in alliterative verse but rarely used elsewhere. Exceptionally, in this one line in *Purity*, the word is used in a non-alliterative position. It has been argued that cases like this show how a good poet can break a traditional stylistic 'rule' for special effect.[22] This is perhaps to find significance where it does not exist. We should think in terms of 'norms', which can be varied, rather than of 'rules' which may be broken only with profound stylistic implications.

Taken as a whole, however, the passage from *Purity* supports the view that the 'chiefly alliterative' words possessed a distinct stylistic status for alliterative poets. The words became a characteristic element in the alliterative style, but they remained 'metrical' words. The feeling seems to have been that they were words introduced into the poetic vocabulary to satisfy a metrical need, and therefore they could not be used freely where the alliterative pattern did not call for them. The implication of this must be that these words continued to be regarded as out of the ordinary. They had a special quality, even though in alliterative positions they became established as a traditional feature of the alliterative style.

Collocations and Set Phrases

Having looked at some of the more characteristic words that provide the basis for the alliterative poetic diction, we may now turn our attention to the relationship existing between the words in the line. It is a striking feature of the alliterative style that words are paired and grouped together in a predictable way, and that as a result one line often recalls lines from other poems. The second line of *Gawain* describes Troy as 'Þe borȝ brittened and brent to brondez and askez'. A search through the alliterative corpus produces numerous examples of the phrase *britten and brenne* in the sense 'destroy and burn'. Among others are Susannah's cry 'I be bretenet and brent in baret to byde' (*Pistill*, 147), Arthur's question to Sir Craddock about his knights at home in Britain, 'Are they brettenede, or brynte, or broughte owte of lyue?' (*Morte Arthure*, 3520), Lady Mede's complaint that Conscience has assembled men 'To brennen and to bruten, to bete adoun strengthes' (*Piers Plowman*, C. iv. 238), and (with one element of the phrase in each half-line) the Duke of Saxony's threat to the Roman Emperor to 'bruttene alle hise burnes and brenne his londes' (*Palerne*, 1133). It is clear from these examples that *britten and brenne* forms a standard collocation in alliterative verse, and one that is entirely typical of the alliterative style, though not often found elsewhere.[23]

The use of well-established collocations has always been part of the language itself. Frequently, even today, collocations are alliterative, and the explanation is that alliteration makes the phrase more memorable and heightens the association between the two words. For example, the adjectives 'spick and span' never occur separately, 'kith' is now always accompanied by 'kin', 'hale' more often than not calls forth 'hearty', and 'the more the merrier' is a phrase in constant use. Collocations, both alliterative and non-alliterative, are also a characteristic feature of medieval English verse-technique. What has aptly been termed the 'doublet-style'[24] is richly illustrated in the opening lines of the tail-rhyme romance *Octavian* (dated *c.* 1350):

Lytyll and mykyll, olde and yonge,
Lystenyth now to my talkynge,
   Of whome Y wyll yow kythe;
Jesu lorde, of hevyn kynge,
Grawnt us all hys blessynge
   And make us gladd and blythe.
Sothe sawys Y wyll yow mynge
Of whom the worde wyde can sprynge,
   Yf ye wyll lystyn and lythe;
Yn bokys of ryme hyt ys tolde
How hyt befelle owre eldurs olde,
   Well oftyn sythe.

(1–12)[25]

The doublet – that is to say the association of two complementary or contrasting words of the same grammatical class, adjective with adjective, verb with verb and so on – is both the most striking and the most common form of collocation. These doublet-phrases, *lytyll and mykyll, olde and yonge, gladd and blythe, lystyn and lythe* are repeated again and again in the romances. When used with restraint and appositeness they help to create an open-textured and relaxed style that does not make excessive demands on the concentration of its audience.

It comes as a surprise to many to observe that the collocation is also very much part of Chaucer's style. Chaucer's indebtedness to English traditions of poetry is now becoming more clearly recognised, and his frequent use of doublet-phrases, often alliterative, such as *holt and heeth, leef nor looth, wepe and waille* and so on, is one aspect of that debt.[26]

It was inevitable that the alliterative poet should seize upon this rhetorical device and exploit it to the full. The collocation had for him qualities and a usefulness that he could not ignore. In his search for three words associated in initial sound and in sense, he accepted with gratitude any established collocation that provided him with the basis for a half-line and sometimes even for a full line. By the same process, any new collocations that he formed would tend to be taken up by other alliterative poets, and so in their turn quickly become established as traditional features of the alliterative style.

This explanation lays emphasis on the poet's convenience, which is an important factor but not the only one. Established phrases such as *merth and mynstralsye* or *he rose up radly* are of great value to the reader also. Because they are traditionally poetic the phrases have a wide range of associations developed from previous contexts; they have a shared meaning which is revealed without the need for ponderous reflection. Because the essential idea is stated in a phrase rather than in a single word the concept emerges with emphasis and clarity. These considerations are particularly important in long narrative poems – as so many alliterative poems are – where the need is for an easygoing, perspicuous style, not too tightly packed with meaning and without hooks and barbs to draw the reader deeper when he wants to be skimming along. Therefore the established collocation helps both reader and poet; it is expected and unsurprising, it fits the metre and fills the line, and it evokes a stock response which – precisely because it is stock – can be calculated by the poet. The style gains by being a shared one, because the poet can communicate more immediately by submerging himself within a common stylistic tradition than by asserting his individuality and parading his idiosyncracies.

King Arthur's speech of lament over the dead body of Gawain in *Morte Arthure* is a passage which illustrates a poet taking full advantage of a traditional style for an occasion that demands all the ceremony of established usage:

> Then the corownde kyng cryes fulle lowde:
> 'Dere kosyne o kynde, in kare am I leuede,
> For nowe my wirchipe es wente and my were endide.
> Here es the hope of my hele, my happynge of armes;
> My herte and my hardynes hale one hym lengede,
> My concelle, my comforthe that kepide myne herte;
> Of alle knyghtes the kynge that vndir Criste lifede,
> Thou was worthy to be kynge, thofe I the corowne bare.
> My wele and my wirchipe of alle this werlde riche
> Was wonnene thourghe sir Gawayne and thourghe his witt one.'   (3955–64)

[kynde – *kindred*; wirchipe – *honour*; hele – *prosperity*; happynge – *fortune*; hale – *completely*; lengede – *depended*; kepide – *controlled*; wele – *wealth*; one – *alone*.]

Here the poet favours the most straightforward collocational pattern of two semantically contiguous words set in parallel to provide the basis for the first half-line. One of the commonest such phrases in alliterative verse is *wele...wirchipe*, and J. P. Oakden's lists of alliterative phrases provide a selection of examples of it.[27] A similarly constructed collocation *herte...hardynes*, though not in Oakden's lists, is also recorded in other poems (e.g. *Wars*, 658). The phrase *concelle...comforthe* conforms to the same pattern, although I do not know of other uses of it. However, it is not necessary to show that a certain phrase occurs in identical form elsewhere in order to establish its traditional nature. The essential feature is that the phrase conforms to an expected pattern, and in this case the conformity of *concelle...comforthe* is emphasised by its position as one of a series of doublet nouns having the same metrical function and all referring to the relationship between the dead hero and his bereaved king. Thus, once the underlying pattern has been established, fresh collocations can be created on the same model.

Another common collocational pattern illustrated here is a first half-line based on two nouns, one as the attribute of the other. Generally the order is as in *hope of my hele* and *kosyne o kynde*, but on occasions the poet reverses this as in *of alle knyghtes the kynge*. In this case the purpose of the reversal is to provide a parallel with the line that follows, although the variation of an over-used pattern is welcome for its own sake. The temptation to fill the second stress of the line by a noun in a prepositional phrase is one to which the alliterative poets succumb with monotonous regularity, and the position provides a favourite resting-place for routine phrases such as 'on bent' and 'uppon grounde' even in the best poets.

The passage from *Morte Arthure* provides a particularly common example of a third pattern, the linking of an adjective with its noun, as in *corownde kyng*. The sense in which this phrase is most frequently used is a good indicator of the character of the alliterative style. *Corownde kyng* nearly always means no more than simply 'king'; the fact of his coronation is quite irrelevant to the context, even if the adjective has some slight effect of enhancing his royal status. However, in the passage from *Morte Arthure* the fact that Arthur is 'the corownde kyng' for once is significant, as is revealed by the echo of the phrase a few lines later:

Thou was worthy to be kynge, thofe I the corowne bare.

Although Arthur is king by virtue of coronation, Gawain is the uncrowned king by strength of character, 'of alle knyghtes the kynge'. This shows the exploitation of one of the most commonly used collocations, where a cliché is unexpectedly filled with significance. This sort of verbal resonance is rare in alliterative verse, for it demands from the reader a special kind of attention to detail, a kind, indeed, which would ultimately be destructive of the traditional narrative style. If the attention of the audience were regularly to be directed away from narrative progression towards verbal detail and echo, then *corownde kyng* ought to mean more than 'king', and when it does not, the poet's use of a pleonasm would become an obtrusive fault of style.

These lines from *Morte Arthure* show in the most straightforward manner how the alliterative poet may use a collocation to form the basis of a first half-line. Alternatively, a collocation may span a line, as *wele...worship* does in:

Þat wele wantid no wegh, ne worship in vrthe.   (*Troy*, 1696)

More interesting is the process whereby a word-cluster may shape the expression of certain stereotyped themes. For example, in the description of daybreak or nightfall, *derk* is most frequently collocated with *day*. Dawn is announced in several poems with the words:

> Whan þe derk was don and the day sprongen.
>
> > (*Siege J.*, 853; *Troy*, 1079, 6061, 7554, 12531; and cf. *Parlement*, 16)

Another poet uses a different verb without altering the sense:

> Sone þe derke ouiredrafe and þe day springis. (*Wars*, 1505)

Around the same alliterating trio the author of *St. Erkenwald* presents a more vivid picture:

> Þe derke ny3t ouerdrofe, and day belle ronge. (117)

All these poets depict daybreak as a balanced contrast between darkness (in the first half-line) and light (in the second), and nightfall may be similarly described:

> Quen it is dreuyn to þe derke, and þe day fynyst. (*Wars*, 687)

Or the *derk...day...drive* cluster may be fitted into the first half-line to allow for an expression of the agency of God, *Dry3ten*:

> The day dryuez to þe derk, as Dry3tyn biddez. (*Gawain*, 1999)

To describe dawn the contrast of the basic *derk...day* collocation may be dropped, while the idea of God's activity is retained:

> And as Dryghtyn the day droue frome þe heuen. (*Parlement*, 6)
> When þe dawande day Dry3tyn con sende. (*Patience*, 445)

In many of the grand set-piece descriptions of alliterative poetry, the feast, the sea-storm and so on, the same tendency may be observed of a group of words orbiting around the central concept and directing the poetic realisation of the theme.[28]

The tendency of words to cluster together in this way inevitably leads to recurrent verbal and conceptual echoes between one poem and another. The structure of the alliterative line encourages the poet to build his half-lines around established collocations in a predictable way, and so in any poem many half-lines are repeated more or less exactly both within that poem and in poems by other writers. The repetition of whole lines is not so common, but it occurs especially when the poet is describing a set topic. Faced with these parallels, earlier critics assumed them to be the result of imitation or identity of authorship. However, it is rarely possible to pin down the 'source' of a collocation, and nearly always it owes its existence to an alliterative school of poetry, or more generally still to the English poetic tradition.

Quite often useful information about the status and history of a collocation may be gained by studying its use outside alliterative poetry, and by tracing the origins of the combination and also of the individual words within it. The very widespread use of collocations in Middle English romances provides good evidence for judging whether a particular phrase had become established generally in English verse.[29] Collocations that are found extremely frequently are, for example: *clip and kiss, game and glee, live in land, man on mold* and *see with sight*. All of these are taken up by the alliterative poets. Many of such phrases are, in fact, of great antiquity and are found first in Old English poetry, as is *clyppe and cysse* in *The Wanderer* and *menn ofer moldan* in *The Dream of the Rood* and elsewhere.

Other phrases that are very common in fourteenth-century verse incorporate words that entered the language after the Conquest. The collocation *romance ... rede* is fitted to the iambic rhythm of *Octavian*, 'In romans as we rede' (15), while in alliterative verse it is adapted to the rhythm of the standard half-line with a disyllabic interval:

> Riche romance to rede and rekken the sothe.   (*Parlement*, 250)
> Ne redde in no romance þat euer renke herde.   (*Wynnere*, 23)

There is a particularly interesting group of collocations derived from Scandinavian usage,[30] and in the fourteenth century these are found much more commonly in alliterative verse than elsewhere. We have already looked at the distribution of one phrase of this sort, *britten and brenne*. This is apparently modelled on the collocation found in Norse as *brjóta ok brenna*, although in the Middle English phrase the first verb descends from Old English.[31] The partial anglicisation of a Scandinavian phrase is a characteristic of numerous collocations. In *Gawain*, *glaum ande gle* recalls Norse *glaumr ok gleði*, but on the model of the very widespread *game and glee* the second element of the Norse phrase is replaced by an English synonym. The first element in *sorȝ and syt* (*Pearl*, 663)[32] is derived from Old English, but *syt*, 'care', is a Scandinavian borrowing, and the whole phrase is based on Norse *sorg ok sút*. The word *mynne* is found only in the phrase *more and mynne* (in *Gawain* and *Piers Plowman*) meaning 'the greater and the smaller'. The origin of this is the Norse tag *meiri ok minni*, with anglicisation of the first element. The Norse phrase *gull ok gørsimar*, 'gold and treasure' gave rise to the expression found in *Morte Arthure* and elsewhere, *gersoms and golde*. The author of *Gawain* remodels the phrase by using the similar-sounding loan-word from French, *garysoun*, 'possessions', instead of *gersom*.[33]

How did these Scandinavian phrases reach the alliterative poets? It is important to note that in general the Norse collocations found in English poems were used in Scandinavian prose rather than in verse. This suggests the probability that they entered the English vocabulary as set phrases in speech, as colloquial expressions or as legal formulas and the like, rather than as part of a shared poetic diction. Phrases modelled on Scandinavian usage are particularly common in the twelfth-century poem *Ormulum*, which was composed in an area where the Scandinavian influence on the language and culture was strong. They were taken up by the alliterative poets in the fourteenth century as valuable additions to their stock of collocations. They demonstrate once again that alliterative poetic diction was not based on a fossilised poetic tradition, but rather that the poets were ready to exploit the vigour of the colloquial expressions in their poetic vocabulary.

The most characteristic position of the alliterating collocation is, as we have seen, in the first half-line, and by using it the poet has the basis for a complete metrical unit:

> Þere watz no mon upon molde of myȝt as hymselven.   (*Purity*, 1656)
> Such glaum ande gle glorious to here.   (*Gawain*, 46)

In the second half-line, however, the pressures of the metre operate differently. Here there is no demand for an alliterating pair of words, but instead for a rhythmic, alliterative and syntactic pattern that will *complete* the first half-line. The stress-pattern is more regular, consisting in the majority of cases of a disyllabic interval between stresses $-(X)'XX'(X)$ – or clashing stress $-(X)''(X)$.

To fit these patterns a number of syntactic structures become stereotyped.[34] They have one verbal element that can be varied to match the alliterating sound of the first half-line, and they are sufficiently adaptable to suit a wide range of contexts. A typical example is a unit made up of an adjective that alliterates with the preceding half-line, followed by an infinitive verb with the sense 'to see'. The phrase is used to indicate or to emphasise the appearance of what has been described in the first half-line. If the adjective is monosyllabic, the preferred rhythmic pattern is created by using the verb *byholde*. So in *The Siege of Jerusalem* the tent of the besiegers is 'britaged aboute, briȝt to byholde' (334), and after the battle the Romans 'kesten ded vpon ded, was deil to byholde' (641). A disyllabic adjective produces an interval between the stresses of three syllables. So when Titus sees the starving population of Jerusalem:

> Þe peple in þe pauyment was pite to byholde. (1243)

Many poets tend to avoid this trisyllabic interval in the second half-line, and this is done by using a monosyllabic verb. In *The Wars of Alexander* the hero meets a massive hart 'was meruale to sene' (1061), and in *Alisaunder of Macedoine* Queen Olympias's legs are 'louely too seene' (192).

It will have been observed that the underlying structure is a syntactic and not a lexical one. It is in this way that the patterns used in the second half-line differ from the collocations that are so characteristic of the first half-line.

Romances and historical poems need a wide variety of phrases for describing warriors. The author of *The Destruction of Troy*, who is always satisfied with the most stereotyped expressions, provides good examples of the standard patterns used in the second half-line to give the sense 'brave (or cowardly etc.) men'. If the alliterating adjective is a monosyllable, the rhythmic structure of the line is maintained by *men of armys*:

> With baners on brede, and bold men of armys. (6866)
> Wenton out wightly wale men of armys. (4716)

A disyllabic adjective stressed on the first syllable is completed by *of dedis*:

> Homer was holden haithill of dedis. (38)
> Telamon full tyte, tristy of dedis. (10938)

The same rhythmic pattern is preserved with a trisyllabic adjective and a noun with the stress on the first syllable:

> With chere for to cherys the chiualrus knightes. (509)[35]

The alternative rhythm with clashing stress is another possibility with *knightes*:

> Dede ys the dragon and the derffe knightes. (948)

Such basic patterns that allow for variations to suit context and rhythm are extremely common. An interesting pattern to observe is one with which the poets express a simile or a comparison of some kind. Here the structure consists of a variable noun or adjective, and the phrase *as it* (*they* etc.) *were*, but the position of the variable within the phrase changes to suit the metrical pattern. In *Patience* Jonah's leafy bower is 'happed vpon ayþer half, a hous as hit were' (450), while Gawain, looking for the Green Chapel, sees only 'a lawe as hit were' (*Gawain*, 2171). A different word-order that preserves the same rhythm is shown in *Purity*, 82, for the lord invites to his feast people from the streets 'as barounez þay were' (the noun is disyllabic), and later in the poem the wise men stare in confusion at the mysterious writings on Belshazzar's wall:

> And alle þat loked on þat letter as lewed þay were
> As þay had loked in þe leþer of my lyft bote.   (1580–1)
>
> [lewed – *ignorant*; lyft bote – *left boot*.]

The rhythm with clashing stress is possible with a monosyllabic adjective or noun, and in such cases the word order is rearranged. So the Green Knight glares 'as he wode were' (*Gawain*, 2289), and Will is arrayed 'as I a shepe were' (*Piers Plowman*, Prol. 2).

These and many other similar syntactic structures were used by poets as an aid to composition. Together with the collocations, they constitute a striking feature of the alliterative style. Unfortunately, the use of set expressions of one kind or another, though not a fault in itself, creates a dangerous temptation for the poet. It is often too easy for him to choose the obvious expression, whether it is appropriate or not, and the result can be a limpness of style, or at its worst an irritating meaninglessness. So many collocations have one element that is entirely otiose; *see with sight* means 'see', *calles and clepes* means 'calls'. It is proper in a narrative poem to put up with a certain degree of emptiness of expression for the sake of avoiding too great a compression of meaning and of smoothing the narrative flow, but at its worst the smoothness of the alliterative style fails to conceal the triteness of what is being said:

> Hee had a suster in sight, seemely to fonde,
> The moste lufsum of life þat euere lud wyst;
> Olympias þe onorable ouer all hue hyght.
> Rose red was hur rode, full riall of schape,
> With large forhed and long loueliche tresses,
> Glisiande as goldwire, growen on length;
> Bryght browse ibent, blisfull of chere,
> Grete yien and graie, gracious lippes,
> Bothe cheekes and chinne choice too beholde;
> Mouth meete þertoo, moste for too praise,
> Hur nose namelich faire, hur necke full scheene...   (*Alisaunder*, 175–85)[36]
>
> [fonde – *examine*; lud – *man*; hue – *she*; rode – *complexion*; Glisiande – *glistening*;
> chere – *appearance*; yien – *eyes*; namelich – *especially*; scheene – *beautiful*.]

Indeed, as Chaucer puts it, she 'hadde a semely nose'! The poet has got hopelessly bogged down in a rhetorical convention, the *descriptio personae*, which starts from the head and finishes (literally, in this case) with the toes 'tidily wrought'.[37] The author feels obliged to provide a description of the beauty of Queen Olympias, but he has no feeling for the subject, as is clear from the tired conventionality of his expressions, the lack of point in the prepositional phrases such as 'in sight', 'of life', and also the second half-lines with their obtrusively regular construction of adjective plus infinitive, 'choice too beholde', 'moste for too praise'. The poet, who is here departing from his Latin source, has formed no picture of the queen in his mind, and has nothing interesting to say about her, but still the machinery of alliterative verse-composition rattles merrily along.

Formulas

In all that has been said so far the term 'formula' has been deliberately avoided. What Oakden in the 1930's referred to as 'alliterative phrases' and 'tags' are now generally known as 'formulas', and although the term had been applied to Old English verse as early as the nineteenth century, it has more recently acquired a new range of associations. The seminal studies in this field were by Milman Parry, who in the 1930's demonstrated the formulaic nature of Homeric verse, and argued that the use of formulas would be of particular value to a poet composing orally. Comparisons were made with oral poetry in Yugoslavia, which was found to be highly formulaic. The debate about the significance of the formula in Homeric verse and about the validity of comparing it with modern Yugoslav poetry still continues.[38]

Parry's observations were applied to heroic verse in various other cultures, among them Old English verse, which, it was maintained, has a large proportion of formulas. However, there is still a vigorous debate in progress about whether Old English poetry really is formulaic, and if it is, whether this tells us anything about the method of composition, oral or otherwise. The central difficulty has always been how to apply Parry's original definition of the Homeric formula as 'a group of words which is regularly employed under the same metrical conditions to express a given essential idea' to the very different conditions of Old English verse-composition. There is no general agreement about what constitutes a formula in Old English verse.[39]

The application of the term 'formula' to Middle English alliterative poetry was made in 1957 by R. A. Waldron.[40] He admitted that the poems as we have them could not possibly be oral, since many of them are close translations of Latin and French works, but nevertheless he argued that the use of formulas in alliterative verse betrayed its oral origins. As an example of a 'complete formulaic first half-line' he gives that built around the alliterating words *ware...wegh*:

$$\overset{x}{(he} \ \overset{x}{was} \ \text{etc.)} \ \overset{/}{ware} \ \overset{x}{of} \ \overset{x}{the} \ (\text{þat, } a) \ \overset{/}{wegh}.$$

Illustrations given of this formula are, among others:

> Vn war of þe weghes þat by the walles lay.   (*Troy*, 1183)
> Þe wylde watz war of þe wyȝe with weppen in honde.   (*Gawain*, 1586)

He continues, 'The half-line can be made to fit a much wider range of contexts by the variation of the word *wegh*', and quotes lines such as:

> Weren ware of hur werk and went for help.   (*Alisaunder*, 414)

But in what way does Waldron's 'complete formulaic first half-line' differ from Oakden's 'alliterative phrase' *ware...wegh*? Given the standard pattern of the first half-line with two alliterating stresses and a disyllabic interval between them, and given the additional factor that *ware* followed by a complement is constructed with *of*, it is difficult to see how else this alliterative phrase could have fitted the metrical structure. The poet constructing his half-line around this collocation would have little option but to use it this way.

If the term 'formula' is to mean more than 'collocation' or 'alliterative phrase' it must be precisely defined, yet there is no precision when the word is applied to Middle English alliterative verse. L. D. Benson's statement that 'a phrase like "brittened and brent" is a formula, a fixed phrase occurring with the same words (or nearly the same) in similar contexts and in the same metrical position in a number of other poems'[41] is too vague to be helpful. What is the minimum length of the 'fixed phrase'? How much allowance has to be made for the qualification 'or nearly the same'? If the phrase is found in a different metrical position, for instance straddling the caesura, is it still the same formula? What force needs to be given to 'similar contexts'?

Inevitably, a term used of Homeric verse will mean something radically different when applied to English verse written on very different principles over 2000 years later. Ideally a 'formula' would denote a complete half-line whose traditional character was demonstrated by exact repetition of that half-line in several other poems. If it were established that alliterative poetry consisted largely of such half-lines, the implication would be that the poet relied on such prefabricated units for his composition, that a trained 'singer' could have drawn on his stock of half-lines for oral composition, and that therefore alliterative verse was, if not oral, at least the inheritor of an oral tradition.

But alliterative verse is not made up of such units. The collocation examined earlier, *wele...wirchipe*, is no more than a collocation. When it is used to provide the stressed syllables of a first half-line, it shows every sort of variation in the surrounding unstressed syllables:

My wele and my wirchipe	(*Morte Arthure*, 3963)
For wele ne for worchyp	(*Gawain*, 2432)
Wyth wele and wyth worschyp	(*Purity*, 651)
Bothe in weile and in worship	(*Troy*, 3356)
Þan with worchip and wele	(*Palerne*, 5046)

This is an habitual collocation that is part of the language. Caxton uses it in prose: 'I am right ioyous of thy wele and worship',[42] and to call this a formula is to broaden the term so that it no longer has useful meaning. Until the term has been precisely defined, and its value (if any) in analysing the structure of fourteenth-century alliterative verse demonstrated, it will merely be confusing and misleading, and it is better to avoid it altogether.

Waldron also examines in his article the frequent occurrence of 'rhythmical-syntactical patterns' of the type:

$$I \ shall....thee \ (you)........$$

For example:

I shall fast the þis forward (*Troy*, 7985)

Phrases of this type are, in a sense, the opposite of a collocation, because it is often the unstressed rather than the stressed elements of the line that are constant or nearly so. It might be observed that the patterns Waldron illustrates are merely a selection of the ordinary grammatical constructions used in prose as well as verse, though in some cases the word-order is not that of prose. Such constructions are particularly useful to the alliterative poet in the throes of composition, because they can so readily be fitted in to the metrical patterns of the half-line, and their lexical elements can be varied to suit a wide variety of contexts. Syntactic 'moulds' of this sort are, as we saw earlier, a common basis for second half-lines. They are less common, or at least less noticeable, in the first half-lines, but there are even some standard constructions that make up the basis for a complete line, such as:

$$....the \ (ADJ)-est \ (NOUN)/that........ever$$

And the semelyeste segge that I seghe euer. (*Parlement*, 135)

It is not surprising that such patterns should have become standardised, for they are the inevitable choice of a conventional poet adapting his syntax to the demands of the metre. Nothing is to be gained by conjuring up an inheritance of oral verse and naming these 'syntactically formulaic phrases'.[43] The term 'grammetrical units', used by R. F. Lawrence,[44] is concise and admirably descriptive, drawing attention as it does to the interplay between metre and grammar that is the fundamental characteristic of such phrases.

Fourteenth-century alliterative poetry cannot, therefore, be described as formulaic in any meaningful sense, even though the style was very much a shared one, and to a greater or lesser extent all the poets made use of a characteristic poetic diction and a range of standard 'grammetrical' patterns. Such practises are neither good or bad of themselves, but they may be used skilfully or incompetently. We have analysed the elements of the alliterative style, but it remains to show, in the work of a few outstanding writers, the power and beauty of the poetry that may be constructed from these basic materials.

Chapter 5

THE ART OF NARRATIVE

Three Narrative Poems

The foregoing chapters have been concerned more with the Revival as a poetic movement than with individual poems within the movement. My discussions of individual poems have emphasised those aspects which are shared by most alliterative works, and although I have tried to demonstrate the wide variety of styles and subjects within the 'school', I have concentrated upon those features which are the common possessions of the poems of the Revival: the basic metrical techniques, the verbal resources and the similarities of approach and attitude.

Ultimately, however, it is the differences and not the similarities which are important to the reader of alliterative poetry. Although it is a necessary (or at least valuable) preliminary to observe and take account of what characteristics a poem has in common with others of the same movement, it is precisely the features that distinguish it from the common run that mark out a poem as an individual work of art. The techniques of alliterative verse were available equally to mediocre and bad poets; it is only the artist who has the skill to fashion the basic materials into a creation that demands attention for what it is rather than for what it illustrates or represents.

It is time, therefore, to study a few poems not primarily in order to illuminate aspects of the Revival (though this may also, I hope, be accomplished), but in order to gain a deeper appreciation of the art of individual poets. There are quite a large number of poems of quality high enough to merit critical examination, and the choice between them is not an obvious one. I have felt that in the presence of such an *embarras de choix* little purpose would be served by displaying once again the supreme qualities of three alliterative poems which are generally acknowledged as masterpieces; *Gawain*, *Pearl* and *Piers Plowman* have received, and will continue to receive, an undue share of critical attention. More is to be gained by choosing poems which, despite their many qualities, have been overlooked for one reason or another, and also poems that are as different from one another as possible, so that the immense range and flexibility of the verse of the Revival will thereby be demonstrated. To represent the many styles and topics of alliterative poetry I will discuss firstly a chronicle of an ancient hero, secondly a religious work that draws on biblical stories to support its homiletic theme, and thirdly a satire on contemporary behaviour and morality. The first is *The Wars of Alexander*, the neglected virtues of which will be illuminated by a comparison with a more famous poem, the alliterative *Morte Arthure*; the second is *Purity*, which because of its subtle structural progression is the least understood of the four masterpieces in the *Gawain* manuscript; the third is *Pierce the Ploughman's Crede*, which ever since the sixteenth century has lived under the long shadow of *Piers Plowman*.

Between them, these three poems cover a remarkable range of alliterative styles and subjects. We shall see richly detailed description as vivid as can be found anywhere in alliterative poetry – descriptions of battles, processions and cataclysms; we shall hear also the informal style of alliterative poetry as it captures the lively tones of the spoken language. We shall observe poets developing the luxuriance of the alliterative vocabulary to its full potential; we shall see for what reasons and to what effect another poet turns his back even on the commoner alliterative expressions. We shall read of the past and of the present, of the heroic and the degraded, of the rich pomp of the rulers of the ancient world and the abject poverty of the fourteenth-century peasant. This range is encompassed by three poets of one school of poetry writing within a few years of one another.

The individual qualities of these three poems will be my central concern, and yet there is a characteristic that unites the three. It is that each owes its success to its narrative technique; they differ widely in the methods by which they tell a story, but each tells its story well. Alliterative poetry is above all else the poetry of narrative, and each of the three poets to be considered in this chapter is, in his individual manner, a consummate storyteller.

The Chronicle Manner: Alexander and Arthur

The Wars of Alexander, an incomplete work of nearly 6000 lines, is certainly the best of the three alliterative Alexander 'fragments', and indeed one of the finest examples of extended alliterative narrative. After describing the extraordinary circumstances of Alexander's conception, the poem deals with his youthful exploits and the early victories after his accession, then with his long struggle against Darius. Following this come the Asian adventures, including Alexander's prolonged debate with Dindimus, king of the ascetic Brahmans, his relations with Queen Candace, and finally his capture of Babylon. At this point the text breaks off, shortly before the Latin source ends its account with the description of Alexander's death by poison.

Several alliterative writers undertook the task of translating a long narrative in Latin or French, and none has greater success than the author of the *Wars*. The poem is often misleadingly classed with the romances, but its approach is soberly historical (which does not, of course, mean that its contents are *true*) and it should rather be described as a chronicle. This accounts for the poet's repeated insistence that he is closely following his source – 'as I fynd wreten', 'for so the text tellis' – and in fact the *Wars* is a remarkably faithful translation of a Latin prose history, the *Historia de Preliis*.[1] Comparisons will here be made not only with the *Historia* but also with another English translation contemporary with the *Wars*, the prose *Life of Alexander* extant in the Thornton manuscript.[2] The prose translation is even more literal (although the writer tends to add explanations here and there to help his readers), so that a comparison between the two English translations brings out very clearly the different narrative techniques of poet and prose author.

Poetic chronicle is a form which we have difficulty in coming to terms with. We can no longer regard it as an accurate source of historical knowledge, and on the other hand its poetic potential is circumscribed by the author's dependence on his original text. Chronicle differs in several respects from romance, though the two forms may shade into one another. In a chronicle incredible events are played down or rationalised. So in the *Wars* Anectanabus can transform himself into a dragon, but this is only because he is an Egyptian, who are 'þe wysest wees of the werd', possessing great scientific knowledge and powers of sorcery. Strange creatures live in distant regions, in Persia and India, but medieval man's capacity for believing the extraordinary was similarly exploited in *Mandeville's Travels*. Because it is chronicle, the *Wars* has, unlike most romances, no interest in love. Alexander is 'wemles for woman touching' (4948), and women are important to him merely as political pawns or threats to his supreme power. His own feelings, if any, are not discussed. Indeed the poet, unlike the author of romance, is scarcely interested in Alexander's motives and emotions; at one point the Greek soldiers complain that Alexander could not live without fighting – 'His flesche is fostard and fedd be fiȝt' (3495) – but this is a tantalising insight into the hero's character which is not explored further. Alexander is a great conqueror and an explorer of distant regions, and his career is seen as an example of martial valour and an opportunity for an exciting travelogue.

The inevitable consequence is that the structure is entirely episodic. If the poet had concentrated on Alexander's personal fortune, he would have had a basic structural pattern, for Alexander's life was considered a classic case of 'tragedie' – of a fall from greatness by the turning of Fortune's wheel, by some moralists as a rebuke for the hero's excessive pride.[3] The poet retains from his source several warnings to Alexander of his impending death, including the remark of an angel that Alexander will be 'diȝt to þe deth of driȝtins ire' (1504), but these hints are not expanded and the poet makes no attempt to evoke an idea of the symmetry of Alexander's rise to greatness and his corresponding fall.[4] As we shall see later, the *Wars* differs in this respect from the alliterative *Morte Arthure*, where Arthur's rise and fall is emphasised by the striking account of his dream of the wheel of Fortune.

The inherent danger of this sort of episodic chronicle is that the result will be mere versified history, like *The Destruction of Troy*. As a poem it ought to have form and shape, some perceivable pattern, but as chronicle it must remain faithful to its source, recording events not because of their significance to a pattern but just because they took place. In order to give the *Wars* at least an elementary structural pattern the poet divides it up into observable sections. Though the poem is incomplete, with the text breaking off in passus 27, it is clear that not much has been lost, and it is likely that there were originally 28 passus in all. If this is so, then the poem falls into two halves, for at the end of passus 14 the poet signals a definite break – 'Now will I tary for a time and tempire my wittis' – before starting off again with 'þe lattir ende of his lyfe'. Though the passus are not of constant length, each consists of a series of 24-line 'paragraphs', and these are subdivided into four-line 'sentences'.[5] Even if this is a superficial patterning, it at least conveys some sense of order and control by a poet conscious of the structure of his work.

By the early fifteenth century English writers were beginning to realise, as French writers had learnt long before, that in many ways prose was a better medium for long narrative than verse. The Thornton *Life of Alexander* is one of the earliest Middle English prose histories. Undoubtedly, translation into prose had much in its favour, as Trevisa says when discussing the matter: 'Prose is more clear than rhyme, more easy and more plain to know and understand'.[6] A verse translation of a prose text will tend to be considerably longer than its original; it will be filled out with padding made necessary by the verse technique and with 'poetic' decoration, and the poet's attempt to transfer a prose statement to verse will, unless he is skilful, lead to contortions of syntax. In some ways, however, the writer of an alliterative work combines the best of both prose and poetic narrative; his verse-form retains much of the flexibility of prose, but yet gives scope for the powerful expressions of poetry. We shall see that the author of the *Wars* is very successful in overcoming the compromises and restrictions of verse-narrative and in developing the potential strengths that verse has over prose.

As a consequence of the increased length of a verse translation over a prose original, the action of the narrative is retarded. Some of the additional length may be a result of the poet's attempt to make his source more vivid and lively, but too often it is simply the demands of the verse-form that lead to meaningless and pointless expansion. Since we are right to think of medieval poets as characteristically expanding their sources, it is interesting to note that the *Wars* is not very much longer than the Thornton *Life*. When we compare the *Wars* with the prose *Life* we can see that the poet chooses some topics for expansion, but on other occasions he unobtrusively simplifies the action and reduces the narrative. Occasionally he reduces too radically, and this leads to obscurity, but more often the process is effective, and the result is a greater tautness and power over the prose version. A good example of this comes near the end of the story, when Alexander arrives at the ocean at the world's end. According to the Thornton *Life*:

> In þat see þay sawe ane ile a littill fra þe lande. And in þat ile þay herde men speke Grewe. And þan Alexander commanded þat sum of his knyghts sulde do off þaire clathes and swyme ouer to þe ile. And þay did soo. And als sone als þay come in þe see þare come gret crabbes vp oute of þe water and pullede þam downne to þe grounde and drownned þam. (105. 17–23)

[Grewe – *Greek*; sulde – *should*.]

The description of this event in the *Wars* is much more concise than either the Latin or the prose translation:

> þar in an ilee he heres
> A grete glauir and a glaam of Grekin tongis.
> Þan bad he kniȝtis þaim vnclethe and to þat kithe swym,
> Bot all at come into þat cole, crabbis has þaim drenchid. (5503–6)

[glauir – *chattering*; glaam – *din*; kithe – *place*; at – *that*; cole – *cold sea*; drenchid – *drowned*.]

The *Wars* retains all the essential details of the prose accounts, and yet relates them in a very much shorter space without giving the effect of undue compression. At the same time the poetic expression is much more vivid than the prose. The Thornton *Life* 'þay herde men speke Grewe' is a literal rendering of the Latin, but the poet takes skilful advantage of the alliterative collocation *glauir and glaam* (cf. *Gawain*, 1426) with his 'A grete glauir and a glaam of Grekin tongis'. The babble of Greek, so startling to Alexander in this outlandish place, is picked out vividly. Thus the poetic description, although shorter, is also more compelling.

Another equally fine example of skilful reduction in the *Wars* is the account of the Basilisk which kills men by its stare. Alexander cunningly fits a mirror to a large shield, so that the Basilisk kills itself in its own reflection. The prose

Life describes the encounter in twelve laborious lines (92. 1–12),[7] which the *Wars* gives in five:

> In bole and in balan buskes he his fotes,
> A blason as a berne-dure þat all þe body schildis,
> And fiches in a fyne glas on þe fere side.
> Þe schrewe in þe schewere his schadow behaldis,
> And so þe slaʒtir of his siʒt into himselfe entris.
>
> (4851–5)

[In bole...schildis – *He covers his feet in wood and whalebone, with a shield as large as a barn-door that protects his whole body*; fiches – *fixes*; fyne – *clear*; fere – *far*; schrewe – *evil creature*; schewere – *mirror*; slaʒtir – *deadly power*.]

Whereas the Thornton *Life* and the Latin give the dimensions of the shield – 'seuen cubites of lenghte and foure on brede' – the *Wars* conveys its size with an effective simile, 'as a berne-dure'. Once again the poet has abbreviated the narrative and yet made an impact with a telling detail.

The kernel of the poet's ability to describe events concisely is his avoidance of verse-padding, which is the bane of mediocre alliterative narrative. An earlier alliterative poet, the author of *Alisaunder of Macedoine*, is much less successful in this respect, and since he is for some of his poem dependent on a text of the Latin similar to that used by the author of the *Wars*, the two poems can be compared to demonstrate the much greater narrative art of the latter. One episode will suffice to illustrate the point. Early in the story, Queen Olympias discovers she is pregnant, and some time later her husband Philip is sitting in his palace when a small bird flies in. The extraordinary event which follows is described by the Latin source of the *Wars* in this way:

> Post paucos vero dies sedens Philippus Rex in palacio suo, apparuit ei parva ac mitis avis volans in gremio eius et generavit ovum et, cadens in terram, divisum est. Et statim ex eo parvulus serpens exivit, cogitavitque ovum intrare, et antequam ibi caput immitteret, extinctus est.[8]

[*A few days later King Philip was sitting in his palace when there appeared to him a small and gentle bird, and it flew into his lap and laid an egg, which fell to the earth and was broken. At once a tiny serpent came out of it, and intended to return to the egg, but before it could put its head there it died.*]

The event is interpreted for Philip by a soothsayer, who explains that the serpent represents the unborn Alexander who, after accomplishing great deeds, will die before he can return to his birthplace.

Both alliterative poets expand on their source to some degree. *Alisaunder of Macedoine* is the longer of the two, but its expansions consist mainly of metrical padding:

> In a somer seasoun soone therafter,
> As Philip satt by hymself, soothe for too tell,
> A faire breeding brid bremlich went
> And in þe lappe of þat lud louely hee sittes.
> Or þis freelich foule farde of þe place
> Hee bredde an ai on his barm, and braides him þan.
> Philip wondred was of this werk quainte,
> And satte still on þe stede, stirred no foote.
> Þe ai fell on þe flore in the frekes sight,
> And þe shell to-shett on þe schire grounde.
> Whan it cofli too-clef, þer crep oute an addre,
> And buskes full boldely aboute þe shell.
> Whan this worme had went wislich aboute
> Hee wolde haue gliden in againe, graithlich and soone,
> But or hee had in his hed hee hastely deide,
> And dreew nere too his denne, but deide biside.
>
> (999–1014)

[bremlich – *boldly*; lud – *man*; louely – *graciously*; Or – *before*; freelich – *excellent*; farde of – *left*; bredde – *laid*; ai – *egg*; barm – *lap*; braides him – *hurries away*; werk quainte – *strange action*; stede – *place*; to-shett – *broke open*; schire – *bright*; cofli too-clef – *quickly broke apart*; buskes – *hurries*; wislich – *indeed*; graithlich – *rapidly*.]

In this passage expressions such as 'In a somer seasoun' and 'soothe for too tell' exist merely to complete the verse-pattern. Much of the additional length is made up of alliterating adjectives and adverbs, which tell us nothing interesting and are sometimes even inappropriate. The bird which is 'faire breeding' and 'freelich' goes 'bremlich' and sits 'louely'. The egg breaks 'cofli' on the 'schire' ground, and the adder 'buskes full boldely', glides 'graithlich' and dies 'hastely'. A two-line expansion pictures Philip rather strangely sitting stock-still as the egg rolls out of his lap. The poet is the slave of his verse-form; to find alliterating letters he is forced to add meaningless and inappropriate detail.

The description in the *Wars* is a little shorter but much more to the point:

Anoþire ferly þar fell within fewe days,
Þe king was sett in his sale, with septer in hand,
Þen come þar-in a litill brid, into his barme floȝe,
And þar hurkils and hydis as scho were hand-tame.
Fast scho flekirs about his fete, and fleȝtirs aboute,
And þar it nestild in a noke, as it a nest were,
Qwill scho had layd in his lape a litill tyne egg,
And þan scho fangis hire fliȝt and floȝe away swyth.
Þis egg, or þe kyng wyst, to þe erth fallis,
Brak, and so it wele burde, and brast all esoundir;
Þan wendis þar-out a litill worm, and wald it eft enter,
And, or scho hit in hire hede, a hard deth suffirs.

(501–12)[9]

[ferly – *marvel*; sale – *hall*; barme – *lap*; floȝe – *flew*; hurkils – *crouches*; flekirs – *flickers*; fleȝtirs – *flutters*; noke – *corner*; Qwill – *until*; tyne – *tiny*; fangis – *takes*; swyth – *quickly*; or – *before*; and so... burde – *inevitably*; brast – *burst*; wald – *wished*.]

The king is pictured 'with septer in hand', but the interest then concentrates on the bird, the description of which emerges from a genuine poetic imagining of the scene; the bird, strangely tame, flutters about Philip's feet, and then taking his lap as a nest, lays an egg there. The poet has taken the trouble to visualise the event, and yet there is no major expansion and the narrative is not interrupted.

An insensitive and inane use of the alliterating words, as seen on occasions in *Alisaunder of Macedoine*, is particularly damaging because the alliteration focuses the attention on the words themselves. These acquire a special emphasis and importance which the poet ignores at his peril, but which a skilful writer can build on to great advantage in developing a particularising and itemising style. The baldest expression of this style is the list, so common as to be a characteristic of the verse of the Revival. An example is the 22-line catalogue of Alexander's conquests that ends the incomplete text of the *Wars*.[10] But the particularising style is often handled with much more discretion to fill out a scene with the vividness of detail. For instance, Alexander's prolonged correspondence with the ascetic Brahmans about their simple, unambitious way of life presents a clash of attitudes which inevitably was viewed in terms of medieval Christian attitudes to asceticism, a medievalisation which is vigorously promoted in the *Wars* by supplying the kind of detail that fitted a fourteenth-century context. The Brahmans, in pursuit of their ascetic ideal, dress simply, telling Alexander (in the words of the prose *Life* translating the Latin): 'Oure wiffes ne are noȝte gayly arayed for to plese vs' (80. 9–10).[11] The *Wars*, typically enough, goes into detail and alludes to the fripperies of medieval dress:

> Oure paramours vs to plese ne pride þaim beweues,
> Nouthire furrers, filetts ne frengs, ne frettis of perle.
> Is þam na surcote of silke, ne serkis of Raynes,
> Ne kirtils of camlyn, bot as þam kynd leues.
>
> (4337–40)[12]

[ne pride þaim beweues – *do not cover themselves in proud array*; furrers –*furs*; frengs – *borders*; frettis – *ornaments*; Is þam – *they have*; serkis of Raynes – *shirts from Rheims*; camlyn – *costly fabric*; bot...leues – *only what Nature provides*.]

A less happy result of the same desire to bring the story up to date arises in the Brahmans' warning to Alexander that men are not permanent residents of this life but merely pilgrims, 'tamquam peregrinantes' says the source; the author of the *Wars* envisages this in terms of a fourteenth-century Christian pilgrimage: 'Bot as qua pas a pilgrymage fra Parysch to Rome' (4649).

All alliterative poets attempted to present their material in terms with which a medieval audience were familiar, and they were undisturbed by the anachronisms this led to. The young Alexander is portrayed as a medieval English boy, and Darius taunts him by saying he is not fit to fight but only 'at þe bowlis as a brode (i.e. 'child') or with a ball playe' (1929), redefining the Latin 'cum pueris puerilia excercere' in medieval terms. As a schoolboy, the Latin tells us, Alexander who was receiving lessons from Aristotle struggled ('pugnabat') with his schoolfellows for mastery in learning. Perhaps taking his cue from the Latin verb, the English poet adds a graphic scene not of mental but of physical tussles in a medieval school:

> In absens of Arystotill, if any of his feris
> Raged with him vnridly or rofe him with harme,
> Him wald he kenely on þe croune knok with his tablis,
> Þat al to-brest wald þe bordis, and þe blode folowe.
> If any scolere in þe scole his skorne at him makis,
> He skapis him full skathely, bot if he skyp better.
>
> (637–42)

[feris – *schoolmates*; Raged – *acted violently*; vnridly –*fiercely*; rofe – *hurt*; tablis – *writing tablets*; to-brest...bordis – *the wooden tablets would break*; skapis... skathely – *escapes with difficulty*; bot if – *unless*.]

It is with the same purpose of relating the distance, not to say outlandish, adventures of Alexander to sights and events within the common experience of the medieval audience that the author of the *Wars* uses the simile. Surprisingly, few alliterative poets are noted for their effective use of similes; the *Gawain*-poet is one and the author of the *Wars* another. The similes in the *Wars* are often characterised by unblushing hyperbole, as with the account of the struggle between Alexander's soldiers and the serpents infesting a high mountain somewhere beyond the Ganges:

> Þare was hurling on hiȝe as it in hell ware,
> Quat of wrestling of wormes and wonding of kniȝtis;
> As gotis out of guttars in golanand wedres,
> So voidis doun þe vemon be vermyns schaftis.
>
> (4794–7)

[hurling – *roaring*; Quat of – *what with*; wormes – *serpents*; wonding – *wounding*; gotis – *streams*; golanand wedres – *tempestuous weather*; voidis – *pours*; schaftis – *jaws*.]

The simile of venom pouring from the serpents' jaws like rainwater streaming from gutters is outrageously exaggerated, but its effectiveness derives from the fact that it likens an outlandish event to a very common one. Nearly always in the *Wars* the similes refer to everyday sights and sounds. Another lot of strange beasts have:

> heuy hedis and hoge, as horses it were,
> And þai ware tacchid full of tethe as tyndis ere of harows,
> And fell flammes as of fire floȝe fra þaire mouthes.   (5572–4)

[hoge – *huge*; tacchid – *set*; tyndis – *prongs*; fell – *fierce*; floȝe – *flew*.]

The three similes in these three lines associate the beasts with common sights, and the image of the harrow-blades is particularly vivid. Elsewhere the poet twice uses the image of cobwebs to good effect. The dying King Darius bitterly likens life to a fragile cobweb 'Þat þis coppis opon kell-wyse knytt in þe woȝes' (3300) – 'that spiders spin in the fashion of a net on the walls'. The basis of this comparison, life is like a cobweb, is in the Latin source, but the English poet brings it home (literally) by visualising the web strung up on the wall. On another occasion Alexander's knights enter a dark and perilous valley:

> A dreȝe dale and a depe, a dym and a thestir;
> Miȝt þare na saule vndire son see to anothire.
> Þai ware vmbethonrid in þat thede with slike a thike cloude
> Þat þai miȝt fele it with þaire fiste as flabband webbis.   (4804–7)

[dreȝe – *dreary*; thestir – *gloomy*; vmbethonrid – *enveloped*; thede – *region*; slike – *such*; flabband webbis – *flapping cobwebs*.]

Because we have all shuddered at cobwebs clinging to our faces on a dark night we can share in the peculiar horror of the simile.

In my analysis of the methods the poet uses to bring to life a chronicle of ancient history and distant regions, I have so far considered techniques which do not involve substantial alterations or additions to the Latin source, and since the poet regards himself as an accurate historian, he cannot allow himself any major departure from his text. However, expansion – that is to say imaginative re-creation of a scene – is permitted to the poetic historian. In the *Wars* this often takes the form of grand set-piece descriptions for which alliterative poetry is so justly famous.[13] The poets realised how wonderfully alliterative verse, with its repeated emphasis on the stressed syllables, evoked the energy of a violent battle or a storm at sea, and some poets seize on every opportunity for a display of this sort. But the danger is that these set-piece descriptions interrupt the narrative flow. *The Siege of Jerusalem* is mainly taken up with endless descriptions of battles. Individually they are fairly powerful, but together they quite overwhelm the story. *The Destruction of Troy* intersperses its battle scenes with a few storms, but the poet is too obviously drawing on a common stock of incidents to construct his descriptions, so that there is a great deal of repetition of the details. The set-piece descriptions in the *Wars* are much more powerful, partly because they are used with considerable restraint, and partly because, even though they deal with the usual topics – battles and storms, as well as a procession – they spring from a genuine and fresh poetic imagination. The most extensive expansion occurs between lines 1137 and 1576, where 450 lines of verse compare with a mere three and a half pages of the Thornton *Life*. The first part of this section gives an account of the 'Foray of Gaders' and the siege of Tyre, and here the expansion is occupied with battle description, reaching a superb climax in the account of Alexander's final and successful assault on the besieged city of Tyre.[14] First we hear the noise of drums and trumpets, and then the attackers press forward, bearing their shields and shooting arrows up at the men on the city walls:

> Now tenelis vp taburs and all þe toun rengis,
> Steryn steuyn vp strake, strakid þar trumpis,
> Blewe bemys of bras, bernes assemblis,
> Seȝes to on ilk syde and a saute ȝeldis.
> Pare presis to with paues peple withouten,
> Archars with arows of atter envemonde
> Schotis vp scharply at shalkis on þe wallis,
> Lasch at þam of loft; many lede floȝen.

(1385–92)

[tenelis – *play*; taburs – *drums*; rengis – *resounds*; Steryn...trumpis – *a fierce noise arose and trumpets sounded there*; bemys – *trumpets*; Seȝes to – *advance*; ilk–every; a saute ȝeldis – *attack*; presis to – *press forward*; paues – *shields*; withouten – *outside the walls*; atter – *poison*; envemonde – *envenomed*; Lasch – *strike*; of loft – *up high*; floȝen – *fled.*]

The attack is fiercely resisted and many of the Greeks fall into the sea or are killed by spears. However, Alexander's soldiers press forward, firing their cross-bows and using their siege-engines, which eventually crush the battle-ments of Tyre:

> Sum braidis to þar bowis, bremely þai schut,
> Quethirs out quarels quikly betwene,
> Strykis vp of þe stoure stanes of engynes,
> Pat þe bretage aboue brast all in soundire;
> Girdis ouir garettis with gomes to þe erthe,
> Tilt torettis doun, toures on hepis,
> Spedely with spryngaldis spilt þaire braynes,
> Many miȝtfull man marris on þe wallis.

(1413–20)

[braidis to – *seize*; bremely – *fiercely*; schut – *shoot*; Quethirs – *whizz*; quarels – *bolts*; betwene – *at intervals*; Strykis – *fly*; stoure – *conflict*; bretage – *battlement*; Girdis – *throw*; garettis – *watch-towers*; Tilt...doun – *overturned turrets*; spryng-aldis – *catapults*; marris – *injure.*]

Even from these brief extracts it may be seen how the bustle and noise and carnage of the battle are captured by the rhythmic agility of the alliterative line.

Having taken Tyre, Alexander approaches Jerusalem, where the high-priest sensibly decides not to resist the conqueror but instead to appease him by a grand display in his honour. The seventy-line description that follows, expanded from a few hints in the source, portrays the cloths laid out on the streets, overshadowed by awnings to ward off the sun, the clothing of those in the procession, the priests in rich robes and the children wearing dazzling white, as white 'as any snyppand snawe þat in þe snape liȝtis' – 'as any freezing snow that falls in the pasture', and then describes the music, the bells and the incense. Here is a small part of that account, the description of the bishop's robes, first his habit brightly coloured and patterned with depictions of birds and animals and set with gleaming stones, then his cape of chestnut colour edged with gold, his violet vestment embroidered with satyrs, and his elaborate gold mitre set with sparkling gems:

> Now passis furth þis prelate with prestis of þe temple,
> Reueschid him rially, and þat in riche wedis,
> With erst an abite vndire all, as I am infourmede,
> Fulle of bridis and of bestis of bise and of purpre;
> And þat was garnest full gay, with golden skirtis,
> Store starand stanes strenkild all ouire,
> Saudid full of safirs and oþire sere gemmes,
> And poudird with perry, was purer þan othire.
> And sithen he castis on a cape of kastans hewe,

With riche ribans of gold railed bi þe hemmes,
A vestoure to vise on of violet floures,
Wroȝt full of wodwose and oþer wild bestis.
And þan him hiȝtild his hede and had on a mitre
Was forgid all of fyne gold and fret full of perrils,
Stiȝt staffull of stanes þat straȝt out bemes
As it ware shemerand shaftis of þe shire son.   (1529–44)[15]

[Reueschid – *dressed*; rially – *splendidly*; erst – *first*; abite – *habit*; bise – *blue*;
garnest – *adorned*; Store…stanes – *large gleaming gems*; strenkild – *sprinkled*;
Saudid – *set*; sere – *different*; poudird – *decorated*; perry – *jewelry*; sithen – *next*;
kastans hewe – *chestnut colour*; railed – *arrayed*; vestoure – *garment*; vise – *gaze*;
wodwose – *satyrs*; hiȝtild – *ornamented*; forgid – *made*; fret – *decked*; Stiȝt staffull –
set very full; straȝt – *radiated*; shemerand – *shimmering*; shire – *bright*.]

Possibly this description quite faithfully represents civic pageants that many
of the original readers would have seen, and to an age in which extravagant
display was not uncommon, this account may not have seemed exaggerated.[16]
The purpose of the description is to exalt the heroic grandeur of Alexander's
exploits and to portray a scene that will root itself in the memory of the reader.
The tendency of alliterative poetry to enumerate is developed to its full potential, as every detail of the procession is visualised and defined. The task the
author of the *Wars* attempts, to construct a lively and vivid poetic chronicle,
is a difficult one, and his success is a mark of the great range of his narrative
gifts.

The *Wars* is much more firmly in the chronicle manner than a more famous
alliterative poem on another hero of the past, *Morte Arthure*, and a comparison
between the two poems reveals the strengths and limitations of both. The
Morte is a free version of the 'historical' Arthurian tradition descending
from Geoffrey of Monmouth and Wace, but it also borrows themes and
incidents from romance, with the aim of enhancing its protagonists, Arthur
and Gawain.[17] As a result, in contrast to the *Wars*, the *Morte* places emphasis
on the motives of its central character. However, in attempting to extend the
bounds of the chronicle manner, the poet takes on new responsibilities which
present him with difficulties he is not prepared to resolve. Though many will
disagree with this judgement, the *Morte* is a most interesting and ambitious
failure, whereas the *Wars*, rather less ambitious, is a triumphant success within
its chosen genre.

While the author of the *Wars* permitted himself no substantial deviation
from his source, the author of the *Morte* adopts a freer approach and shapes
his narrative much more consciously and prominently. The poem is balanced
around Arthur's two dreams, the first (ll. 760 ff.) foretelling the hero's rise to
prosperity, and the second (ll. 3222 ff.) signalling his downfall. The second dream
is particularly powerful, and the detail in which it is described shows that the
poet intended to emphasise its significance to the narrative. Arthur, glorying
in his victories in Tuscany, falls asleep and dreams that he is in a wood full of
cruel beasts that are lapping up the blood of his knights. Fleeing from there he
enters a beautiful meadow, where he meets a richly dressed lady with a wheel,
Lady Fortune herself. Around the wheel, some attempting to climb it and some
having fallen from it, are eight of the Nine Worthies. Arthur is lifted onto the
top of the wheel and treated with great favour, but at midday the lady's mood
abruptly changes, and she turns the wheel crushing Arthur beneath it. The
message of the dream is clearly that all the Worthies, Arthur among them,
achieve greatness and then fall, not through their own fault but merely at the
whim of fickle Fortune. However, the philosophers who interpret Arthur's

dream for him warn him of the need to prepare his soul for his approaching death, and take the opportunity to chide him for his sinful pride and cruelty:

> Thow has schedde myche blode and schalkes distroyede,
> Sakeles, in cirquytrie, in sere kynges landis;
> Schryfe the of thy schame, and schape for thyne ende. (3398–400)

[Sakeles – *innocent*; cirquytrie – *pride*; sere – *many*; schape – *prepare*.]

Several modern readers have seen the condemnation expressed in these lines as the key to the poem, and have elevated to prominence a few other hints in the poem where Arthur is accused, or even accuses himself, of sin. It has therefore been maintained that Arthur's fall is caused by his vaunting pride and his unjust and cruel wars, but no two commentators are agreed on when Arthur's wars become unjust. Are they unjust from the outset, or after his defeat of the Roman Emperor Lucius (ll. 2386 ff.), or as he fights with great cruelty in Tuscany (ll. 3150 ff)?[18] This difference of opinion is quite understandable, because there is no discussion in the poem of the concept of the 'just war', no explicit comment on when and why Arthur's wars become sinful, and no consistent attitude towards the warriors' reckless ambition. It is anachronistic, however, to apply liberal, twentieth-century views of warfare to *Morte Arthure*. Though the code of chivalry may seem a fine ideal when compared to the barbarities of our own wars, even within this code actions which to us seem unpardonably cruel were acceptable to contemporaries, particularly in the case of siege warfare.[19] Despite occasional criticisms of Arthur's actions, as a rule the poet exalts the knights' heroic deeds, glorying in the cruel slaughter of giants and pagans, in the 'genitales...jaggede...in sondre', and in gory descriptions such as:

> That alle the filthe of the freke and fele of the guttes
> Foloes his fole fotte whene he furthe rydes. (2782–3)

[fele – *many*; fole – *horse's*.]

In a chronicle like the *Wars*, glorification of such actions is acceptable because we are not asked to explore the hero's conduct and motives. By raising the moral issue of the hero's attitude to war, by suggesting fitfully that Arthur's pride is not the noble courage underlying all heroic action but rather the most heinous of sins, the *Morte* poses questions which are nowhere resolved. The two contrasting attitudes to Arthur are not presented in such a way as to interact and to develop tensions, as is sometimes argued, because to praise Arthur for heroic pride in one breath and condemn him for sinful arrogance in the next is ultimately self-defeating. The poet juggles with two possible views of reckless bravery; while his approach is essentially one of glorification, he is unable to resist alluding to the attitude of disapproval. The explanation suggested for the hero's fall by his philosophers, and taken up at various points in the poem, simply does not accord with the tone of the poem as a whole.

The poet's occasional inconsistencies of attitude should not, however, be allowed to obscure the many real virtues of one of the better-known alliterative poems. The *Morte* is vigorous, with touches of grim humour, although it is a grimness that often tends to crude violence. The poet is able to handle his verse in a lively manner, but unfortunately he hits on the idea of running groups of lines on one alliterative letter when describing episodes of violence and excitement. This involves him in some repetition and leads to a superficially clever search for alliterating words that becomes tedious. This is especially true of the battle descriptions. In a scene such as the following the poet shows his considerable skill at portraying the rapid action and multi-farious brutalities of the battlefield:

> Swerdez swangene in two sweltand knyghtez,
> Lyes wyde opyne welterande one walopande stedez,
> Wondes of wale mene, werkande sydys,
> Facez feteled vnfaire in filterede lakes,
> Alle craysed fortrodyne with trappede stedez. (2146–50)

[swangene – *strike*; sweltand – *dying*; Lyes – *they lie*; welterande – *writhing*; walopande – *galloping*; Wondes – *wounds*; wale – *fine*; werkande – *aching*; Facez... stedez – *faces gruesomely jumbled together in pools of blood, all crushed and trodden down by caparisoned horses.*]

But one battle, one bloody and meaningless death, follows close on the heels of another, because the poet, though a writer of unusual talent, has none of the restraint of the author of the *Wars*.

Narrative Structure in Purity

Just as the world of ancient heroes in the *Wars* and in *Morte Arthure* is given a medieval setting, the world of the Old Testament is by the same method vividly brought to life in *Patience* and *Purity*. The biblical accounts which are often sparse and allusive are filled out with detail and colour, so that Jonah, Abraham and Belshazzar are portrayed in terms of fourteenth-century manners. The poet is justified in reworking the Bible narrative in this way because his purpose is to use the Old Testament stories as illustrations of moral principles which concern men of his own time.

Patience is a fairly short poem constructed with powerful simplicity, giving a most lively and attractive version of the story of Jonah and the Whale. The story is told as an example of impatience, which is defined in a brief ex-pository prologue as the inability to submit patiently and obediently to the will of God. The elaborations on the biblical account are principally to portray Jonah's state of mind, so that we may learn from this example of an impatient man and recognise the folly of his querulous complaints about the duties God has demanded of him.[20] The poem depicts an all-powerful and all-seeing God – 'Hit may not be þat he is blynde þat bigged (i.e. 'made') vche yȝe' (124) – but one who is ultimately merciful in his use of this power. God rescues Jonah from drowning and takes pity on the repentant sinners of Nineve. *Purity* is also concerned with the almighty power of God, but it gives a much sterner and more terrifying picture of the destructive force of this power. Here God destroys individuals, cities, the whole world, in his fury at man's sinfulness.

This uncomforting picture of a wrathful God as seen in *Purity* is very much out of line with the emphasis of modern theology, and it is no doubt partly for this reason that *Purity* is a far less widely admired poem than *Patience*. *Purity* has lacked admirers also because its structure, so much more complex than that of *Patience*, has not been understood. The poem is not the tenu-ously-linked assemblage of biblical stories that some readers have regarded it, but a tightly-controlled work devoted to a single theme and bound by a number of recurrent symbols and motifs.

The multifarious incidents of *Purity* are all directed to the exposition of one lesson, which is that the defilement of sin – especially sexual sin – destroys man's relationship with God and awakens God's wrath.[21] The emphasis is therefore properly on God's anger, even though there are several points in the poem which stress God's mercy towards the just and the repentant. The theme is developed through three episodes from the Old Testament which illustrate God's vengeance; they are the drowning of the world by the Flood, the destruction of Sodom and Gomorrah, and the death of Belshazzar. These episodes might almost have been chosen for their suitability for vivid alliterative description. All the accustomed topics are there – the storms, floods, destruction of cities by natural causes and by man, the feasts – all described in the full vigour of the alliterative manner. Perhaps the most dramatic of them is the description of the destruction of the cities:

> Clowdez clustered bytwene, kesten up torres,
> Þat þe þik þunder-þrast þirled hem ofte.
> Þe rayn rueled adoun, ridlande þikke,
> Of felle flaunkes of fyr and flakes of soufre,
> Al in smolderande smoke smachande ful ille,
> Swe aboute Sodamas and hit sydez alle,
> Gorde to Gomorra þat þe grounde laused,
> Abdama and Syboym, þise ceteis alle faure,
> Al birolled wyth þe rayn, rostted and brenned,
> And ferly flayed þat folk þat in þose fees lenged.
> For when þat þe helle herde þe houndez of heven
> He watz ferlyly fayn, unfolded bylyve;
> Þe grete barrez of þe abyme he barst up at onez,
> Þat alle þe regioun torof in riftes ful grete,
> And cloven alle in lyttel cloutes þe clyffez aywhere,
> As lauce levez of þe boke þat lepes in twynne
> Þe brethe of þe brynston bi þat hit blende were
> Al þo citees and her sydes sunkken to helle.   (951–68)[22]

[kesten up torres – *threw up mountainous cumulus*; þe þik...þirled hem – *the frequent thunderbolts pierced them*; rueled – *poured*; ridlande – *falling*; felle flaunkes – *terrible sparks*; soufre – *sulphur*; smachande – *smelling*; Swe – *drifted*; hit – *its*; Gorde – *rushed*; laused – *split open*; birolled – *drenched*; brenned – *burnt*; ferly flayed – *greatly terrified*; fees – *places*; lenged – *lived*; He watz...bylyve – *he was very glad and opened at once*; abyme – *abyss*; barst up – *broke open*; torof – *split apart*; cloven – *split*; cloutes – *pieces*; As lauce...twynne – *like loose leaves from a book that springs apart*; Þe brethe...were – *by the time the smell of the brimstone was stirred up.*]

This magnificent description effectively evokes the terrifying vengeance of God and his power to destroy what displeases him. It is 'fylþe of þe flesch' which makes God 'forȝet alle his fre þewez' – his gracious manner of action – and the poet demonstrates this by the examples of the Flood, provoked by sexual promiscuity, and the destruction of Sodom and Gomorrah, brought on by homosexuality. Although it is only fleshly sin that awakens destruction on this vast scale, all sinfulness is a stain of uncleanness on man's soul, and will deprive the individual sinner of his eternal reward. This is a message which the poet states clearly at the beginning of his work, basing himself on 'blessed are the clean of heart' from the Sermon on the Mount:

> Me mynez on one amonge oþer as Maþew recordez,
> Þat þus of clannesse unclosez a ful cler speche:
> Þe haþel clene of his hert hapenez ful fayre,
> For he schal loke on oure Lorde wyth a bone chere.   (25–8)

[Me mynez on – *I remember*; unclosez – *discloses*; bone chere – *happy face*.]

The message of the individual's loss of God through the stain of sin is reiterated in the last of the three biblical episodes that illustrate the poet's theme. This differs from the previous two because it involves not universal destruction but the death of an individual, Belshazzar, and also because it is not concerned with sexual sin specifically, though that is also involved, but with the stain of sin in general, with a man who defiles his own soul which is sacred to God. Belshazzar misuses the holy vessels; these, as we shall see, stand as an image of man's soul.

These three central episodes, set in their chronological order, are each preceded by a description of the events which historically led up to them. These associated incidents also reveal God's power for vengeance or for mercy, and by contrasting his reaction to other situations they highlight God's attitude to impurity.

The preamble to the first episode, Noah's Flood, repeats the lesson that 'For fele fautez may a freke forfete his blysse/Þat he þe Soverayn ne se' (177–8), and lists a variety of such mortal sins, but it was only for sins of the flesh that God 'wex wod to þe wrache for wrath at his hert' (204). Two examples of God acting *without* anger are then given: God sent the wicked angels from Heaven and drove Adam and Eve out of Eden, and both judgements were based on a just decision tempered by mercy and willingness to forgive. God's absolute power over the wicked angels is brilliantly demonstrated by likening the wicked angels falling from Heaven to a snow shower, to a swarm of bees and to flour forming a thick dust beneath a sieve. God's action follows immediately on Lucifer's vain thoughts:

> As sone as Dryʒtynez dome drof to hymselven,
> Þikke þowsandez þro þrwen þeroute,
> Fellen fro þe fyrmament fendez ful blake,
> Sweved at þe fyrst swap as þe snaw þikke,
> Hurled into helle-hole as þe hyve swarmez;
> Fylter fenden folk forty dayez lencþe
> Er þat styngande storme stynt ne myʒt,
> Bot as smylt mele under smal sive smokez forþikke
> So fro heven to helle þat hatel schor laste,
> On uche syde of þe worlde aywhere ilyche.
> Þis hit watz a brem brest and a byge wrache,
> And ʒet wrathed not þe Wyʒ, ne þe wrech saʒtled.　　　　　　(219–30)

[As sone...hymselven – *as soon as God's decree came upon him*; þro – *violently*; þrwen – *were flung*; fendez – *devils*; Sweved – *whirled*; swap – *blow*; Fylter...folk – *fiends huddle together*; Er – *before*; stynt ne myʒt – *stopped*; as smylt...forþikke – *as strained meal smokes very thickly under a fine sieve*; hatel schor – *fierce shower*; aywhere ilyche – *the same everywhere*; brem brest – *fierce destruction*; wrache – *punishment*; And ʒet...saʒtled – *and yet God did not become angry, and nor did wretched Satan make peace*.]

Satan was too proud to ask for mercy and forgiveness.

Adam's sin was one of disobedience, and once again God's vengeance was exacted with restraint, and eventually remedied through the grace of the Virgin Mary:

> Al in mesure and meþe watz mad þe vengaunce,
> And efte amended wyth a mayden þat make had never.　　　　　(247–8)

[meþe – *moderation*; make – *equal*.]

Adam's descendants were the most beautiful of beings, who were commanded only to observe the natural law and keep it cleanly. But 'þenne founden þay fylþe in fleschlych dedez' (265), and this corruption opened the gate to the influence of the Devil, who engendered on the daughters of the earth a new perverted race of men, so that evils of all kinds multiplied. God repented of having ever created man, and resolved to destroy the world utterly. The poet sees initial sexual uncleanness as the root of general corruption.

Noah represents for the poet the just and obedient man, totally submissive to God's will, and on account of his goodness God extended mercy to him.

For the rest of the world, however, repentance came too late, and God's anger was so aroused that he looked on pitilessly as the people drowned:

> Bi þat þe flod to her fete floȝed and waxed,
> Þen uche a segge seȝ wel þat synk hym byhoved.
> Frendez fellen in fere and faþmed togeder
> To dryȝ her delful deystyne and dyȝen alle samen,
> Luf lokez to luf and his leve takez
> For to ende alle at onez and for ever twynne.   (397–402)

[Bi þat – *when*; seȝ – *saw*; fere – *companionship*; faþmed – *embraced*; dryȝ – *endure*; delful – *sad*; samen – *together*; twynne – *separate*.]

This cluster of stories – the episode of the Flood preceded by the Fall of the Angels and the Banishment from Eden – defines with precision God's reaction to 'fylþe of þe flesch'. This is no distant and aloof Godhead, but a Creator who descends to human passion in his fury at the sinfulness of his creation:

> Felle temptande tene towched his hert,
> As wyȝe, wo hym withinne...   (283–4)

[Felle...tene – *cruel afflicting anger*; As wyȝe – *as if he were a man*.]

By the same method the lesson of the second episode, the Destruction of Sodom and Gomorrah, is sharpened by the poet's extended account of the events that led up to it. There is first an account of the visit of the angels to Abraham. The poet emphasises (as in the Bible) that the angels are a physical manifestation of God, and he portrays the warmth of the relationship between God and his favoured Abraham. Abraham busies himself to serve God with wholesome food 'in plater honest', and this simple meal will contrast effectively with the excess of Belshazzar's Feast.

> And God as a glad gest mad god chere,
> Þat watz fayn of his frende, and his fest praysed.   (641–2)

Sarah, to the Middle Ages the image of the faithful wife,[23] is promised a son whose blessed descendants will people the world, and at her laugh of disbelief God stresses his absolute power:

> Hopez ho oȝt may be harde my hondez to work?   (663)

[Hopez ho – *does she imagine*; oȝt – *anything*.]

God then reveals to Abraham his decision to destroy the cities because:

> þay han founden in her flesch of fautez þe werst,
> Uch male matz his mach a man as hymselven,
> And fylter folyly in fere on femmalez wyse.   (694–6)

[matz – *makes*; mach – *companion*; fylter...fere – *foolishly cling together*; wyse – *fashion*.]

Abraham pleads for God to show mercy, and God promises to withhold vengeance if as few as ten good men may be found there.

God's messengers to Sodom are treated with great courtesy by Lot, who, like both Abraham and Noah, represents the just man who will be saved for his obedience to God. Lot's wife, however, acts as a contrast to Lot and to Sarah, for she disobeys her husband's explicit instructions not to salt the meal prepared for the angels, and thereby 'wrathed oure Lorde'. The Sodomites reveal their propensities by making indecent advances on the angels, and Lot and his family are persuaded by the angels to leave the city. Again disobeying instructions, Lot's wife looks back at the burning town, and is turned into a pillar of salt. The poet comments that this is

> For two fautes þat þe fol watz founde in mistrauþe:
> On, ho served at þe soper salt bifore Dryȝtyn,
> And syþen, ho blusched hir bihynde, þaȝ hir forboden were. (996–8)

[mistrauþe – *unfaithfulness*; ho – *she*; Dryȝtyn – *God*; syþen – *next*; blusched – *looked*; þaȝ – *though*.]

So the preamble to this second episode highlights themes that are to be important in the episode itself. God's favour is extended to Abraham for his obedience and also to Sarah his wife despite her incredulity. In the kindred family, Lot's willing obedience and his ready welcome of the angels are rewarded, but his wife's disobedience to her husband and to God is punished. Beyond this pattern of just reward and punishment of individuals lies God's revulsion at the sins of Sodom, and his 'vengaunce violent þat voyded þise places' (1013).

The linking of these two main episodes, the Flood and the destruction of the cities, is natural enough since both exemplify God's wrath against sexual sin and in both one family is saved while all else is destroyed by convulsions of nature. The two stories are several times linked in the Bible itself.[24] The third *exemplum*, however, is not obviously related, and its significance has puzzled those who have failed to recognise that the poet has progressed to a new step in his argument. Up to this point the theme of the punishment of the pride or disobedience of the individual – Lucifer, Adam and Lot's wife – has been subordinate to that of the destruction of whole communities as a result of sexual sin. In the story of Belshazzar's Feast the punishment of the individual becomes the major theme. Having dealt specifically with the vengeance attending sexual sin, the poet goes on to show that all sin is uncleanness, and that God who is himself so clean cannot bear to see something of his made dirty, whether it be an object as precious as man's eternal soul, or one as insignificant as a holy vessel. Belshazzar defiles the holy vessels taken from the Temple of Jerusalem by using them at his feast; the holy vessels are significant because they represent all those things that are sacred to God, and the most precious of these is man's eternal soul. The image of the soul as a vessel sanctified to God, which once clean must not be stained again, was a well-known one.[25] The poet makes the parallel explicit before embarking on his account of Belshazzar's Feast. The soul, he says, may be cleansed by the waters of Penance, but if it is subsequently defiled God's anger will be aroused:

> Bot war þe wel if þou be waschen wyth water of schryfte,
> And polysed als playn as parchmen schaven,
> Sulp no more þenne in synne þy saule þerafter,
> For þenne þou Dryȝtyn dyspleses wyth dedes ful sore,
> And entyses hym to tene more trayþly þen ever,
> And wel hatter to hate þen hade þou not waschen.
> For when a sawele is saȝtled and sakred to Dryȝtyn,
> He holly haldes hit his, and have hit he wolde;
> Þenne efte lastes hit likkes, he loses hit ille,
> As hit were rafte wyth unryȝt and robbed wyth þewes.
> War þe þenne for þe wrake; his wrath is achaufed
> For þat þat ones watz his schulde efte be unclene. (1133–44)

[playn – *smooth*; Sulp – *defile*; entyses – *provoke*; tene – *anger*; trayþly – *quickly* (?); hatter – *more hotly*; saȝtled – *reconciled*; Dryȝtyn – *God*; Þenne... likkes – *if sins then please it once again*; ille – *with ill-will*; rafte wyth unryȝt – *snatched wrongfully*; þewes – *thieves*; wrake – *vengeance*; achaufed – *aroused*.]

Merely defiling a holy vessel incurs God's wrath, so violently does he hate the profanation of anything sacred to him:

> Þaȝ hit be bot a bassyn, a bolle oþer a scole,
> A dysche oþer a dobler þat Dryȝten onez served,
> To defowle hit ever upon folde fast he forbedes. (1145–7)

[Þaȝ – *even if*; a bolle...scole – *a bowl or a cup*; dobler – *plate*; þat...served – *that once served God*; upon folde – *anywhere*; fast – *firmly*.]

This lesson, the poet concludes, was revealed in the time of Belshazzar.

Up to this point the broad outline of the argument of the poem runs therefore as follows. All sin defiles man and destroys his relationship with God, and as a consequence man is deprived of the sight of God in Heaven (ll. 177–92). Sins of the flesh are particularly displeasing to God, and on two occasions they provoked God to such violent anger that he destroyed the whole community that was tainted by them (ll. 249 ff., 781 ff.). However, God is merciful to those who repent and cleanse themselves through Penance, but if, having done this, they defile their souls again, they provoke God's anger more than if they had never been cleansed (ll. 1113–44).

The view that it is particularly culpable to pollute a soul which has once been cleansed has good biblical authority. It is given, for example, in the Second Epistle of St. Peter, in a chapter which also mentions as instances of God's vengeance on sinners three of the *exempla* used by the poet. It can scarcely be doubted that it is this chapter that provided the poet with the basis of his argument:[26]

> God spared not the angels that sinned, but delivered them, drawn down by infernal ropes to the lower hell, unto torments, to be reserved unto judgement; and spared not the original world, but preserved Noe, the eighth person, the preacher of justice, bringing in the flood upon the world of the ungodly. And, reducing the cities of the Sodomites and of the Gomorrhites into ashes, condemned them to be overthrown, making them an example to those that should after act wickedly, and delivered just Lot, oppressed by the injustice and lewd conversation of the wicked...By whom a man is overcome, of the same also is he the slave. For if, flying from the pollutions of the world, through the knowledge of our Lord and Saviour Jesus Christ, they be again entangled in them and overcome; their latter state is become unto them worse than the former. For it had been better for them not to have known the way of justice than, after they have known it, to turn back from that holy commandment which was delivered to them. For, that of the true proverb has happened to them: The dog is returned to his vomit; and: The sow that was washed, to her wallowing in the mire. (2 Peter ii. 4–7, 19–22)

Having understood how the poet's argument develops, we may approach his final *exemplum*, Belshazzar's Feast, and see how its accompanying preamble underlines the lesson of the *exemplum* itself. The poet tells us that it is because the ruler of Jerusalem, Sedecias, sitting on Solomon's throne, turned aside from the faith to which he owed allegiance as Solomon's successor and 'used abominaciones of idolatrye' (1173) that Jerusalem was sacked. Their oppressor was Nabuchodonosar, a pagan, but yet the agent chosen by God, because the Jews who were once consecrated to God ('halȝed for his') had fallen back into the uncleanness of sin (ll. 1161–8). The severity of their punishment is underlined by this grisly description of Nabuchodonosar's massacre of the Jews:

> Þay slowen of swettest semlych burdes,
> Baþed barnes in blod and her brayn spylled,
> Prestes and prelates þay presed to deþe,
> Wyves and wenches her wombes tocorven
> Þat her boweles outborst aboute þe diches. (1247–51)

[Þay...burdes – *they slew the sweetest lovely women*; her – *their*; wom͞es – *stomachs*; tocorven – *cut open*; outborst – *spilled out*.]

The pillage and burning of Jerusalem echoes the destruction of Sodom, but it also looks forward to the next stage in the argument, for the Jews represent the poet's first example of God's anger at those who defile what was once pure by falling from true allegiance into idolatry. This is the essential theme taken up in Belshazzar's Feast.

Nabuchodonosar pressed on into Jerusalem and seized the vessels that Solomon had assembled in the worship of God, yet the pagan prince treated them 'wyth reverens'. For many years afterwards he ruled as a powerful king, and gradually he came to acknowledge the true God. Later the poet recalls that (like Lucifer) Nabuchodonosar grew proud and thought himself equal to God. For this he was humbled so that he became like a beast, until he recognised 'who wroȝt alle myȝtes', and because he repented he was restored to his former state.

He is contrasted with his son Belshazzar, who handled the holy vessels with disrespect and who did not repent of his pride. Like the Jews, Belshazzar reverted to idolatry. His desecration of the vessels is a symbolic re-enactment of this defilement of his own soul, and at the same time the poet's description of the feast at which the desecration takes place is carefully directed to show that Belshazzar's symbolic act is a reflection of the corruption of his way of life. The elaborate account of the feast tellingly conveys an atmosphere of luxury and uncleanness. Belshazzar, surrounded by his concubines and tippling wine from the holy vessels, is guilty of lechery, drunkenness and pride (ll. 1349–50). The loving description of the vessels made in God's honour, decorated with all the art that man could devise (ll. 1453–92) underlines the magnitude of Belshazzar's irreverence in using them for his unclean pleasures:

> Þer watz rynging on ryȝt of ryche metalles,
> Quen renkkes in þat ryche rok rennen hit to cache,
> Clatering of covaclez þat kesten þo burdes,
> As sonet out of sauteray songe als myry.
> Þen þe dotel on dece drank þat he myȝt,
> And þenne drinkez arn dressed to dukez and prynces,
> Concubines and knyȝtes, bicause of þat merthe,
> As uch on hade hym inhelde, he haled of þe cuppe.   (1513–20)

[on ryȝt – *truly*; rok – *castle*; cache – *take (the wine)*; Clatering...myry – *the clatter of the cup-covers which the ladies threw around rang out as merrily as music from a psaltery*; dotel – *fool*; dece – *dais*; dressed – *served*; hade hym inhelde – *had wine poured out for him*; haled of – *drank off*.]

And so Belshazzar, whose death is foretold by the finger writing on the wall, is 'corsed for his unclannes' and bloodily beaten to death in his bed by the invading Persians.

The episode of Belshazzar's Feast, which at first strikes the reader as rather a startling divergence from the poet's theme, in fact consolidates the imagery of the poem and draws together its separate threads. It is linked especially to the poet's introductory discussion of uncleanness, which had argued that *all* kinds of uncleanness, not only sexual, are displeasing to God. Sexual uncleanness which provokes God's particular wrath was the subject of the first two episodes, but Belshazzar is guilty of defilement by sin in general. The poem opens with the admonition that priests handling God's own body at Mass must pay particular attention to their spiritual cleanness if they are not to displease God in his heavenly court,[27] and this is reflected in Belshazzar's inversion of the Mass as, glorying in the corrupt pomp of his earthly court, he handles God's holy vessels in uncleanness. The second section of the poet's introduction gives a brief account of the parable of the wedding feast adapted from the Gospels of Matthew and Luke. This wedding feast is God's feast:

> Thus comparisunez Kryst þe kyndom of heven
> To þis frelych feste þat fele arn to called. (161–2)

[comparisunez – *compares*; frelych – *noble*; fele – *many*.]

Belshazzar's Feast is the obverse; not a wedding feast, for he has put aside his wife for his concubines; not God's feast, but a feast to serve the Devil:

> Þe gay coroun of golde gered on lofte,
> Þat hade ben blessed bifore wyth bischopes hondes,
> And wyth besten blod busily anoynted
> In þe solempne sacrefyce, þat goud savor hade
> Bifore þe Lorde of þe lyfte in lovyng hymselven,
> Now is sette for to serve Satanas þe blake. (1444–9)

[gered on lofte – *set up high*; besten – *beasts'*; busily – *assiduously*; lyfte – *Heaven*; lovyng hymselven – *praising him*.]

In the poem's two feasts material objects have spiritual significance. The wedding guest is cast into darkness for the uncleanness of his clothes, which represent his deeds:

> Wich arn þenne þy wedez þou wrappez þe inne,
> Þat schal schewe hem so schene, schrowde of þe best?
> Hit arn þy werkez, wyterly, þat þou wroȝt havez. (169–71)

[schewe hem – *appear*; schene – *beautiful*; schrowde – *clothes*; wyterly – *truly*.]

Similarly we have seen how the poet associates the holy vessels with man's pure soul. The image of clothes as outward representations of inner qualities or vices is a focal symbol that runs through the poem and helps to direct the whole ambitious structure to one point. At the beginning of the poem the Heavenly King and his court are enveloped 'in alle þat is clene/Boþe wythinne and wythouten in wedez ful bryȝt' (19–20). Lucifer before his fall wears 'fayre wedez' (217), and the radiant angels that visit Lot are dressed in fine white clothes – 'wlonk whit watz her wede' (793). Significantly, Belshazzar's mind is set not on wholesome objects but on 'þe clernes of his concubines and curious (i.e. 'exquisite') wedez' (1353), so that when, right at the end of the poem, the poet prays for grace that we may 'gon gay in oure gere' (1811) we recognise the same image of outward beauty to symbolise inner purity picked up for the last time.

The narrative of *Purity* is an intricate structure of parallels and contrasts, of images and inverted images, a poem in which the narrative and descriptive powers of the verse are directed towards the portrayal of a God stung to anger by the uncleanness and sinfulness of his creation.

Satiric Technique in Pierce the Ploughman's Crede

In style, outlook and technique no alliterative poem could be less like those we have looked at so far in this chapter than *Pierce the Ploughman's Crede*, and yet this poem, in its own way, demonstrates the art of telling a story as effectively as *The Wars of Alexander* or *Purity*. The *Crede*, like Langland's *Piers Plowman* to which it is indebted, is a keen satire on ecclesiastical degeneracy, though the object of its criticism is much more limited than Langland's, for it is a singleminded attack on the friars. Like *Piers Plowman* again, the *Crede's* attack is set in a narrative framework, and in this way it differs from other poems on the friars, such as the poem beginning 'Of þes frer mynours me thenkes moch wonder/Þat waxen are þus hauteyn',[28] which launches immediately into direct assault. The *Crede* adopts a more subtle and oblique approach, and this strengthens the satire immeasurably. The evils of the friars are seen through the eyes of an unbiased and naive narrator and heard from the lips of the friars themselves as the narrator questions one after the other in his search for someone who will teach him the Creed. The narrator is a fascinating and complex figure in so many fourteenth-century poems, and it is significant that he appears in all the satiric poems of the Revival. Through such a figure the satire can emerge much more powerfully than from a direct attack by the poet *in propria persona*. The narrator has no axe to grind; he merely reports what happened, his story. We can see that the *author* of the *Crede* is a Lollard, but the narrator of the poem is not; he has no ulterior motive for attacking the friars. So, too, the dreamer of *Wynnere and Wastoure*, though perturbed by the degeneracies he sees all around him, is an impartial reporter of his dream, even if his creator has a very serious moral lesson to put across; Will the dreamer in *Piers Plowman* stumbles confusedly towards Truth, discovering and disclosing the decaying moral state of society on his way, and, in the closest parallel to the *Crede*, the narrator in *Mum and the Sothsegger* wanders in an increasingly bemused state from one supposed authority to another in search of someone who will speak out truthfully. All these poems make their satiric and moral points within a narrative framework, whether it is a dream-vision, a quest or (in *Piers Plowman*) both, and the story maintains our interest in the satire, sets the objects of contempt within a context where they display their evil in action, and most important, by separating (however incompletely) narrator from poet, permits the corruptions of the world to proclaim themselves without the intervention of an omniscient and committed author.

At the outset of his quest, the narrator in the *Crede* has no prejudice against the friars. Indeed, it is to them he turns to learn his Creed, and no-one could be more surprised than he by what he sees and hears. One after another friars of each of the four orders attack the corruption, greed and ignorance of their fellow orders, and, as they sit at ease in their palaces or in the tavern, unable to teach the narrator the Creed but for a small donation willing to absolve him for not knowing it, they unmask in themselves precisely those vices they have censured in their fellows. The Dominicans live in regal splendour, and their minster is described in all the detail we are by now accustomed to find in alliterative verse:

Wiþ arches on eueriche half and belliche y-corven,
Wiþ crochetes on corners wiþ knottes of golde,
Wyde wyndowes y-wrouȝt, y-written full þikke,
Schynen wiþ schapen scheldes to schewen aboute,
Wiþ merkes of marchauntes y-medled bytwene.   (173–7)

[belliche y-corven – *beautifully carved*; crochetes – *decorated projecting stonework*; y-written – *inscribed*; merkes – *badges*; y-medled – *intermingled*.]

In the midst of this luxury sits a grotesque friar, described in a series of vivid similes:

A greet cherl and a grym, growen as a tonne,
Wiþ a face as fat as a full bledder,
Blowen bretfull of breþ, and as a bagge honged
On boþen his chekes, and his chyn wiþ a chol lollede
As greet as a gos eye, growen all of grece,
Þat all wagged his fleche as a quyk myre.   (221–6)

[tonne – *barrel*; bretfull – *quite full*; chol – *jowl, i.e. double chin*; lollede – *wagged about*; eye – *egg*; grece – *fat*; quyk myre – *quagmire*.]

The only information that the narrator is able to extract from this bloated Dominican is that the Austin Friars love money and carry out their 'duties' among whores and thieves; so he turns next to an Austin Friar, who tells him that a Franciscan, instead of dressing simply and going barefoot as St. Francis had instructed, will wear a fine coat:

> Wiþ foyns or wiþ fitchewes oþer fyn beuer,
> And þat is cutted to þe kne and queyntly y-botend,
> Lest any spirituall man aspie þat gile.
> Fraunces bad his breþeren barfote to wenden;
> Nou han þei bucled schon for bleynynge of her heles,
> And hosen in harde weder, y-hamled by þe ancle. (295–300)

[foyns or fitchewes – *marten or polecat fur*; queyntly y-botend – *craftily buttoned up*; schon – *shoes*; for bleynynge – *to avoid sores*; hosen – *socks*; y-hamled – *cut short*.]

Eventually defeated and demoralised in his fruitless search for enlightenment from the friars, the narrator comes across the ploughman Pierce, whose dreadful poverty contrasts starkly with the riches of the supposedly poor friars:

> His hod was full of holes and his heer oute,
> Wiþ his knopped schon clouted full þykke;
> His ton toteden out as he þe londe treddede,
> His hosen ouerhongen his hokschynes on eueriche a side,
> All beslombred in fen as he þe plow folwede. (423–7)

[knopped – *knobbly*; clouted full þykke – *much patched*; ton – *toes*; toteden – *peeped*; hokschynes – *lower part of legs*; beslombred – *bedaubed*; fen – *mud*.]

His wife and child present an equally miserable picture:

> Wrapped in a wynwe schete to weren hire fro weders,
> Barfote on þe bare ijs, þat þe blod folwede;
> And at þe londes ende laye a litell crom-bolle,
> And þeron lay a litell childe lapped in cloutes. (435–8)

[wynwe schete – *sheet used for winnowing corn*; weren – *protect*; ijs – *ice*; crom-bolle – *large bowl*; lapped – *wrapped*; cloutes – *rags*.]

And yet instead of demanding money as the friars had done, the ploughman immediately offers food. The narrator tells him wearily that he merely needs someone to teach him the Creed, and recounts the experiences he has had with the friars. The ploughman is a convinced Lollard, fierce in his denunciation of the evils of the friars, reminding the narrator of the way they persecuted Wycliffe and one of his followers, Walter Brute, a stubborn and courageous Lollard who proselytised in the Herefordshire area until 1393.[29]

The ploughman is obviously the mouthpiece for the views of the poet, views which could more easily have been dismissed if they had stood on their own. However, in the context of the narrator's quest it becomes clear that the ploughman is stating no more than the truth, and the fact that he alone is able to teach the narrator his Creed demonstrates his superiority, poor though he is, over the corrupt friars.

This, then, is a poem about the honesty of the humble man. The narrator is ignorant and poor; the ploughman is equally destitute but has enough learning and understanding to teach others the elements of his Christian faith. Against honest poverty stand the greed and corruption of the rich friars. For a poem extolling the virtues of the plain man, the high style of alliterative verse with its rich and elaborate diction and poetic expressions would be thoroughly inappropriate. So the poet banishes every trace of the characteristic alliterative vocabulary, and writes instead in an informal style which attempts to convey the vigour of the spoken language and the vividness of colloquial expressions. As a lesser poet, the author of the *Crede* does not achieve Langland's outstanding success in this, but he has, nevertheless, a fine ability to capture the homely expression, as in the Carmelite's astonishment at the narrator's refusal to buy absolution:

> A fol y þe holde!
> Þou woldest not weten þy fote and woldest fich kacchen!　　　　　　(404–5)

Or the same friar's attack on the Dominicans:

> Þey ben digne as dich water þat dogges in bayteþ.　　　　　　(375)[30]

[digne – *haughty*; in bayteþ – *rummage in.*]

This is a poem that immerses itself in the realities of everyday life:

> For her kynde were more to y-clense diches
> Þan ben to sopers y-set first and serued wiþ siluer.
> A great bolle full of benen were betere in his wombe,
> And wiþ þe randes of bakun his baly for to fillen,
> Þan pertriches or plouers or pekokes y-rosted.　　　　　　(760–4)

[her kynde – *the natural position (of friars)*; diches – *dishes*; benen – *beans*; wombe – *belly*; randes – *rinds.*]

The subject-matter thus provides the most important motive for the poet to use a plain style, but we should also bear in mind that the poem was in all probability written to encourage the Lollards of the south-west midlands, where for some years in the late fourteenth century there was great Lollard sympathy and activity, principally among ordinary laymen who would perhaps have little patience with an elaborately poetical work.[31] Therefore both the poet's audience and his subject demand an easy and straightforward style, a style which has to sacrifice many of the grander effects achieved by the verse of the *Wars* in favour of a naturalness and simplicity which the *Wars* does not seek to achieve. Of course neither style is inherently better than the other; rather each is appropriate to its context. The range of the alliterative style is as wide as the subjects chosen by the poets, and we have observed something of this range in this chapter; what the poets have in common is a supreme ability to tell a story well.

Chapter 6

EPILOGUE: AFTER THE REVIVAL

The Context of Dunbar's Tretis
In England the impetus of the Revival waned in the fifteenth century, but in Scotland it gained a new lease of life. After about 1450 a number of interesting alliterative works were composed by Scottish writers, and quite quickly the style and the vocabulary of the poems became more distinctively Scottish. The outstanding work of this later alliterative movement is Dunbar's *Tretis of the Tua Mariit Wemen and the Wedo* written in about 1500. There is no poem that better demonstrates the value of studying a literary work in its context rather than taking it in isolation, because the *Tretis* derives its strength from English, Scottish and French traditions. It is the first two of these that I am here concerned with. Dunbar looks over his shoulder to the poems of the Revival of the fourteenth century in England, and yet he is essentially a Scottish writer working within a Scottish tradition of alliterative poetry that had diverged considerably from the English school from which it sprang. An understanding of these later developments in Scotland is therefore very valuable for an appreciation of the *Tretis*.[1]

The unrhymed alliterative line was not favoured by Scottish writers, and the preferred form was the thirteen-line stanza, for which the model (with the long ninth line instead of a 'bob' line) was *The Awntyrs off Arthure* and perhaps other poems like it that have since been lost. Probably the first of the Scottish rhyming alliterative poems was *The Buke of the Howlat*, written by Richard Holland in 1446 or not long after,[2] a clumsily constructed eulogy of the House of Douglas. The frame-story describes how the howlat (owl), aggrieved because Nature has not blessed him with physical beauty, is granted a feather from every other bird, and thus decked in borrowed plumes becomes 'so pomposs, impertinat and reprovable' (924) that Nature deprives him of his feathers again. The whole action is overheard by a poet strolling through a beautiful forest 'in the myddis of May'. Into this structure are thrust an account of the Douglases and their history, as well as descriptions of sixty-four different birds. Despite the incongruous juxtaposition of some of the material, the difficult stanza is quite skilfully handled and there is some good incidental writing, particularly in the picture of the owl before and after, first gloomily regarding his crooked beak in the water, 'My neb is netherit as a nok, I am bot ane Owle' (57), but later strutting about 'In breth as a batall-wricht full of bost blawin' (916) – 'angry as a warmonger puffed up with pride'.

Arthurian romance is represented in the second half of the fifteenth century by *Golagros and Gawane* which is in the same thirteen-line stanza. The poem retells two episodes, taken from the First Continuation of Chrétien's *Perceval*, that exhibit the courtesy and valour of Gawain in contrast to Kay's lack of these qualities. There are vigorous descriptions of combat:

> Thai gird one tva grete horse, on grund quhil thai grane,
> The trew helmys and traist in tathis thai ta,
> The rochis reirdit vith the rasch, quhen thai samyne rane,
> Thair speris in the feild in flendris gart ga.
> The stedis stakerit in the stour, for streking on stray,
> The bernys bowit abak,
> Sa woundir rude wes the rak;
> Quhilk that happynnit the lak
> Couth na leid say. (912–20)

[gird one – *spur on*; quhil – *until*; grane – *groan*; traist – *trusty*; in...ta – *they cut to pieces*; rochis – *rocks*; reirdit – *rang*; rasch – *clash*; samyne – *together*; flendris – *splinters*; stakerit – *staggered*; stour – *encounter*; streking on stray – *dashing about*; bowit – *went*; rude – *violent*; rak – *encounter*; Quhilk...say – *no-one could say who came off worse*.]

In its praise of Gawain and its dignified treatment of knightly courtesy, the poem inherits the traditional attitudes of the fourteenth-century English alliterative romances. Quite different and more interesting is the approach taken by another Scottish romance of the same period, *Rauf Coilȝear*. This, though it has no identifiable source, is set in the time of Charlemagne. The emperor loses his way in a violent storm, and Rauf the Collier, unaware of Charlemagne's identity, offers him shelter. This leads to a farcical scene, played out often enough to this day, as the rough collier and his royal guest debate the niceties of who should allow whom to go through the door first. Rauf loses his temper and, accusing the emperor of discourtesy, throws him inside by the scruff of the neck:

> The Coilȝear, gudlie in feir, tuke him be the hand,
> And put him befoir him, as ressoun had bene;
> Quhen thay come to the dure the King begouth to stand,
> To put the Coilȝear in befoir maid him to mene.
> He said: 'Thow art vncourtes, that sall I warrand'.
> He tyt the King by the nek, twa part in tene;
> 'Gif thow at bidding suld be boun or obeysand,
> And gif thow of courtasie couth, thow hes forȝet it clene.' (118–25)

[gudlie in feir – *in a friendly manner*; begouth to stand – *stood back*; maid...mene – *he intended to indicate*; tyt – *caught*; twa...tene – *very angrily*; boun – *prompt*; obeysand – *obedient*; couth – *knew*.]

Charlemagne is intrigued at this abrupt introduction to rustic manners, and even though Rauf is once again obliged to reprove him for bad behaviour 'and hit him vnder the eir', Charlemagne invites him to the court to sell his charcoal there. The next day Rauf sets out for the court, managing to quarrel with Roland on the way. On his arrival in Paris he is knighted by the emperor, and the following day the new-made knight encounters, of all things, a Saracen on a camel. When the 'steeds' have been slain, the knights fight hand-to-hand, in a fine burlesque of chivalric combat:

> He gaue ane braid with his brand to the beirne by,
> Till the blude of his browis brest out abufe.
> The kene knicht in that steid stakerit sturely,
> The lenth of ane rude braid he gart him remufe;
> Schir Rauf ruschit vp agane and hit him in hy,
> Thay preis furth properly thair pithis to prufe. (858–63)

[braid – *blow*; stakerit – *staggered*; sturely – *greatly*; The lenth...remufe – *made him retreat a couple of yards*; in hy – *quickly*; pithis – *strength*.]

Although stock themes of romance are present, they are, for the first time in alliterative poetry, treated lightheartedly. In *Sir Gawain and the Green Knight* 'cortaysye' is a Christian virtue of deep significance both to the poet and to his audience. In *Rauf Coilȝear* it has become a question of who goes through a doorway first – an occasion for comedy. The poet is no longer committed to the idealised world of chivalry, and so cannot use it as a vehicle for serious moral and social comment; instead he views it from a distance with an amused tolerance. Though this lively poem is not a parody of romance, it contains the seeds of parody that were to germinate in later Scottish writings. Because it anticipated later attitudes, *Rauf Coilȝear* became a popular poem. Several allusions are made to it in the first half of the sixteenth century,[3] and it was still regarded highly enough in 1572 to be printed at St. Andrews by Robert Lekpreuik.

Rauf Coilȝear may be seen as a bridge between the sober moral reflections of *The Awntyrs off Arthure* and, in the same stanza-form, the scatological humour of Henryson's *Sum Practysis of Medecyne*, in which singularly unpalatable remedies are prescribed for various afflictions. Henryson appears to have been the first of several Scottish poets to use the stanza for ridicule and abuse.

The form was used with more serious intent by Gavin Douglas for the prologue to the eighth book of his translation of the *Aeneid*,[4] completed in 1513. Other prologues in different metres deal with such topics as the sorrows of love, the seasons, the nature of translation and literary criticism, but significantly Douglas reserves the thirteen-line stanza for an attack on the degeneracy of the age. Alliterative verse has by this time become the language of insult:

> Swengeouris and scurryvagis, swankeis and swanys,
> Gevis na cur to cun craft, nor comptis for na cryme,
> With berdis as beggaris, thocht byg be thar banys,
> Na laubour list thai luk till, thar luffis ar byrd lyme.   (68–71)

> [*Rogues and vagabonds, strong lads and young fellows, don't bother to learn a craft, and, with beards like beggars, don't consider it a crime, even though they are sturdily built, not to bother to look for work, for they have sticky fingers.*]

Of course, satire is no new subject for alliterative verse. A history of the ancestry of this passage would look back to *Wynnere and Wastoure* and *Piers Plowman*, and further back still to poems written some two centuries before Douglas's *Aeneid*, such as the Harley Lyric *On the Retinues of the Great*, which directs its satire at the same objects:

> Whil God wes on erthe and wondrede wyde,
> Whet wes þe resoun why he nolde ryde?
> For he nolde no grom to go by ys syde,
> Ne grucchyng of no gedelyng to chaule ne to chyde!   (33–6)[5]

> [*While God travelled widely on earth, what was the reason he would not ride? Because he did not want an attendant at his side, nor the complaints of a servant chattering and chiding him!*]

Nevertheless, it is a significant fact that from the end of the fifteenth century the thirteen-line alliterative stanza was only used for ribaldry and satire. A cheerful example of the type is *The Gyre Carling*, a short and engaging piece of nonsense about the love of a certain Blasour for 'an grit gyre carling' (ogress) who smacks her admirer over the head with an iron club, and in the process of this violent exercise 'lut fart North Berwick Law'. The poem has the additional interest of being in part a direct parody of earlier alliterative verse. The opening lines of *The Siege of Jerusalem* run:

> In Tiberyus tyme þe trewe emperour,
> Sir Sesar hymsulf, seysed in Rome,
> Whyle Pylat was prouost vnder þat prince riche...   (1–3)

This is deftly echoed in the first lines of *The Gyre Carling*:

> In Tiberus tyme the trew Imperiour,
> Quhen Tynto hillis fra skraiping of toun henis wes keipit...   (1–2)

The use of the alliterative stanza for satire and abuse is extended by Alexander Montgomerie, whose lampoon *Ane Anser to ane Helandmanis Invectiue* was regarded by its Victorian editor as so obscene that he refused to elucidate it, remarking: 'It is with a feeling akin to disgust that we read this scurrilous pasquin.... Fortunately the piece is not only obscure, but also seems to be in great part unintelligible'.[6]

Polwart and Montgomerie's Flyting of 1582 contains the last examples of the stanza. The work consists of unrelieved abuse hurled from each side. It was quoted approvingly by the young James VI, who is one of the earliest critics of alliterative verse. In his 'Reulis and Cautelis to be Obseruit and Eschewit in Scottis Poesie' of 1584 he makes the point that the thirteen-line stanza is reserved for abuse and satire:

> Let all your verse be *Literall*, sa far as may be, quhatsumeuer kynde they be of, bot speciallie *Tumbling* verse for flyting. Be *Literall* I meane that that the maist pairt of your lyne sall rynne vpon a letter, as this tumbling lyne rynnis vpon F.
>   *Fetching fude for to feid it fast furth of the Farie.*
> Ye man obserue that thir *Tumbling* verse flowis not on that fassoun as vtheris dois. For all vtheris keipis the reule quhilk I gaue before, to wit, the first fute short, the sec-ound lang, and sa furth. Quhair as thir hes twa short and ane lang throuch all the lyne, quhen they keip ordour: albeit the maist pairt of thame be out of ordour, and keipis na kynde nor reule of *Flowing*, and for that cause are callit *Tumbling* verse.[7]

Some pages later he advises: 'For flyting, or Inuectiues, vse this kynde of verse following, callit *Rouncefallis* or *Tumbling* verse',[8] and quotes a stanza from *Polwart and Montgomerie's Flyting*.

It is evident, therefore, that when Dunbar was writing in the early years of the sixteenth century the thirteen-line alliterative stanza had come to be re-garded as most fitted for lampoons and invective. *Kynd Kittok* (which some have considered to be by Dunbar) is a short and good-humoured poem in this stanza, very much in the vein of *The Gyre Carling*. The 'gudame' Kynd Kittok 'deit of thirst, and maid a gud end' (5), slipping into Heaven while St. Peter's back was turned. But the attractions of the alehouse outside the celestial gates were too strong to be resisted, and on her return from a visit there 'Saint Petir hat hir with a club' (32) – which seems almost a traditional greeting in this sort of poem. So she went back to the alehouse.

> Frendis, I pray yow hertfully,
> Gif ye be thristy or dry,
> Drink with my Guddame as ye ga by,
>   Anys for my saik.   (36–9)

Dunbar's unrhymed alliterative poem, *The Tretis of the Tua Mariit Wemen and the Wedo* written in about 1500, is of major importance.[9] The setting of the poem is an idyllic garden full of flowers, around midnight on a Midsummer Night's Eve. The narrator hides in a hawthorn hedge to overhear the intimate conversation of three most lovely ladies. The first two speakers are wives, who recount in the frankest detail their experiences, erotic and otherwise, with their despised husbands. Then the third of the ladies, the Widow, reproves her comrades for lack of subtlety in the conduct of their love-lives, and relates the story of her experiences with her two former husbands, both of whom, to her profound relief, are now dead, allowing her to lead her life as an amorous widow unhindered. As the sun rises on this conversation, and the throstles begin to sing and the mists to disperse, these finely dressed ladies rise and return home, leaving us alone with the narrator, who asks:

Quhilk wald ȝe waill to ȝour wif, gif ȝe suld wed one? (530)

[Quhilk – *which*; waill – *choose*.]

In the light of the traditions of Scottish alliterative poetry at this time, it is a striking feature of Dunbar's *Tretis* that it is written not in the thirteen-line stanza but in unrhymed alliterative lines. The only other examples of this in Scotland are some political prophecies,[10] which are of no literary value, though as late as 1603 the Scottish printer Robert Waldegrave considered the genre of sufficient interest to merit a collection under the title *The Whole Prophesie of Scotland*.[11] The implication of Dunbar's choice of metre – and it is an implication reinforced by the quotation of *The Siege of Jerusalem* in *The Gyre Carling* – is that fourteenth-century alliterative poetry was much more familiar to Scottish readers than we now suspect, and that Dunbar is deliberately recalling that tradition.

The *Tretis* combines the older tradition of alliterative verse with the more recent developments of the Scottish poets. So Dunbar's vocabulary, though distinguished from that of the poets of the Revival by a rich fund of Scottish expressions, at the same time preserves many of the traditional alliterative elements, in particular the words for 'man' – *freke, leid, sege* – and the frequent use of the absolute adjective – *the semely, the tothir wlonk, this amyable.* And yet all is used with a satiric purpose, for the ladies are anything but *wlonk* and *amyable*. The combination of old and new is especially marked in the tone and subject-matter of the poem. The poets of the Revival handled weighty subjects in a serious and dignified manner; fabliau and burlesque were subjects for other metres. The idea that alliterative verse was only suited for invective, ribaldry and obscenity is a Scottish development on which the *Tretis* depends heavily. However, if the English poets did not care to write in this vein as a general rule, they were quite capable of adopting the style when the need arose. The emphasis of alliteration is a powerful reinforcer of insults, as we see in *The Wars of Alexander* when Alexander is described by Darius as:

Ane amlaȝe, ane asaleny, ane ape of all othire,
A wirling, a wayryngle, a wawil-eȝid shrewe,
Þe caitifeste creatour þat cried was euire. (1705–7)

[amlaȝe – *worthless fellow*; asaleny – *little ass*; of – *above*; wirling – *dwarf*; wayryngle – *lit. butcher-bird, i.e. villain*; wawil-eȝid – *wall-eyed*; caitifeste – *most despicable*; cried – *created*.]

The difference between this and the abuse of the *Tretis* is only a matter of degree:

I have ane wallidrag, ane worm, ane auld wobat carle,
A waistit wolroun, na worth bot wourdis to clatter;
Ane bumbart, ane dron bee, ane bag full of flewme,
Ane scabbit skarth, ane scorpioun, ane scutarde behind;
To see him scart his awin skyn grit scunner I think.
Quhen kissis me that carybald, than kyndillis all my sorow,

As birs of ane brym bair his berd is als stif,
Bot soft and soupill as the silk is his sary lume;
He may weill to the syn assent, bot sakles is his deidis.
With gor his tua grym ene are gladderrit all about,
And gorgeit lyk tua gutaris that war with glar stoppit. (89–99)

[wallidrag – *weakling*; wobat carle – *caterpillar-man*; waistit wolroun – *decayed boar*; bumbart – *drone*; flewme – *phlegm*; scabbit skarth – *scabby monster*; scutarde – *discharger*; scart – *scratch*; scunner – *disgust*; carybald – *monster*; birs – *bristles*; brym – *fierce*; sary lume – *feeble tool*; sakles – *blameless*; gor – *filth*; ene – *eyes*; gladderrit – *besmeared*; gorgeit – *filled*; glar – *muck*.]

Dunbar's powerful and repulsive simile in the last line also finds a parallel in the practices of the best alliterative poets, as may conveniently be illustrated, again from the *Wars*, by the use of the same image of gutters in a description of the venom pouring from serpents' jaws 'as gotis out of guttars in golanand wedres' (4796).

The revelations of the three ladies in the *Tretis* take place in a 'plesand garding' which is described in some detail both at the beginning and at the end of the poem. Fifty years previously Holland had given *The Buke of the Howlat* a similar setting,[12] but any reader of fourteenth-century alliterative verse will be reminded more immediately of the dream-vision poems such as *Wynnere and Wastoure* and *The Parlement of the Thre Ages*, which preface a debate on grave moral issues with a spring scene. The *Tretis*, like *The Gyre Carling*, underlines its points by burlesquing a certain kind of alliterative verse, the moral dream-vision debate in a vernal setting.

Dunbar's purpose in alluding to this kind of poetry is to expose the depravity of the ladies' attitudes. The *Tretis* is not, as some have seen it, an amoral poem, for its moral is implicit in the contrasts expressed by the poem, in the contrast between the *Tretis* and the moral vision-poems of the Revival, and in the contrast within the poem itself between dissimulation and reality, a theme encapsulated in the Widow's boast of her hypocrisy: 'I wes dissymblit suttelly in a sanctis liknes' (254). Hypocrisy is the Widow's watchword, and her art is to cloak depravity beneath a demure exterior. The ladies' outward appearance is at one with the beauty of the natural setting. They are:

All full of flurist fairheid as flouris in June,
Quhyt, seimlie and soft as the sweit lillies,
New upspred upon spray as new spynist rose. (27–9)

[flurist fairheid – *blooming beauty*; Quhyt – *white*; spynist – *opened*.]

The idyllic setting and this outward beauty constitute an ironic introduction to the boastful accounts of shameless deceit and unbridled lust, and the point is made again at the end of the poem when the scene reverts to the natural beauty as the 'ryall roises' rise and leave. Dunbar leads those readers acquainted with the earlier tradition of alliterative verse to expect a moral vision, but appearances are deceptive, just as the Widow advises that they should be:

I haif a wattir spunge for wa, within my wyde clokis,
Than wring I it full wylely and wetis my chekis,
With that watteris myn ene and welteris doune teris. (437–9)

Dunbar's idyllic opening is as false as the tears shed by the Widow's 'wattir spunge'.

The similarities in structure and theme between the *Tretis* and the French tradition of *chanson de mal mariée* have long been recognised,[13] but it might also be noted that the *Tretis* is strikingly close in its structural outlines to *The Parlement of the Thre Ages*. The natural setting of the two poems is conventional enough, and so the parallels at this point are not especially significant in themselves, though each poem opens with a similar statement:

In the monethe of Maye when mirthes bene fele...   (*Parlement*, 1)
Apon the Midsummer evin, mirriest of nichtis...   (*Tretis*, 1)

and continues with descriptions of how the dew 'donkede', the birds sang happily and the flowers bloomed beside the river. But what is more significant is that in each poem three characters (in one poem men, in the other women) discuss the conduct of their lives. It is unusual for the debate form (to which both poets are indebted) to accommodate three disputants, since issues can most clearly be set forth by opposing *two* points of view. In both the *Parlement* and the *Tretis* the problem is resolved by pairing the first two disputants, so that they represent what is essentially the same position; this is then contrasted with the position of the third disputant. Youth and Middle Elde stand for worldly values, but Elde has rejected the things of this world as vain;[14] the Widow is distinguished from the two wives by her age ('ʒe woddit wemen ʒing', 41) and her widowhood, and drawing on her rich experience of life she is able to instruct her companions that it is expedient to 'counterfeit gud maneris'. The structure of both debates is that the first two speakers are dismissed comparatively quickly, and the main part of the action concentrates on the statement of the third, who turns to the previous two and admonishes them in moral (or mock-moral) tones. Elde, borrowing a phrase from the Office of the Dead,[15] warns his companions that Death comes unannounced to all. The Widow blasphemously represents herself as a preacher, correcting the false conduct of her listeners:

God my spreit now inspir and my speche quykkin,
And send me sentence to say, substantious and noble,
Sa that my preching may pers ʒour perverst hertis,
And mak ʒow mekar to men in maneris and conditiounis.   (247–50)

However, the views on the sacrament of marriage that she subsequently expresses represent those of La Vieille in *Le Roman de la Rose* rather than those of the Church.

Which of these ladies, asks Dunbar, would *we* choose as a wife? The author of the *Parlement* does not explicitly ask us to make a choice between the Ages, but it is a choice that must nevertheless be made.

It seems highly probable that, to underline his ironic purpose, Dunbar took over the structure of the *Parlement*, and did so in the expectation that at least some of his readers would know the poem well enough to recognise the parallels between the *Parlement* and the *Tretis*, and from the contrast set up by these parallels to draw their own conclusions about the corrupt values the women stand for. This is, admittedly, presupposing a closer knowledge in Scotland at this time of the verse of the Revival than there is firm evidence to support, but in any case it is clear that the *Tretis* is alluding to the *type* of moral debate represented by the *Parlement*, and is playing off the attitudes which are appropriate in that sort of poetry against the Scottish vein of ribaldry. The poem's opening setting in the beauty of the natural scene suggests at first that Dunbar is writing within an older tradition of sober social and moral criticism. The overturning of these expectations provides its own comment on the 'thre gay ladeis'.

The Survival of Alliterative Verse in England

Alliterative poetry continued in high popularity in England throughout the fifteenth century. The majority of the surviving manuscripts are from this period, and many of them are from areas outside the west midlands, showing that interest in alliterative poetry was quite widespread. Even so, with the un-doubted loss of so many manuscripts we are apt to underestimate the extent of the continued interest in alliterative poems; only one manuscript of *Morte Arthure*, copied in the mid-fifteenth century in East Yorkshire, is now extant, but there is evidence to suggest that another copy was circulating in Lincoln-shire slightly earlier,[16] and when Malory came to write his account of Arthur's wars with Lucius, he took his material from *Morte Arthure*, using a text which differed to some extent from the one that survives.[17]

Strangely, despite the widespread popularity of alliterative poetry, it seems likely that little of any importance was written after the first decade or so of the fifteenth century, although the problem of dating most of the poems makes it difficult to be sure of this. A case in point is *Death and Liffe*, preserved only in the seventeenth-century Percy Folio Manuscript, inevitably a very corrupt version. Some parts of the poem seem to depend on *Piers Plowman*,[18] which provides a likely *terminus a quo*, but, apart from the date of the manuscript, there is nothing to provide a *terminus ad quem*. So, too, several important poems such as *The Destruction of Troy* and *The Wars of Alexander* could conceivably be fifteenth-century compositions. The decline in the creative impulse of the Revival is the more difficult to date because there is no obvious explanation for it. All that can be said is that the poems of the Revival which can be dated with certainty fall within the period 1352–1415, and that alliterative works known to be written later than this seem from their style and approach to represent departures from the mainstream of the Revival.

Several of these derivative pieces are very feeble, melancholy pointers to the decay of the alliterative style. *The ABC of Aristotle*, a dreary alphabetical list of admonitions that even Polonius would have despised, was dispiritingly popular, to judge from the large number of manuscripts in which it is preserved. The Lollard controversies provoked three unattractive works, *Jack Upland*, *Friar Daw's Reply* and *Upland's Rejoinder*, the first in alliterative prose, and the last two, probably dating from about 1420 and 1450 respectively,[19] in very weak alliterative verse. Much livelier, however, is the *Second Burlesque*, an amusing parody of alliterative verse, with its nonsensical account of the 'batell of Brakonwete':[20]

> The hare and harthestone hurtuld togeydur,
> Whyle the honbul-be hod was hacked al to cloutus.   (12–13)

The reader of alliterative verse will recognise the echo of *Wynnere and Wastoure's* 'hares appon herthe-stones' (14), though this is a collocation which appears regularly in political prophecies.

More accomplished fifteenth-century writers built upon the poetry of the Revival to develop new and interesting types of alliterative verse. The in-fluence of the Revival is expressed in a number of the best dramatic works of this period, and is particularly strong in the York Plays. Some thirteen of the York Plays were entirely rewritten in alliterative rhyming stanzas, a revision which took place some time after 1415.[21] Whereas the other York Plays are written in verses of fairly regular stress-patterns with ornamental alliteration, the revised plays, which include the work of the so-called York Realist,[22] are composed in lines that are accentual in rhythm and in which alliteration is metrically functional. The revisers adopt the commoner alliterative expressions, and they use a wide variety of stanza-forms, some of which, such as the very impressive thirteen-line stanzas of *The Appearance of Our Lady to Thomas*, were forms which had been used by poets of the Revival. Other stanza-forms appear to be innovations, and often the modifications of the traditional alliterative style and vocabulary are so great that the poetry of the Revival is only faintly recalled. *The Judgement of Jesus* is in twelve-line bob-and-wheel stanzas, consisting of a quatrain of four-stress lines followed by lines of three stresses. This passage portrays Pilate's anger and incredulity as the soldiers' spears involuntarily bow down at the entry of Jesus:

> *Cayphas.* A! sir, saugh ʒe noʒt þis sight, how þat þer schaftes schuke,
> And theʒ baneres to this brothell þai bowde all on brede?
> *Anna.* ʒa, ther cursed knyghtes by crafte lete them croke
> To worshippe þis warlowe vnworthy in wede.
> *Pilate.* Was it dewly done þus in dede?
> *Cayphas.* ʒa, ʒa, sir, oure selfe we it sawe.
> *Pilate.* We! spitte on them, ill mott þai spede!
> Say, dastard, þe deuyll mote ʒou drawe.
>   How dar ʒe
> Þer baners on brede þat her blawe
> Lat lowte to þis lurdan so lawe?
> O faytouris, with falshed how fare ʒe?[23]

[brothell – *scoundrel* (*i.e. Jesus*); on brede – *far and wide*; croke – *bend*; warlowe – *villain*; mott – *may*; spede – *prosper*; þe deuyll...drawe – *may the Devil take you*; lowte – *bow*; lurdan – *rascal*; faytouris – *liars*.]

The rhythms and verse patterns of the Revival have here undergone a remarkable metamorphosis, and out of them the playwright has fashioned a very effective vehicle for dramatic dialogue.

Alliterative verse in rhyming stanzas was also used elsewhere in fifteenth-century drama, for example in the morality play *The Castle of Perseverance*,[24] which is composed mainly in thirteen-line stanzas. Interestingly enough, the Chester Plays, written in the home of the Alliterative Revival, are composed predominantly in regular syllabic verse with little ornamental alliteration. The Chester cycle is generally regarded as the earliest, which bears out the implication of the revision of the York Plays, that alliterative verse-forms were a later development in the mystery cycles, dating from a period when the alliterative line had elsewhere fallen into disuse.

As we have observed, the manuscripts show that throughout this century alliterative verse was still widely read and copied, and even in the sixteenth century the activity of scribes continued to some extent, but for the most part it now became geographically limited to the Cheshire area where alliterative verse had always been strong. Humphrey Newton of Pownall in Cheshire, who died in 1536, copied into his commonplace book (along with poems of his own composition) *The ABC of Aristotle* and, more interesting, two alliterative poems in intricate pararhyme stanzas.[25] The first, 'On clife þat castell so knetered', describes a lonely and impregnable fortress, and the poem consists of a sixteen-line bob-and-wheel stanza alliterating in pairs of lines and rhyming alternately as follows: *knetered/knatered/betered/batered*, etc.[26] The second, 'Wyntre that snartely snewes', is a mildly salacious tale about tupping a young lady in a meadow; it also alliterates in pairs, and runs for the first thirty-two lines on two rhymes only. Both poems appear to be late exercises in alliterative verse in complex rhyme-patterns, imitating much earlier works such as *De*

Tribus Regibus Mortuis in similar pararhyme stanzas. The second poem in particular shows many verbal parallels with older alliterative poetry of that area, especially with *Gawain*.

A truly massive task was undertaken by Thomas Chetham of Nuthurst in south Lancashire, who in about 1540 transcribed the 14,000 lines of *The Destruction of Troy*, and on his death in 1546 left the fruit of his great labours to his son 'to be an heyrelome at Notehurst'.[27] Like Newton, Chetham was a minor landowner of the north-west midlands, and was bailiff of Thomas and Edward Stanley, earls of Derby. Also associated with the Stanleys is the remarkable poem *Scotish Ffeilde*, an account of the Battle of Flodden in 1513. The poem, which seems to draw its information from an historical account bearing some resemblance to Edward Hall's *Chronicle*, may have been written many years after the battle, but within the reign of Henry VIII who is spoken of as still living.[28] The author of the poem was one of the Legh family living at Baguley in Cheshire:

> He was a gentleman, by Iesu, that this iest made....
> Att Bagily that bearne his bidding place had,
> And his ancetors of old time haue yearded their longe. (416–19)

[iest – *story*; bidding place – *dwelling place*; yearded – *lived*.]

Scotish Ffeilde is an extraordinary witness to how well alliterative verse was still remembered and understood in some circles. If it were not a description of a datable event, the poem might easily pass for a slightly modernised transcription of a fourteenth-century poem, so completely does Legh capture the style and habits of the alliterative tradition. It is a deliberate and skilful re-creation of alliterative battle poetry, with its vocabulary including *burne, freake, gome, hattell, leede, rincke, sege* and *wye*, its collocations such as *dungen to death*, and *buske and bowne*, its correct alliterative patterns, its opening address to God reminiscent of the opening of *Morte Arthure*, and its routine descriptions of the natural scene as a prelude to battle, which is again paralleled in *Morte Arthure*.[29]

The character of its battle-description may be compared, in style if not in quality, with that of fourteenth-century poetry. A passage from *The Wars of Alexander* (ll. 1385–92) quoted in the previous chapter provides a good standpoint from which to judge the description in *Scotish Ffeilde* of the forces joining battle at Flodden:

> Then trumpetts full truly they tryden together,
> Many shames in that shawe with theire shrill pipes;
> Heauenly was theire melody, their mirth to heare,
> How thé songen with a showte all the shawes ouer!
> There was gurding forth of gunns with many great stones,
> Archers vttered out their arrowes and egerlie they shotten. (319–24)

[tryden – *sounded* (?); shames – *horns*; gurding – *discharging*; vttered – *shot*.]

Though this is not first-rate poetry, it is a remarkably competent and faithful imitation of verse written more than a century earlier. The poem is one of a number written to honour the Stanleys at about this time, and together with several others in praise of that family, it is preserved in the Percy Folio Manuscript,[30] compiled by a seventeenth-century collector working in the north-west midlands,[31] who also copied *Death and Liffe* and a ballad version of *Gawain* called *The Grene Knight*.

There is therefore strong evidence of the interest taken in alliterative verse in a small area of the north-west midlands during the first half of the sixteenth century. However, a few alliterative poems attracted interest elsewhere. A rather surprising case of this is *Alisaunder of Macedoine*, for we owe the survival of this work to the humanist poet and scholar Nicholas Grimald, who copied out the text in his notebook.[32] Grimald's only known connection with the west midlands is that in 1551–2 he was licensed as a preacher in Eccles in south Lancashire, where, twenty years previously, the priest Thomas Bowker had recorded his ownership of the manuscript containing *St. Erkenwald*.[33] Perhaps it was here that Grimald found his text of *Alisaunder of Macedoine*. He was attracted by some of the distinctive features of the alliterative vocabulary, and incorporated a number of these words, such as the synonyms for 'man', into his own verse published in 1557 in Tottel's *Miscellany*, as this passage from *The Death of Zoroas*, one of the earliest blank-verse poems, shows:

One, Meleager, could not bear this sight,
But ran vpon the sayd Egyptian renk
And cut him in both kneez; he fell to ground,
Wherwith a hole route came of souldiours stern,
and all in peeces hewed the silly seg.[34]

Nevertheless, the only alliterative poems that captured widespread attention were *Piers Plowman* and *Pierce the Ploughman's Crede*. There are sixteenth-century manuscripts of all three versions of *Piers Plowman*, including a mixed A and C Version copied in 1532 by Sir Adrian Fortescue, whose unswerving devotion to Catholicism resulted in his execution seven years afterwards. Many later readers, on the other hand, regarded Langland as a Protestant before his time, and their demand for a text of the poem was answered in 1550 by Robert Crowley, who printed a B Version of the poem, remarking in his preface that Langland was one of those bold enough 'to open their mouthes and crye oute agaynste the worckes of darckenes, as did Iohn wicklefe'.[35] Crowley makes brief but sensible comments on the metre, and adds encouragingly: 'The Englishe is according to the time it was written in, and the sence somewhat darcke, but not so harde, but that it may be vnderstande of suche as will not sticke to breake the shell of the nutte for the kernelles sake'. Three years later, following Crowley's example, Reynold Wolfe brought out an edition of *Pierce the Ploughman's Crede*, and both poems were reprinted in 1561.

If it had not been for the prints of these two works, alliterative poetry would have been entirely forgotten by the end of the sixteenth century. As it was, *Piers Plowman* and *Pierce the Ploughman's Crede* were still available to those interested in the ecclesiastical corruptions of a former age. All other alliterative poems lay neglected in manuscripts, and vanished for a long time from the literary scene.

The Rediscovery of Alliterative Verse

By the late sixteenth century, as we have seen, interest in alliterative poetry had reached a very low ebb. Only *Piers Plowman* still occasionally provoked a passing remark from humanist critics, essentially because it was regarded as an unmedieval poem. It was, so they thought, anti-Papist, and furthermore it did not rhyme, a point which was in its favour, for medieval writers were to be blamed, as William Webbe maintained in his *Discourse of English Poetrie* (1586), in that they 'conuerted the naturall property of the sweete Latine verse to be a balde kinde of ryming, thinking nothing to be learnedly written in verse which fell not out in ryme'.[36] With a fine disregard for accuracy, Webbe refers to the poet Pierce Ploughman who followed Lydgate, and 'who in hys dooinges is somewhat harshe and obscure, but indeede a very pithy wryter, and (to hys commendation I speake it) was the first that I haue seene that obserued the quantity of our verse without the curiosity of Ryme'.[37] Clearly Webbe knew very little about *Piers Plowman*. Since he was intent on reforming English verse on Classical models, he had a passing interest in a poem that was unrhymed, but yet the metre certainly did not follow the rules of Latin verse, and was therefore not worth his detailed attention. George Puttenham in *The Arte of English Poesie* (1589) referred to 'that nameles who wrote the *Satyre* called Piers Plowman' as a 'malcontent' who 'bent himselfe wholy to taxe the disorders of that age, and specially the pride of the Romane Clergy, of whose fall he seemeth to be a very true Prophet; his verse is but loose meetre, and his termes hard and obscure, so as in them is little pleasure to be taken'.[38] Spenser, however, had genuflected before the 'high steppes' of *Piers Plowman* in the Epilogue to *The Shepheardes Calender* (1579), and later Milton praised the poem as a satire in his *Apology for Smectymnuus* (1642), though it is not necessary to suppose that either poet knew Langland's work at all well.[39]

It was not until the middle of the eighteenth century that the contempt of most scholars and critics for the barbarisms of the Middle Ages began to be replaced by a renewed interest in medieval literature, more particularly in medieval romance. Writers became aware that in their wholehearted devotion to Augustan models, 'what we have lost is a world of fine fabling'.[40] As a young man Thomas Percy had rescued his Folio Manuscript from the Shropshire household of Humphrey Pitt, where it was 'being used by the maids to light the fire'.[41] In the poems that he saved from the flames he found a wealth of fascinating information about the Middle Ages, which would 'show the gradation of our language, exhibit the progress of popular opinions, display the peculiar manners and customs of former ages, or throw light on our earlier classical poets'.[42] Among the contents of the Percy Folio Manuscript were two alliterative poems, *Scotish Ffeilde* and *Death and Liffe*, and although Percy published neither of these in the *Reliques of Ancient English Poetry* (1765), he was sufficiently interested in their style to include an essay 'On the Alliterative Metre without Rhyme in Pierce Plowman's Vision'. His understanding of the metrical principles was, not surprisingly, very imperfect, but in the course of his essay he mentioned other alliterative poems that he knew were still preserved in manuscript, including *The Siege of Jerusalem* and *Cheuelere Assigne*.

The first serious attempt at a critical account of the poems of the Revival was by Thomas Warton in his *History of English Poetry*, the first volume of which was published in 1774. Though Warton, like his contemporaries, was interested most of all in the medieval romances, he recognised the importance of *Piers Plowman*, and devoted Section VIII to a discussion of the poem and long extracts from it. He regarded the alliteration of the poem as a drawback in that it necessitated the 'constraint of seeking identical initials, and the affectation of obsolete English', which 'while it circumscribed the powers of our author's genius, contributed also to render his manner extremely perplexed, and to disgust the reader with obscurities'. Nevertheless, Warton praises Langland's imagination, his observation of life, his strokes of humour, and the sublimity of his imagery. The next section of the *History* discusses the satire of *Pierce the Ploughman's Crede*, again with long quotations from the poem. Section X quotes from *Alexander and Dindimus*, *The Wars of Alexander* and *The Siege of Jerusalem*, and refers the reader to Percy's essay on alliterative verse.

While he was working on a later section of the *History*, Warton came across MS. Cotton Nero A.x, the *Gawain* manuscript, which had passed from the collection of the sixteenth-century bibliophile Henry Savile of Banke in York-shire[43] to the library of Sir Robert Cotton and eventually, having survived a disastrous fire in 1731, to the British Museum. Although it was too late for Warton to mention its contents in the appropriate place in the *History*, his discussion in Section XLIII of the verse of *The Tournament of Tottenham* (which he erroneously supposed to be a sixteenth-century composition) allowed a digression on the use of alliteration, and in a footnote 'for the use of those who collect specimens of alliteration' he quoted lines from *Pearl* and *Purity*. But it was Richard Price, in his revision of Warton's *History* in 1824, who first mentioned and quoted *Sir Gawain and the Green Knight* in a note on *Sir Tristrem*, with the aim of illustrating the use of 'strange ryme' and 'selcouth names'. His promise to edit the poem was never fulfilled. It was Price also who first stated that *Piers Plowman* existed in three versions, a fact which was prompt-ly forgotten and had to be rediscovered by Skeat.

Despite the work by Percy, Warton and others such as Joseph Ritson, no alliterative poems had appeared in print. The honour of being the first for over two centuries to publish alliterative poetry fell to the unscrupulous John Pinkerton, in whose *Scotish Poems* of 1792 were included *The Buke of the Howlat* and *Golagros and Gawane*, and also *The Awntyrs off Arthure*, the text of which was taken from a transcript of a manuscript owned by Ritson, which had been lent to Pinkerton on the understanding that he would not print it.[44]

Not until the nineteenth century did alliterative poems become more widely available. The first C Version of *Piers Plowman* was edited by T. H. Whitaker in 1813, who a year later published *Pierce the Ploughman's Crede*. The Rox-burgh Club brought out *Cheuelere Assigne* in 1820, and in 1822 David Laing's *Select Remains of Ancient Popular Poetry* included the principal Scottish alliterative poems. Even so, the masterpiece of alliterative romance had to wait until 1839 for an edition, when, prompted by the enthusiasm of Sir Walter Scott, Sir Frederick Madden edited *Gawain*, together with other Arthurian poems, for the Bannatyne Club. The three other poems in the Cotton Nero manuscript did not appear in print until 1864, when the Early English Text Society very appropriately devoted its first volume to an edition by Richard Morris of all the Cotton Nero poems. In the later years of the nineteenth cen-tury very valuable editions of a large number of alliterative poems, including the three versions of *Piers Plowman*, were brought out by W. W. Skeat, whose work still stands as an example of excellence to modern editors.

The rediscovery of alliterative verse has, for the most part, been confined to the learned world, and it is associated particularly with the emergence of English as a respectable university subject. It is surprising that poets of the last hundred years, with all their metrical experimentation, have paid so little attention to alliterative verse. Gerard Manley Hopkins became interested in the techniques of alliterative verse as a consequence of his own experiments in diction and 'sprung rhythm', but when he came to read *Piers Plowman* he was disappointed by it. Writing to Robert Bridges in 1882, nearly seven years after composing *The Wreck of the Deutschland*, he said of 'sprung rhythm': 'So far as I know – I am enquiring and presently I shall be able to speak more decidedly – it existed in full force in Anglo saxon verse and in great beauty; in a degraded and doggrel shape in *Piers Ploughman* (I am reading that famous poem and am coming to the conclusion that it is not worth reading).'[45]

The only poet of this century who has made a serious attempt to adapt the alliterative line as a way of organising accentual verse is W. H. Auden.[46] His most significant work in alliterative verse, *The Age of Anxiety*, 'a baroque eclogue', has been coolly received by most of its critics. If not successful in every way, it is nevertheless a remarkable metrical experiment which achieves passages of great beauty. Auden drew on his reading of both Old and Middle English verse. His line is marked by the frequent enjambment so characteristic of the Old English line, but inevitably the rhythms and the alliterative patterns are rather more reminiscent of Middle English verse, with an occasional deliberate echo of *Piers Plowman*:

> When in wan hope I wandered away and alone,
> How brag were the birds, how buxom the sky,
> But sad were the sallows and slow were the brooks
> And how dismal that day when I danced with my dear.[47]

Rosetta, imagining 'those lovely innocent countrysides inhabited by charming eccentrics with independent means', has undoubtedly been reading some of the medieval descriptions of the *locus amoenus*:

> Fat cattle brooded
> In the shade of great oaks, sheep grazed in
> The ancient hollows of meander scars and
> Long-legged ladies with little-legged dogs
> Lolled with their lovers by lapsing brooks.[48]

But perhaps even more successful, and more significant in that it demonstrates the potential of the alliterative line for modern poetry, is this fine evocation of a train-journey:

> Autumn has come early; evening falls;
> Our train is traversing at top speed
> A pallid province of puddles and stumps
> Where helpless objects, an orphaned quarry,
> A waif of a works, a widowed engine,
> For a sorry second sigh and are gone
> As we race through the rain with rattling windows.[49]

If there is any future for long narrative verse, modern poets might do worse than to look back to the practices of the poets of the fourteenth-century Revival, for the alliterative line gives the scope and flexibility that many poets search for, and yet contains them within that framework of control which is so helpful for an easy, long-poem style. It may be time for a second alliterative revival.

NOTES

Chapter 1

1. For fuller discussion of the date see Gollancz's edition of the poem, and J. M. Steadman, 'The Date of *Winnere and Wastoure*', *M.P.*, xix (1921–2), 211–19. However J. R. Hulbert, 'The Problems of Authorship and Date of *Wynnere and Wastoure*', *M.P.*, xviii (1920–1), 31–40, thought that the poem could not be dated so precisely. Individually many of the references used to determine the date might be questioned, but cumulatively the evidence is strong. For more general studies of *Wynnere and Wastoure* see J. Speirs, *Medieval English Poetry: The Non-Chaucerian Tradition* (London, 1957), pp. 263–89; and T. H. Bestul, *Satire and Allegory in Wynnere and Wastoure* (Lincoln, Nebraska, 1974).
2. For *tauerne* (l. 477) Gollancz's 1st edn. reads *tonne*, corrected in his 2nd edn. (1931).
3. This is put forward with confidence by N. Coghill, 'The Pardon of Piers Plowman', *P.B.A.*, xxx (1944), 303–57; with more hesitation by S. S. Hussey, 'Langland's Reading of Alliterative Poetry', *M.L.R.*, lx (1965), 163–70.
4. Some have argued that *Wynnere and Wastoure* is by the same author as the *Parlement*, though this seems to me unlikely. But see J. P. Oakden, 'A Note on the Unity of Authorship of *Wynnere and Wastoure* and *The Parlement of the Thre Ages*', *R.E.S.*, x (1934), 200–2.
5. Some guide to the range of vocabulary in different poems is given by J. P. Oakden, *Alliterative Poetry in Middle English* (Manchester 1930–5), vol. ii, pp. 175–93.
6. Comparative statistics of metrical patterns, which should, however, be treated with caution, are given by Oakden, ibid., i, 153–200.
7. Cf. also *Piers Plowman*, x. 48–9: 'Ac murthe and mynstralcye amonges men is nouthe/Leccherye, losengerye and loseles tales'.
8. Ed. J. Earle and C. Plummer, *Two of the Saxon Chronicles Parallel*, 2 vols. (Oxford, 1892–9). Most of the verse annals are also ed. E. van K. Dobbie, *The Anglo-Saxon Minor Poems* (London, 1942), from which my quotations are taken.
9. For a classification of these different styles see A. McIntosh, 'Wulfstan's Prose', *P.B.A.*, xxxv (1949), 109–42.
10. Used by McIntosh, ibid., who admits the dangers of the term.
11. This is analysed by W. P. Lehmann, *The Development of Germanic Verse Form* (Austin, 1956), pp. 98–123. See also M. M. R. Stobie, 'The Influence of Morphology on Middle English Alliterative Poetry', *J.E.G.P.*, xxxix (1940), 319–36.
12. Demonstrated by T. A. Shippey, *Old English Verse* (London, 1972), pp. 188–9.

13. J. C. Pope, *Homilies of Ælfric*, vol. i, E.E.T.S. 259 (1967), p. 112.
14. The blurring of the distinction between prose and verse in the Middle English period is emphasised by N. F. Blake, 'Rhythmical Alliteration', *M.P.*, lxvii (1969–70), 118–24. One aspect of the question is illustrated by S. M. Kuhn, 'Was Ælfric a Poet?', *Philological Quarterly*, lii (1973), 643–62.
15. Previously *Durham* was dated 1104–9, but for the suggestion that it might be a little earlier than this see H. S. Offler, 'The Date of *Durham*', *J.E.G.P.*, lxi (1962), 591–4. The poem is edited by Dobbie, *The Anglo-Saxon Minor Poems*.
16. For this see Shippey, op. cit., 177.
17. See M. Schlauch, 'An Old English *Encomium Urbis*', *J.E.G.P.*, xl (1941), 14–28.
18. See N. R. Ker, *Catalogue of Manuscripts Containing Anglo-Saxon* (Oxford, 1957), p. 368. The poem is edited by R. Buchholz, 'Die Fragmente der Reden der Seele an den Leichnam', *Erlanger Beiträge zur englischen Philologie*, vi (1890), p. 11.
19. See Oakden, op. cit., i, 41–2.
20. Ed. Buchholz, art. cit., 1–10.
21. Demonstrated by L. Dudley, 'The Grave', *M.P.*, xi (1913–14), 429–42; and by E. K. Heningham, 'Old English Precursors of *The Worcester Fragments*', *PMLA*, lv (1940), 291–307.
22. Ed. B. Dickins and R. M. Wilson, *Early Middle English Texts* (London, 1951), p. 2.
23. For a list of the activities of this, the 'tremulous Worcester hand', see Ker, op. cit., lvii; and for a discussion of this scribe's interests as compared with those of Laȝamon see E. G. Stanley, 'Laȝamon's Antiquarian Sentiments', *M.Æ.*, xxxviii (1969), 23–37.
24. For discussion of the date of Laȝamon's *Brut* see E. G. Stanley, *N. & Q.*, ccxiii (1968), 85–8, where it is maintained that the poem may be dated between 1189 and the first half of the thirteenth century.
25. At present the only complete edition of Laȝamon's *Brut* is by F. Madden (London, 1847). This passage is quoted from *Laȝamon: Brut*, vol. i, ed. G. L. Brook and R. F. Leslie, E.E.T.S. 250 (1963).
26. A detailed analysis is presented by W. Hilker, *Der Vers in Layamons Brut* (Münster, 1965).
27. This is l. 41 in G. L. Brook's *Selections from Laȝamon's Brut* (Oxford, 1963).
28. See Hilker, op. cit.; and also H. Pilch, *Layamons Brut* (Heidelberg, 1960), pp. 135–47.
29. I quote from the selection in J. A. W. Bennett and G. V. Smithers, *Early Middle English Verse and Prose* (2nd edn., Oxford, 1968), pp. 156–7, ll. 313–22.
30. Useful material for a study of Laȝamon's vocabulary is provided by H. C. Wyld, 'Studies in the Diction of Layamon's Brut', *Language*, vi (1930), 1–24; ix (1933), 47–71, 171–91; x (1934), 149–201; xiii (1937), 29–59, 194–237.
31. This is suggested by Stanley, 'Laȝamon's Antiquarian Sentiments'.
32. Laȝamon's compounds are listed and analysed by Oakden, op. cit. ii, 130–65.
33. See Stanley, art. cit.

34. Oral tradition is suggested by, e.g., D. Everett, *Essays on Middle English Literature* (Oxford, 1955), pp. 37–8.
35. See E. van K. Dobbie, *The Manuscripts of Cædmon's Hymn and Bede's Death Song* (New York, 1937); and for addenda see K. W. Humphreys and A. S. C. Ross, *N. & Q.*, ccxx (1975), 50–5.
36. On the origins of this style see D. Bethurum, 'The Connection of the Katherine Group with Old English Prose', *J.E.G.P.*, xxxiv (1935), 553–64; and for a literary analysis see C. Clarke, 'Early Middle English Prose', *Essays in Criticism*, xviii (1968), 361–82. For full discussion of the dialect, see the edn. of *Þe Liflade ant te Passiun of Seinte Iuliene* by S. R. T. O. d'Ardenne, E.E.T.S. 248 (1961), pp. 177 ff.
37. *Seinte Marherete*, ed. F. M. Mack, E.E.T.S. 193 (1934), pp. 20–2.
38. *Þe Wohunge of Ure Lauerd*, ed. W. M. Thompson, E.E.T.S. 241 (1958), p. 21, ll. 32–7. On the 'Wooing Group' see the editor's remarks, pp. xv–xxx.
39. See the edition by O. Arngart (Lund, 1942–55), vol. i, pp. 137–41.
40. See Oakden, op. cit., i, 45. The poem is edited by R. Morris, *An Old English Miscellany*, E.E.T.S. 49 (1872), pp. 1–25.
41. The reasons for this are explored by R. M. Wilson, *Early Middle English Literature* (3rd edn., London, 1969), 112–15.
42. This essay was first published as the introduction to *Harpsfield's Life of More*, ed. E. V. Hitchcock, E.E.T.S. 186 (1932). The passage quoted is on p. lxvii. For the same view see Oakden, op. cit., i, 3, *et passim*.
43. A. C. Spearing, *The Gawain-Poet* (Cambridge, 1970), p. 20.
44. The observations of Milman Parry and A. B. Lord on the characteristics of Homeric and Yugoslav oral verse were applied to Old English verse by F. P. Magoun, 'The Oral-Formulaic Character of Anglo-Saxon Narrative Poetry', *Speculum*, xxviii (1953), 446–67. Magoun in turn influenced R. A. Waldron, 'Oral-Formulaic Technique and Middle English Alliterative Poetry', *Speculum*, xxxii (1957), 792–804. The oral character of English alliterative verse has since been questioned by a large number of critics; see especially L. D. Benson, 'The Literary Character of Anglo-Saxon Formulaic Poetry', *PMLA*, lxxxi (1966), 334–41; and R. F. Lawrence, 'The Formulaic Theory and its Application to English Alliterative Poetry' in *Essays on Style and Language*, ed. R. Fowler (London, 1966), pp. 166–83.
45. See R. M. Wilson, *The Lost Literature of Medieval England* (2nd edn., London, 1970).
46. Wilson, ibid., makes several references to lost alliterative verse, but these may be misleading. E.g., the well-known statement of Giraldus Cambrensis on the Englishman's love of alliteration (quoted by Wilson, p. 161) is not to be taken as a reference to alliterative verse, since the three 'alliterative lines' Giraldus cites are all proverbial sayings rather than extracts from poems, and are quoted as proverbs by other Middle English writers. They may be followed up in B. J. Whiting, *Proverbs, Sentences and Proverbial Phrases* (Cambridge, Mass., 1968). Proverbial sayings, even today, are frequently alliterative. Also obviously proverbial is the saying on the wolf quoted by Odo of Cheriton (Wilson, p. 125). Other snatches, such as the couplet on St. Kenelm (ibid., 99), or that on Lothbrog's sons (ibid., 38), appear to be commemorative or mnemonic lines, complete in themselves. In any case, both are recorded as early as the twelfth century, before the written tradition of unrhymed alliterative verse had died, and

are irrelevant to the question of the composition of alliterative verse in the later thirteenth century.

47. The manuscript date suggested by *M.E.D.* is *ante* 1300.
48. Previously the Cotton Caligula manuscript of the *Brut* was thought to be earlier, but it is now dated *post* 1250; see N. R. Ker, *The Owl and the Nightingale*, E.E.T.S. 251 (1963), p. ix.
49. Ed. R. Morris, *An Old English Miscellany*, E.E.T.S. 49 (1872), pp. 90–2.
50. For this dating and localisation see N. R. Ker, E.E.T.S. 255 (1965), pp. xxi ff.
51. Ed. G. L. Brook, *The Harley Lyrics* (4th edn., Manchester, 1968), pp. 35–6; and earlier by K. Böddeker, *Altenglische Dichtungen* (Berlin, 1878), pp. 150–4.
52. Ed. R. H. Robbins, *Historical Poems of the XIVth and XVth Centuries* (New York, 1959), pp. 27–9.
53. Ed. Bennett and Smithers, op. cit., 127–8.
54. Ed. Robbins, op. cit., 24–7.
55. Ed. ibid., 7–9. I have, however, incorporated the emendations of the earlier edition by Böddeker.
56. E.g. *The Four Foes of Mankind* (Auchinleck ms.), ed. C. Brown, *Religious Lyrics of the XIV Century* (2nd edn., Oxford, 1957), p. 32; *Old Age* (MS. Harley 913), ed. T. Wright and J. O. Halliwell, *Reliquiae Antiquae* (London, 1843), vol. ii, pp. 210–12. The amusing *Chorister's Lament* (ed. F. L. Utley, *Speculum*, xxi (1946), 194–202) may also date from this period, though critics have generally argued that it is later.
57. Ed. Robbins, *Historical Poems*, p. 29. In l. 15 the reading of the ms. is probably *leuedis* rather than *louedis* as Robbins prints.
58. In l. 16 the ms. reads *lede hir at will*, emended by Gollancz to *lede at hir will*.
59. Ed. C. M. Westra (The Hague, 1950), p. 2. For discussion of the term 'cadence' see L. K. Smedick, 'Cursus in Middle English: *A Talkyng of þe Loue of God* Reconsidered', *M.S.*, xxxvii (1975), 387–406.
60. See Westra, ed. cit., xvii ff.; and M. M. Morgan, '*A Talking of the Love of God* and the Continuity of Stylistic Tradition in Middle English Prose Meditations', *R.E.S.*, n.s. iii (1952), 97–116.
61. See Morgan, art. cit.
62. For full details see H. E. Allen, *Writings Ascribed to Richard Rolle* (London, 1927).
63. Ed. E. J. F. Arnould, *The Melos Amoris of Richard Rolle of Hampole* (Oxford, 1957), who quotes the passage on p. lviii.
64. For some illustration of the relevance of the 'arts of discourse' to the English writings of the mystics see M. M. Morgan, 'A Treatise in Cadence', *M.L.R.*, xlvii (1952), 156–64; and for a more general study see J. J. Murphy, 'The Arts of Discourse 1050–1400', *M.S.*, xxiii (1961), 194–205.
65. Ed. H. E. Allen, *English Writings of Richard Rolle* (Oxford, 1931), pp. 19–36. For the view that the work is not certainly by Rolle see M. M. Morgan, 'Versions of the Meditations on the Passion ascribed to Richard Rolle', *M.Æ.*, xxii (1953), 93–103.
66. Ed. Allen, 61–72. The quotation is on p. 64.
67. However, the authenticity of the lines is to some extent supported by a similar passage in one of Rolle's Latin works in alliterative prose. See Allen, p. 147.

68. Statistics given by Oakden, op. cit., i, 153–200.
69. The poem *Cheuelere Assigne* shows similar metrical irregularities. Like *Joseph of Arimathie* it is a condensation of the opening section of a huge thirteenth-century French romance-cycle. See W. R. J. Barron, '*Chevalere Assigne* and the *Naissance du Chevalier au Cygne*', *M.Æ.*, xxxvi (1967), 25–37. The manuscript (B. M. Cotton Caligula A.ii) is dated about 1460, but there are no firm grounds for dating the composition of the poem.

Chapter 2

1. See M. B. Parkes, 'The Literacy of the Laity', in *The Mediaeval World*, ed. D. Daiches and A. Thorlby (London, 1973), pp. 555–77.
2. Commented on by G. Shepherd, 'The Nature of Alliterative Poetry in Late Medieval England', *P.B.A.*, lvi (1970), 57–76.
3. For an account and a refutation of the theory see H. N. MacCracken, 'Concerning Huchown', *PMLA*, xxv (1910), 507–34.
4. J. P. Oakden, op. cit., ii, 90–103.
5. This is the reading of the Douce ms.
6. See *The Conflict of Wit and Will*, ed. B. Dickins (Leeds, 1937).
7. All quotations from Chaucer are from F. N. Robinson's 2nd edition of the *Complete Works* (London, 1957).
8. For an account of this see A. McIntosh, 'A New Approach to Middle English Dialectology', *E.Sts.*, xliv (1963), 1–11, esp. 8–9.
9. Ibid., 5.
10. This point is raised in the edition of *Sir Gawain and the Green Knight* by Tolkien, Gordon and Davis, p. xxvii.
11. Another satiric poem of the early fourteenth century that Langland may have known is *The Simonie* (or *On the Evil Times of Edward II*) which is composed in rhyming stanzas with sporadic alliteration. The earliest text of this is the Auchinleck ms. (*c.* 1330), ed. T. Wright, *The Political Songs of England* (Camden Soc., vi, 1839), pp. 323–45. See E. Salter, 'Piers Plowman and "The Simonie"', *Archiv für das Studium der neueren Sprachen und Literaturen*, cciii (1967), 241–54.
12. The position is carefully examined by D. Embree, '"Richard the Redeless" and "Mum and the Sothsegger": A Case of Mistaken Identity', *N. & Q.*, ccxx (1975), 4–12.
13. The common approach taken by the four poems is lucidly discussed by A. C. Spearing, *The Gawain-Poet*.
14. These hints in *The Destruction of Troy* are firstly an ambiguous reference to 'Troilus' (l. 8054) which might denote either a poem (not necessarily Chaucer's) or – more probably in the context – the hero himself, and secondly an allusion to Diomede holding Briseide's rein (l. 8078) which might be a borrowing from the scene in Chaucer or an independent addition by the alliterative poet. See C. Spurgeon, *Five Hundred Years of Chaucer Criticism and Allusion* (Cambridge, 1925), vol. i, p. 14; C. D. Benson, 'Chaucerian Allusion and the Date of the Alliterative "Destruction of Troy"', *N. & Q.*, ccxix (1974), 206–7; M. Sundwall, 'The *Destruction of Troy*, Chaucer's *Troilus and Criseyde* and Lydgate's *Troy Book*', *R.E.S.*, n.s. xxvi (1975), 313–17.

15. See C. A. Luttrell, 'Three North-West Midland Manuscripts', *Neophilologus*, xlii (1958), 38–50.
16. See P. Moe, 'The French Source of the Alliterative *Siege of Jerusalem*', *M.Æ.*, xxxix (1970), 147–54.
17. B.M. Add. MS. 31042 (the Thornton manuscript).
18. MSS. B.M. Cotton Caligula A.ii; Camb. Univ. Lib. Mm. v.14.; Huntington HM 128.
19. Lambeth Palace MS. 491, on which see A. G. Hooper, 'The Lambeth Palace MS. of *The Awntyrs off Arthure*', *L.S.E.*, iii (1934), 37–43.
20. See A. McIntosh, 'The Textual Transmission of the Alliterative *Morte Arthure*' in *English and Medieval Studies Presented to J. R. R. Tolkien*, ed. N. Davis and C. L. Wrenn (London, 1962), pp. 231–40.
21. On the dialect of *The Pistill of Susan* (from the evidence of the rhymes) see E. J. Dobson, *N. & Q.*, ccxvi (1971), 110.
22. Parallels are given by W. Matthews, *The Tragedy of Arthur* (Berkeley, 1960), pp. 156–63, 208–9.
23. The possible influence of *Piers Plowman* on *The Canterbury Tales* is explored most thoroughly by J. Mann, *Chaucer and Medieval Estates Satire* (Cambridge, 1973), esp. pp. 208–12.
24. For the suggestion that Chaucer's battle-scenes are indebted in a general way to the alliterative poets see D. Everett, *Essays in Middle English Literature*, pp. 139–48; and also R. W. V. Elliott, *Chaucer's English* (London, 1974), pp. 102–5. C. O. Chapman, 'Chaucer and the *Gawain*-Poet: A Conjecture', *M.L.N.*, lxviii (1953), 521–4, proposed that Chaucer borrowed from *Gawain* for the opening of *The Squire's Tale*, but his arguments are not convincing.
25. Particularly relevant on the similarities of outlook in poetry of the two traditions are J. A. Burrow, *Ricardian Poetry* (London, 1971), and J. A. W. Bennett, 'Chaucer's Contemporary' in *Piers Plowman: Critical Approaches*, ed. S. S. Hussey (London, 1969), pp. 310–24.
26. Parallels are listed by A. C. Baugh, 'The Middle English Romance: Some Questions of Creation, Presentation and Preservation', *Speculum*, xlii (1967), 1–31.
27. For a discussion of this *Troilus* frontispiece and the narrator of the poem see D. S. Brewer, '*Troilus and Criseyde*' in *Sphere History of Literature in the English Language*, vol. i, ed. W. F. Bolton (London, 1970), pp. 195–201.
28. 'The poem, as it were, creates its own audience'. D. Mehl, 'The Audience of Chaucer's *Troilus and Criseyde*', in *Chaucer and Middle English Studies*, ed. B. Rowland (London, 1974), p. 176.
29. For this sort of evidence see two articles by R. Crosby: 'Oral Delivery in the Middle Ages', *Speculum*, xi (1936), 88–110, and 'Chaucer and the Custom of Oral Delivery', *Speculum*, xiii (1938), 413–32. During the fifteenth century authors were more willing to admit the possibility that their works might be read in private as well as listened to; see *Partonope of Blois*, ll. 18–20, ed. A. Bödtker, E.E.T.S. E.S. 109 (1912).
30. We learn from Froissart that it took him ten weeks to read his romance *Meliador* (over 30,000 lines) to the court of Foix. See G. Mathew, *The Court of Richard II* (London, 1968), pp. 29–30.
31. For fuller references on this subject see T. Turville-Petre, 'Humphrey de Bohun and *William of Palerne*', *N.M.*, lxxv (1974), 250–2.

32. The mention of Gloucester in *William of Palerne* (l. 166) refers not, as once thought, to Humphrey's residence there (for there are no records that he held property in the town) but rather to the tomb of Humphrey's uncle, Edward II, in what is now Gloucester Cathedral.

33. See M. R. James and E. G. Millar, *The Bohun Manuscripts* (Oxford, 1936), and M. Rickert, *Painting in Britain: the Middle Ages* (2nd edn., London, 1965), pp. 149–50.

34. E. Salter, 'The Alliterative Revival', *M.P.*, lxiv (1966–7), 146. Professor Salter here states what has long been a general view.

35. 'Si le franceis ne soit pas bon, jeo doie estre escusee, pur ceo qe jeo sui engleis et n'ai pas moelt hauntee le franceis', *Le Livre de Seyntz Medicines*, ed. E. J. Arnould, Anglo-Norman Text Society (1940), p. 239.

36. Her will is printed in J. Nichols, *A Collection of all the Wills, now Known to be Extant, of the Kings and Queens of England* (London, 1780), pp. 177-86.

37. MS. Royal 20.D.iv. See M. Rickert, *The Reconstructed Carmelite Missal* (London, 1952), p. 75.

38. For details see G. A. Holmes, *The Estates of the Higher Nobility in Four-teenth-Century England* (Cambridge, 1957), pp. 7–40.

39. A good picture of the position of the Beauchamps in the west midlands at this date is given by R. H. Hilton, *A Medieval Society* (London, 1966), pp. 42–5. On Guy Beauchamp see *The Complete Peerage*, vol. xii, part ii, pp. 370–2. For his books see M. Blaess, 'L'abbaye de Bordesley et les livres de Guy de Beauchamp', *Romania*, lxxviii (1957). 511–18.

40. *The Complete Peerage*, vol. xii, part ii, pp. 372–4.

41. Ibid., viii, 442–5.

42. On the education and literary tastes of the nobility see further K. B. McFarlane, *The Nobility of Later Medieval England* (Oxford, 1973), pp. 228–47.

43. See Viscount Dillon and W. H. St. John Hope, 'Inventory of the Goods and Chattels belonging to Thomas, Duke of Gloucester', *Archaeological Journal*, liv (1897), 275–308.

44. Ed. A. W. Pollard, *Fifteenth Century Prose and Verse* (London, 1903), pp. 203-8.

45. See *Trevisa's Dialogus*, ed. A. J. Perry, E.E.T.S. 167 (1925), pp. xix–xxii.

46. For full details see Skeat's edn. of *Alexander and Dindimus*, pp. viii–ix; F. P. Magoun, *The Gests of King Alexander of Macedon* (Cambridge, Mass., 1929); M. R. James, *The Romance of Alexander. A Collotype Facsimile of MS. Bodley 264* (Oxford, 1933); S. K. Davenport, 'Illustra-tions Direct and Oblique in the Margins of an Alexander Romance at Oxford', *Journal of the Warburg and Courtauld Institutes*, xxxiv (1971), 83–95.

47. On the identity of Robert Thornton see M. S. Ogden, *The Liber de Diversis Medicinis*, E.E.T.S. 207 (1938), pp. viii–xv. D. Mehl makes interesting comments on the Thornton manuscripts in *The Middle English Romances of the Thirteenth and Fourteenth Centuries* (London, 1969), pp. 259–60.

48. For discussion see K. Sajavaara, 'The Relationship of the Vernon and Simeon Manuscripts', *N.M.*, lxviii (1967), 428–39; and A. I. Doyle, 'The Shaping of the Vernon and Simeon Manuscripts' in *Chaucer and Middle English Studies*, ed. B. Rowland, pp. 328–41. Vernon also contains *Joseph of Arimathie* and *Piers Plowman*.

49. R. S. Loomis, *Arthurian Legends in Medieval Art* (New York, 1938), p. 138.
50. See G. Mathew, *The Court of Richard II*, p. 117.
51. See W. W. Greg, *M.L.R.*, xix (1924), 226–7.
52. The information in this paragraph is taken from J. A. Burrow, 'The Audience of Piers Plowman', *Anglia*, lxxv (1957), 373–84.
53. See McFarlane, op. cit., 237–8.
54. For a corrective to the view that the *Morte Arthure* offers *specific* comment on Edward III see G. R. Keiser, 'Edward III and the Alliterative *Morte Arthure*', *Speculum*, xlviii (1973), 37–51.
55. On the Franklin in his social setting see G. H. Gerould, 'The Social Status of Chaucer's Franklin', *PMLA*, xli (1926), 262–79. For a wider view see N. Denholm-Young, *The Country Gentry in the Fourteenth Century* (Oxford, 1969), esp. pp. 23 ff. (on franklins). An instructive account of the social structure in a part of the west midlands is given by R. H. Hilton, 'Lord and Peasant in Staffordshire in the Middle Ages', *North Staffordshire Journal of Field Studies*, x (1970), 1–20.

Chapter 3

1. E.g.: 'The couplet is the most economical and perspicuous; the alliterative line, most impressionistic and powerful in impact; the stanza, most lyrical and best suited to express emotion.' M. Mills, introduction to *Six Middle English Romances* (London, 1973), p. viii.
2. *Sir Launfal*, ed. A. J. Bliss (London, 1960), ll. 301–12.
3. W. W. Skeat, 'An Essay on Alliterative Poetry', in *Bishop Percy's Folio Manuscript*, ed. J. W. Hales and F. J. Furnivall (London, 1867–8), vol. iii, pp. xi–xxxix. Skeat states this view with more precision in the introduction to his edition of *Joseph of Arimathie*, p. x.
4. Oakden gives comparative statistics of aa/ax lines, op. cit., i, 168–9.
5. It has been suggested that some details of the storm scenes in *Patience* and *The Siege of Jerusalem* may conceivably have been borrowed from *The Destruction of Troy*. See N. Jacobs, 'Alliterative Storms: A Topos in Middle English', *Speculum*, xlvii (1972), p. 701. On the other hand there are tentative indications that the poem may be *post* 1385; see above, p. 34.
6. My discussion relies heavily upon the study by J. Turville-Petre, 'The Metre of *Sir Gawain and the Green Knight*', *E.Sts.*, lvii (1976), 310–28. Other notable studies are Oakden, op. cit., i, 131–241, and M. Borroff, *Sir Gawain and the Green Knight: A Stylistic and Metrical Study* (New Haven, 1962). For a bibliography of earlier studies see Borroff, pp. 279 f. The most important of these is K. Luick, 'Die englische Stabreimzeile im XIV., XV. und XVI. Jahrhundert', *Anglia*, xi (1889), 392–443, 553–618.
7. For discussion and references with regard to Chaucer see T. F. Mustanoja, 'Chaucer's Prosody', in *Companion to Chaucer Studies*, ed. B. Rowland (Toronto, 1968) pp. 58–84. There is a detailed analysis of the question with regard to *Gawain* in Borroff, pp. 182–9.
8. See R. Jordan, *Handbuch der mittelenglischen Grammatik* (2nd edn., Heidelberg, 1934), p. 131.

9. This rhythm is also characteristic of many of the alliterative *Harley Lyrics*; see e.g. the quotations from *The Song of the Husbandman* and *On the Retinues of the Great* above, p. 19.

10. The study by R. F. Lawrence, 'Formula and Rhythm in *The Wars of Alexander*', *E.Sts.*, li (1970), 97–112, shows how in that poem the alternating pattern of stresses is avoided by changing the word-order.

11. Aspects of this passage are discussed by Borroff, pp. 190–200.

12. In conversational style enjambment may be even more marked; see *Gawain*, ll. 1541–4.

13. The author of *Gawain* observes this principle more strictly than most. Davis, edn. p. 150, is probably right to suggest that the few examples in *Gawain* of aa/xx lines are corrupt.

14. See J. Turville-Petre, art. cit., 320. Borroff, though with more hesitation, and differing in detail, comes to the same conclusion, *viz.*, that 'in all the first half-lines, however heavy, it is possible to subordinate one out of three stressed syllables' (p. 198).

15. For a straightforward account of this principle see J. McAuley, *A Primer of English Versification* (Sydney, 1966).

16. See e.g. Oakden, i, 181–200. Oakden's statistics are valuable as a general guide to the practices of the various alliterative poets, but they are vitiated by their lack of precision and accuracy.

17. For a full analysis of this line see J. Turville-Petre, art. cit., 321, and also Borroff, p. 193.

18. The list of contents in the manuscript of *The Destruction of Troy* promises 'the nome of the knight þat causet it to be made, and the nome of hym that translatid it out of latyn into englysshe'. Unfortunately neither promise is fulfilled in the text as it now stands.

19. Illuminating studies of the metre in relation to the style and themes of the poem are J. Lawlor, *Piers Plowman: An Essay in Criticism* (London, 1962), pp. 189–239; and E. Salter, *Piers Plowman: An Introduction* (Oxford, 1962), pp. 13–24. Quite a different view of Langland's metrical practice is put forward by G. Kane and E. T. Donaldson in their edition of *Piers Plowman: The B Version* (London, 1975), pp. 131–40.

20. Oakden, op. cit., i, 171, gives the following percentages of 'extended' half-lines: *St. Erkenwald* 17.5, *Gawain* 15.3, *Piers Plowman* 9, *Pierce the Ploughman's Crede* 7. He finds none at all in *The Destruction of Troy*.

21. *The Note-Books and Papers of Gerard Manley Hopkins*, ed. H. House (London, 1937), p. 235.

22. For purposes of metrical analysis I quote from Kane's edition of the A Version, on the assumption that it more closely approaches what Langland wrote than any present edition of the B Version.

23. The line also illustrates a practice found frequently in *Piers Plowman* but only exceptionally in *Gawain* of alliterating *v* with *f*. The explanation is, at least in part, a matter of dialect.

24. This is very occasionally found in *Gawain*, e.g.,: 'Er me wont þe wede, with help of my frendez' (987). See Borroff, pp. 170–1.

25. In his edition for the E.E.T.S. in 1886, Skeat unfortunately adhered to the faulty line-numbering of Stevenson's edition of 1849 'for the sake of convenience of reference'. As a result, when Kaluza pointed out the 24-line grouping, his arguments appeared so contrived that they were, and have ever since been, ignored. See M. Kaluza, 'Strophische Gliederung in

der mittelenglischen rein alliterirenden Dichtung', *Englische Studien*, xvi (1892), 169–80.

26. It is this confusion of terminology that has led to much fruitless discussion on the existence of so-called 'quatrains' in alliterative verse. The arguments are soberly assessed by M. Day, 'Strophic Division in Middle English Alliterative Verse', *Englische Studien*, lxvi (1931), 245–8. See also J. R. Hulbert, 'Quatrains in Middle English Alliterative Poems', *M.P.*, xlviii (1950), 73–81; and W. Vantuono, 'The Question of Quatrains in *Patience*', *Manuscripta*, xvi (1972), 24–30.

27. See Sir I. Gollancz, *Cleanness* (reissued Cambridge, 1974), p. x. Gollancz regards this as the poet correcting his 'error', but this can hardly be the explanation.

28. In this respect compare Gollancz's *Cleanness* with Menner's *Purity*.

29. E.g. *On the Follies of Fashion*, in C. Brown, *English Lyrics of the XIIIth Century* (Oxford, 1932), pp. 133–4. For a list of poems with 'bob' lines see E. G. Stanley, 'The Use of Bob-Lines in *Sir Thopas*', *N.M.*, lxxiii (1972), 417–26.

30. See T. Turville–Petre, 'Three Poems in the Thirteen-Line Stanza', *R.E.S.*, n.s. xxv (1974), 1–14.

31. The same device is found earlier in the Harley Lyric *The Poet's Repentance*, discussed above, p. 18.

32. In line 4 I have emended ms. *þoзt* to *roзt*.

33. On the relationship between *Summer Sunday*, *De Tribus Regibus Mortuis* and *The Awntyrs off Arthure* see Turville-Petre, art. cit.

34. In his edition of the poem (Manchester, 1974), R. Hanna maintains that the *Awntyrs* consists of two separate works, but the evidence he adduces for this is unconvincing.

35. The evidence for this is that the same curious manuscript-roll (Bodley Rolls 22) contains a second poem with the acrostic 'Pipwel'. See C. Brown, *Religious Lyrics of the XVth Century* (Oxford, 1939), pp. 303–4.

36. MS. Digby 102 provides two further examples of the 14-line stanza: *A Remembraunce of LII Folyes* (which mingles alliterative stanzas with stanzas of iambic tetrameter; the sestet rhymes *ccdddc*), and *A Good Steryng to Heuenward* (not alliterative). Both are edited by J. Kail, E.E.T.S. 124 (1904), and the former also by R. H. Robbins, *Historical Poems*, pp. 50–3.

37. For a list of these see Gordon's edition of *Pearl*, p. 87.

38. Further discussion of this point is in M.-S. Røstvig, 'Numerical Composition in Pearl' *E.Sts.*, xlviii (1967), 326–32.

39. See O. D. Macrae-Gibson, '*Pearl*: The Link-Words and the Thematic Structure', *Neophilologus*, lii (1968), 54–64, reprinted in *The Middle English Pearl*, ed. J. Conley (Notre Dame, 1970), 203–19.

Chapter 4

1. However, that Langland sometimes uses conventional alliterative vocabulary to ironic effect is shown by Burrow, *Ricardian Poetry*, p. 34.

2. Or emend *enclosed* to *enclowed*, 'fastened'. For the same scribal error in a closely similar (and probably derivative) passage, see the manuscript variants in the *Awntyrs*, 382.

3. A handy guide, giving information on acton, jesserant, jupon, bascinet, crest, visor and aventail, is C. Blair, *European Armour* (London, 1958). Another useful short account is by Sir James Mann, 'Arms and Armour', in *Medieval England*, ed. A. L. Poole (Oxford, 1958), vol. i, pp. 314–37.

4. Now in the Tower is the finest late fourteenth-century bascinet, with its visor and aventail. For an illustration see A. R. Dufty, *European Armour in the Tower of London* (London, 1968), pl. lxxii.

5. *The Chronicle of Pierre de Langtoft*, ed. T. Wright, Rolls Series (1866–8), vol. ii, p. 248.

6. *The English Dialect Dictionary*, s.v. *donk*.

7. See A. H. Smith, *English Place-Name Elements* (Cambridge, 1970), s.v. **clōh* and **cnearr*.

8. My discussion here is much indebted to R. W. V. Elliott, 'Some Northern Landscape Features in *Sir Gawain and the Green Knight*', in *Iceland and the Mediaeval World*, ed. G. Turville-Petre and J. S. Martin (Melbourne, 1974), pp. 132–43.

9. For this suggestion see ibid., 137.

10. See K. Cameron, *The Place-Names of Derbyshire*, English Place-Name Society 29 (Cambridge, 1959), part iii, pp. 709–10.

11. A. H. Smith, op. cit., s.v. *gil*.

12. For a discussion of these synonyms in *Gawain* see Borroff, op. cit., chapter 3. This includes a close examination of *freke* and *schalk*, from which many of the details discussed below are taken.

13. Ibid., 54–5.

14. Ibid., 56.

15. According to *The English Dialect Dictionary*, s.v. *shalk*, which, however, does not give a quotation for this. Nor is there confirmation of the survival of the word in *The Scottish National Dictionary*.

16. See Oakden, op. cit., ii, 172–4; and H. C. Wyld, 'Studies in the Diction of Layamon's Brut', *Language*, vi (1930), 1–24.

17. See V. Krishna, 'Archaic Nouns in the *Alliterative Morte Arthure*', *N.M.*, lxxvi (1975), 439–45.

18. See L. D. Benson, *Art and Tradition in Sir Gawain and the Green Knight* (New Brunswick, 1965), pp. 129–31.

19. *M.E.D.*, s.v. *blank*, gives an example which seems on the face of it to suggest that *blonk* was, after all, an everyday word. An entry in the Close Rolls for 1412 orders customs officers to allow William de la Forest of Brittany to ship in a number of items including two pairs of 'blanke herneys'. However, this can hardly mean 'horse armour', but is rather to be taken as Englishman's French for 'white armour'.

20. This was first demonstrated by A. Brink, *Stab und Wort im Gawain* (Halle, 1920), and his conclusions are fully reproduced by Borroff, op. cit., 52–90.

21. *Gnede* is an emendation both in *Purity* and in *The Romance of the Rose*, 6002. It appears to be a word more common in northern works.

22. Thus Borroff, op. cit., 65, argues that *freke* has ironic connotations in *Gawain*, 241, where it is used non-alliteratively.

23. See E. S. Olszewska, 'ME. "Brittene and Brenne"', *N. & Q.*, ccxix (1974), 207–9.

24. By D. S. Brewer, *Chaucer and Chaucerians* (London, 1966), pp. 6–7. See further Burrow, *Ricardian Poetry*, pp. 19–20.

25. *Octavian*, ed. M. Mills, *Six Middle English Romances* (London, 1973).
26. This is discussed by Brewer, op. cit., and by R. W. V. Elliott, *Chaucer's English* (London, 1974), pp. 99 ff.
27. Oakden, op. cit., ii, 195–379.
28. For the feast see Spearing, *The Gawain-Poet*, pp. 21–2; and for the storm at sea N. Jacobs, 'Alliterative Storms: A Topos in Middle English', *Speculum*, xlvii (1972), 695–719.
29. On the use of collocations in the romances see A. C. Baugh, 'Improvisation in the Middle English Romance', *Proceedings of the American Philosophical Society*, ciii (1959), 418–54; and W. E. Holland, 'Formulaic Diction and the Descent of a Middle English Romance', *Speculum*, xlviii (1973), 89–109. There are lists of phrases in Oakden, op. cit., ii, 312–43, and in *Sir Beues of Hamtoun*, ed. E. Kölbing, E.E.T.S. E.S. 46 (1885), pp. xlv–lxiv.
30. On this see the various studies by E. S. Olszewska. The most relevant here are: 'Norse Alliterative Tradition in Middle English', *L.S.E.*, vi (1937), 50–64; 'Alliterative Phrases in the *Ormulum*: Some Norse Parallels', in *English and Medieval Studies Presented to J. R. R. Tolkien*, ed. N. Davis and C. L. Wrenn, pp. 112–27; and notes in *N. & Q.*, ccxix (1974), 207–9, 323–6.
31. In the late fourteenth century the verb *britten* appears in several forms, for the origins of which see B. Sandahl, 'On Old Norse *jó, jú* in English', *Studia Neophilologica*, xxxvi (1964), p. 266, n. 7.
32. See *Pearl*, ed. Gordon, p. 98.
33. Discussed in *Gawain*, ed. Tolkien, Gordon and Davis, l. 1255 n.
34. See R. F. Lawrence, 'Formula and Rhythm in *The Wars of Alexander*', *E.Sts.*, li (1970), 97–112. This is an excellent study of the way an alliterative poet modifies syntactic structures to fit preferred rhythmic patterns.
35. The text, which I have emended, reads *for cherys*.
36. For *fonde* (l. 175) the text reads *sonde*.
37. 'Let the radiant description descend from the top of her head to her toe'. Geoffrey of Vinsauf, *Poetria Nova*, translated M. F. Nims (Toronto, 1967), ll. 598–9.
38. Milman Parry's articles are collected in *The Making of Homeric Verse*, ed. A. Parry (Oxford, 1971). His work was continued by A. B. Lord, *The Singer of Tales* (Harvard, 1960). For more recent developments in the subject see A. Parry's introduction, pp. xxxii–xli.
39. Parry's thesis was first applied to Old English verse by F. P. Magoun, 'Oral-Formulaic Character of Anglo-Saxon Narrative Poetry', *Speculum*, xxviii (1953), 446–67. For a review of the voluminous debate that ensued, see A. C. Watts, *The Lyre and the Harp* (New Haven, 1969), pp. 46–125.
40. R. A. Waldron, 'Oral-Formulaic Technique and Middle English Alliterative Poetry', *Speculum*, xxxii (1957), 792–804.
41. L. D. Benson, op. cit., 121.
42. Quoted in *O.E.D.*, s.v. *weal*.
43. Benson, op. cit., 121.
44. R. F. Lawrence, 'The Formulaic Theory and its Application to English Alliterative Poetry', in *Essays on Style and Language*, ed. R. Fowler (London, 1966), pp. 166–83.

Chapter 5

1. G. L. Hamilton, 'A New Redaction (J^{3a}) of the *Historia de Preliis*', *Speculum*, ii (1927), 113–46, argues that the source of both the *Wars* and the Thornton *Life of Alexander* is a lost variant of the I^3 (or J^3) version of the *Historia de Preliis*. However, as I hope to show elsewhere, there is no need to posit an unrecorded redaction, since manuscripts of the I^3 version such as Cambridge Univ. Lib. MS. Mm.v.14 and Glasgow Univ. Lib. MS. Hunter 84 give a text very close to that used by the two English translators. (Interestingly, the Cambridge ms. contains a copy of *The Siege of Jerusalem* in the same hand.) My quotations from the *Historia de Preliis* are based on a collation of these two mss. Unfortunately, the text from which Skeat quotes in his edition of the *Wars* is a late and very corrupt version of the *Historia*.
2. Ed. J. S. Westlake, E.E.T.S. 143 (1913). References are to page and line.
3. See G. Cary, *The Medieval Alexander* (Cambridge, 1956), pp. 103–5.
4. In order to give the chronicle a 'moral', some versions of the *Historia* end with pious remarks by seven philosophers over Alexander's tomb, commenting on his fall from greatness. It has always been assumed that this episode would have been included in the missing conclusion of the *Wars*, but it is not in either of the Latin texts in the Cambridge and Glasgow mss., nor in the Thornton *Life*.
5. I discuss this in detail above, pp. 60–1.
6. Trevisa's *Dialogue between a Lord and a Clerk*, ed. A. W. Pollard, *Fifteenth Century Prose and Verse* (London, 1903), p. 207.
7. The Latin is even more circumstantial and varies in some details from the Thornton *Life*.
8. Camb. Univ. Lib. MS. Mm.v.14, fol. 142r; and Glasgow MS. Hunter 84, fols. 128v–129r. *Alisaunder of Macedoine* follows the I^2 version of the *Historia*, ed. A. Hilka, *Der altfranzösische Prosa-Alexanderroman* (Halle, 1920), pp. 27–8. The two versions do not differ significantly.
9. On grounds of sense and metre I have emended the ms. reading *arme* (l. 503) to *barme*, a reading confirmed by the Latin source.
10. Commented on by G. Shepherd, 'The Nature of Alliterative Poetry in Late Medieval England', *P.B.A.*, lvi (1970), 60; though he does not point out that the catalogue is translated from the Latin source.
11. The Latin has 'Femine nostre non ornantur ut placeant'.
12. For *beweues* (l. 4337) Skeat's text reads *bewenes*, corrected in his glossary.
13. Shepherd, art. cit., 60–1.
14. The Latin source of this episode is edited in E.C. Armstrong and A. Foulet, *The Medieval French Roman d'Alexandre*, vol. iv (Elliott Monographs, xxxix, Princeton, 1942), pp. 11–13.
15. The Ashmole ms. is rather corrupt at this point, and I have emended the text in line with the readings of the Dublin ms.
16. Many of the details of the procession are paralleled closely in Richard of Maidstone's account of Richard II's entry into London in 1392, *De Concordia inter Regem Ricardum Secundum et Civitatem London*. For the text see T. Wright, *Political Poems and Songs* (London, Rolls Ser., 1859), vol. i, pp. 282–300; and for a translation of the relevant parts of it see E. Rickert, *Chaucer's World* (New York, 1948), pp. 35–9. I owe this reference to Derek Brewer.

17. See J. Finlayson, 'The Alliterative *Morte Arthure* and *Sir Ferumbras*', *Anglia*, xcii (1974), 380–6; and also the introduction to Finlayson's selections from *Morte Arthure* (London, 1967).
18. Views put forward respectively by W. Matthews, *The Tragedy of Arthur* (Berkeley, 1960), pp. 125 ff.; J. Finlayson (ed.) *Morte Arthure*, pp. 14 ff. and 81; R. M. Lumiansky, 'The Alliterative *Morte Arthure* and the Concept of Medieval Tragedy', in *Medieval and Renaissance Studies*, iii, ed. J. M. Headley (Chapel Hill, 1968), pp. 95–118. For a summary of these and other views see G. R. Keiser, 'Edward III and the Alliterative *Morte Arthure*', *Speculum*, xlviii (1973), 37–51.
19. On medieval definitions of the 'just war' and the cruelties acceptable within it see M. H. Keen, *The Laws of War in the Late Middle Ages* (London, 1965), pp. 63–133.
20. Valuable studies of *Patience* are A. C. Spearing, *The Gawain-Poet*, pp. 74–95; and also the introduction to J. J. Anderson's edition.
21. In my discussion of *Purity* I have profited greatly from the stimulating article by T. D. Kelly and J. T. Irwin, 'The Meaning of *Cleanness*: Parable as Effective Sign', *M.S.*, xxxv (1973), 232–60. Other helpful studies of *Purity* are Spearing, op. cit., 41–73; and C. C. Morse, 'The Image of the Vessel in *Cleanness*', *Univ. of Toronto Quarterly*, xl (1971), 202–16.
22. In l. 966 I adopt the reading of Sir I. Gollancz's edition of *Cleanness* (reissued Cambridge, 1974) of *lauce* in preference to Menner's *lance*.
23. In the Nuptual Mass the priest prayed that the bride might be 'longeva et fidelis ut Sara'. See J. S. P. Tatlock, 'The Marriage Service in Chaucer's *Merchant's Tale*', *M.L.N.*, xxxii (1917), 373–4.
24. E.g. in Luke xvii. 26–9.
25. See Kelly and Irwin, art. cit., 247; and for examples from the Old Testament onwards of the image of man's soul as a vessel see Morse, art. cit., 207–11.
26. This text is referred to by Gollancz in his edition of *Cleanness*, footnote on p. xxii, but he does not recognise its significance.
27. On the importance of the image of the court in *Purity* see D. S. Brewer, 'Courtesy and the *Gawain*-Poet', in *Patterns of Love and Courtesy*, ed. J. Lawlor (London, 1966), pp. 58–62.
28. *On the Minorites*, ed. Robbins, *Historical Poems*, pp. 163–4.
29. For Brute's career in the Welsh marches see K. B. McFarlane, *John Wycliffe and the Beginnings of English Nonconformity* (London, 1952), pp. 135–8.
30. 'Digne as ditch water' is a proverbial expression used also in Chaucer's *Reeve's Tale*, 3964.
31. See McFarlane, op. cit., 126–38.

Chapter 6

1. Helpful guides to the Scottish material are Sir William Craigie, 'The Scottish Alliterative Poems', *P.B.A.*, xxviii (1942), 217–36; and J. Kinsley, *Scottish Poetry: A Critical Survey* (London, 1955), pp. 1–32.
2. See M. P. McDiarmid, 'Richard Holland's *Buke of the Howlat*: an Interpretation', *M.Æ.*, xxxviii (1969), 277–90. McDiarmid judges the poem more favourably than I do.

3. For details see F. J. Amours, *Scottish Alliterative Poems*, S.T.S. 27, 38 (1897), pp. xxxv f.

4. Ed. D. F. C. Coldwell, S.T.S. 3rd Ser. 25–8 and 30 (1957–64).

5. Ed. R. H. Robbins, *Historical Poems*, pp. 27–9.

6. J. Cranstoun, *The Poems of Alexander Montgomerie*, S.T.S. 9–11 (1887), p. 380. A more determined attempt to interpret the poem is made by H. Harvey Wood in his edition of Montgomerie's *The Cherrie and the Slae* (London, 1937), pp. 86–9.

7. Text in G. Gregory Smith, *Elizabethan Critical Essays* (Oxford, 1904), vol. i, pp. 218–19.

8. Ibid., 223.

9. For criticism of the poem see, in particular, J. Kinsley, 'The Tretis of the Tua Mariit Wemen and the Wedo', *M.Æ.*, xxiii (1954), 31–5. See also C. Singh, 'The Alliterative Ancestry of Dunbar's "The Tretis of the Tua Mariit Wemen and the Wedo"', *L.S.E.*, n.s. vii (1974), 22–54. I have emended my quotations from the *Tretis* in line with Professor Kinsley's forthcoming edition of Dunbar's poems.

10. Such prophecies, some originating in England and some probably in Scotland, were adapted for particular political situations, and appear in different versions on both sides of the Border during the fifteenth century. See the brief but valuable discussion in Robbins, *Historical Poems*, pp. 309–10. Some of these alliterative prophecies have still to be edited, and there are many unresolved questions concerning the whole genre. For some that have been edited see as follows: *The Cock in the North* (in alternating quatrains), ed. Robbins, ed. cit., 115–17; *When Rome is Removed* (mostly unrhymed), ibid., 118–20; *Thomas à Becket's Prophecies* (unrhymed), ed. J. R. Lumby, E.E.T.S. 42 (1870), pp. 23–31; 'In þe seson of somer' (unrhymed), ed. V. J. Scattergood, *Politics and Poetry in the Fifteenth Century* (London, 1971), pp. 391–3; 'And lx yen barons' (unrhymed), ed. M. Day, *R.E.S.*, xv (1939), 63–6.

11. Reprinted for the Bannatyne Club (Edinburgh, 1833).

12. There is a striking verbal parallel between *Howlat* l. 6 and *Tretis* l. 27.

13. For discussion of this, including a reference to a French *chanson* involving three married ladies, see H. E. Sandison, *The Chanson D'Aventure in Middle English* (Bryn Mawr, 1913), pp. 13, 54–6; and further J. M. Smith, *The French Background of Middle Scots Literature* (Edinburgh, 1934), pp. 39–40, where the *chanson* is printed.

14. I discuss the structure of the *Parlement* in relation to its meaning and to other examples of the debate form in 'The Ages of Man in *The Parlement of the Thre Ages*', *M.Æ.*, xlvi (1977).

15. 'Quia in inferno nulla est redempcio' (*Parlement*, 642). For the source see *Breviarium ad Usum Sarum*, ed. F. Procter and C. Wordsworth (Cambridge, 1879), fasc. ii, p. 278.

16. See A. McIntosh, 'The Textual Transmission of the Alliterative *Morte Arthure*' in *English and Medieval Studies Presented to J. R. R. Tolkien*, ed. N. Davis and C. L. Wrenn (London, 1962), pp. 231–40.

17. Demonstrated by E. V. Gordon and E. Vinaver, 'New Light on the Text of the Alliterative *Morte Arthure*', *M.Æ.*, vi (1937), 81–98.

18. See J. H. Hanford, 'Dame Nature and Lady Life', *M.P.*, xv (1918), 313 ff.

19. See P. L. Heyworth's edition, pp. 9–19.

20. This is probably Brackenthwaite (now Brackenfield) in east Derbys.,

which lies not far from Holbrook and (in west Notts.) Radford, both of which are named in the poem. I am indebted to Professor Kenneth Cameron for localising this group of places; for the forms of Brackenthwaite see his *The Place-Names of Derbyshire*, English Place-Name Society, xxviii (Cambridge, 1959), part ii, p. 217.

21. See J. B. Reese, 'Alliterative Verse in the York Cycle', *Studies in Philology*, xlviii (1951), 639–68; also H. Craig, *English Religious Drama of the Middle Ages* (Oxford, 1955), pp. 224–33.

22. See J. W. Robinson, 'The Art of the York Realist', *M.P.*, lx (1962–3), 241–51.

23. Ed. L. Toulmin Smith, *York Mystery Plays* (Oxford, 1885), XXXIII, ll. 169–80.

24. Ed. M. Eccles, *The Macro Plays*, E.E.T.S. 262 (1969).

25. For text and discussion see R. H. Robbins, 'A Gawain Epigone', *M.L.N.*, lviii (1943), 361–6; and for the other contents of the manuscript see *PMLA*, lxv (1950), 249–81. Robbins prints the two poems as one.

26. The stanza-form of this is analysed by J. L. Cutler, 'The Versification of the "Gawain Epigone"', *J.E.G.P.*, li (1952), 562–70.

27. See C. A. Luttrell, 'Three North-West Midland Manuscripts', *Neophilologus*, xlii (1958), 38–50.

28. Compare l. 49 with ll. 42–4. The poem is not earlier than 1515, the date of the death of the Bishop of Ely which is referred to in l. 285.

29. See J. Finlayson, 'Rhetorical "Descriptio" of Place in the Alliterative *Morte Arthure*', *M.P.*, lxi (1963–4), 1–11.

30. An earlier copy of *Scotish Ffeilde* is in the Lyme manuscript (1580–1600), preserved by the Legh family.

31. See J. W. Hales and F. J. Furnivall, *Bishop Percy's Folio Manuscript* (London, 1867), vol. i, p. xiii.

32. See T. Turville-Petre, 'Nicholas Grimald and *Alexander A*', *English Literary Renaissance*, vi (1976), 180–6.

33. Luttrell, art. cit., 40.

34. *Tottel's Miscellany*, ed. H. E. Rollins (Cambridge, Mass., 1928), p. 117, ll. 28–32.

35. Crowley's preface is quoted in Skeat's edition of *Piers Plowman*, pp. lxxiii–lxxv. See J. N. King, 'Robert Crowley's Editions of *Piers Plowman*: A Tudor Apocalypse', *M.P.*, lxxiii (1976), 342–52.

36. Text ed. G. Gregory Smith, *Elizabethan Critical Essays*, i, 239–40. For humanist attitudes to English metre and rhyme see D. Attridge, *Well-weighed Syllables* (Cambridge, 1974), 89–162.

37. Ed. Smith, i, 242.

38. Ed. Smith, ii, 65.

39. See, however, A. C. Hamilton, 'Spenser and Langland', *Studies in Philology*, lv (1958), 533–48. W. W. Skeat collects allusions to the poem in *The Vision of William Concerning Piers Plowman*, part iv, E.E.T.S. 81 (1885), pp. 863–74.

40. Richard Hurd, *Letters on Chivalry and Romance* (1762), ed. H. Trowbridge, Augustan Reprint Society (Los Angeles, 1963), p. 120. For an account of the eighteenth-century interest in medieval romance see A. Johnston, *Enchanted Ground* (London, 1964).

41. Percy's note in his manuscript; quoted by Hales and Furnivall, i, xii.

42. Percy's Preface to the *Reliques*.

43. See A. G. Watson, *The Manuscripts of Henry Savile of Banke* (London, 1969).

44. See R. Hanna's edition of the *Awntyrs*, p. 10.

45. *The Letters of Gerard Manley Hopkins to Robert Bridges*, ed. C. C. Abbott (London, 1935), p. 156. For a discussion of the origins of Hopkins' metrics see E. W. Schneider, 'Sprung Rhythm: A Chapter in the Evolution of Nineteenth-Century Verse', *PMLA*, lxxx (1965), 237–53.

46. Ezra Pound in his translation of *The Seafarer* and at the opening of the *Cantos* loosely imitates the alliteration of Old English verse.

47. W. H. Auden, *Collected Longer Poems* (London, 1968), p. 334.

48. Ibid., 260.

49. Ibid., 307.

EDITIONS OF POEMS OF THE ALLITERATIVE REVIVAL

References to poems of the Alliterative Revival are to the editions listed below. The edition used is not necessarily the most recent, if an earlier edition provides what I consider to be a more accurate text. When quoting, I have as far as possible brought punctuation, word-division and capitalisation in line with modern practice, and I have expanded abbreviations.

In some cases a poem is known by more than one title. I have followed the title of the edition used (e.g. *Purity* rather than *Cleanness*).

The ABC of Aristotle, ed. F. J. Furnivall, *Queene Elizabethes Achademy*, E.E.T.S. E.S. 8 (1869), pp. 65–7.

Alexander and Dindimus (or *Alexander B*), ed. W. W. Skeat, E.E.T.S. E.S. 31 (1878).

Alisaunder of Macedoine (or *Alexander A*), ed. W. W. Skeat, E.E.T.S. E.S. 1 (1867).

Ane Anser to ane Helandmanis Invectiue, ed. H. Harvey Wood, *The Cherrie and the Slae* (London, 1937), pp. 86–9.

The Awntyrs off Arthure, ed. R. Hanna III (Manchester, 1974).

The Blacksmiths, ed. R. H. Robbins, *Secular Lyrics of the XIVth and XVth Centuries* (2nd edn., Oxford, 1955), pp. 106–7.

The Buke of the Howlat, ed. F. J. Amours, *Scottish Alliterative Poems*, S.T.S. 27 and 38 (1897).

Cheuelere Assigne, ed. H. H. Gibbs, E.E.T.S. E.S. 6 (1868).

The Crowned King, ed. R. H. Robbins, *Historical Poems of the XIVth and XVth Centuries* (New York, 1959), pp. 227–32.

Death and Liffe, ed. J. H. Hanford and J. M. Steadman, *Studies in Philology*, xv, no. 3 (North Carolina, 1918).

The Destruction of Troy, ed. G. A. Panton and D. Donaldson, E.E.T.S. 39 and 56 (1869–74).

De Tribus Regibus Mortuis, ed. E. K. Whiting, *The Poems of John Audelay*, E.E.T.S. 184 (1931), pp. 217–23.

Friar Daw's Reply, see *Jack Upland*.

Golagros and Gawane, ed. F. J. Amours, *Scottish Alliterative Poems*, S.T.S. 27 and 38 (1897).

The Gyre Carling, ed. W. Tod Ritchie, *The Bannatyne Manuscript*, vol. iii, S.T.S. 2nd ser. 23 (1928), pp. 13–14.

Jack Upland, Friar Daw's Reply and Upland's Rejoinder, ed. P. L. Heyworth (Oxford, 1968).

Joseph of Arimathie, ed. W. W. Skeat, E.E.T.S. 44 (1871).

Kynd Kittok, ed. J. Kinsley, *William Dunbar: Poems* (Oxford, 1958) pp. 101–2.

Morte Arthure, ed. E. Brock, E.E.T.S. 8 (2nd edn., 1871).

Mum and the Sothsegger, ed. M. Day and R. Steele, E.E.T.S. 199 (1936), pp. 27 ff.

The Parlement of the Thre Ages, ed. M. Y. Offord, E.E.T.S. 246 (1959).

Patience, ed. J. J. Anderson (Manchester, 1969).

Pearl, ed. E. V. Gordon (Oxford, 1953).

Pierce the Ploughman's Crede, ed. W. W. Skeat, E.E.T.S. 30 (1867).

Piers Plowman, the A Version, ed. G. Kane (London, 1960). The B and C Versions, ed. W. W. Skeat (Oxford, 1886). Unless otherwise stated, quotations are from the B Version.

The Pistill of Susan (or *Susannah*), ed. F. J. Amours, *Scottish Alliterative Poems*, S.T.S. 27 and 38 (1897). Quotations are from the Vernon text.

Polwart and Montgomerie's Flyting, ed. J. Cranstoun, *The Poems of Alexander Montgomerie*, S.T.S. 9–11 (1887).

Purity (or *Cleanness*), ed. R. J. Menner (New Haven, 1920).

The Quatrefoil of Love, ed. Sir Israel Gollancz and M. M. Weale, E.E.T.S. 195 (1935).

Rauf Coilȝear, ed. F. J. Amours, *Scottish Alliterative Poems*, S.T.S. 27 and 38 (1897).

Richard the Redeless, ed. (as the first part of *Mum and the Sothsegger*) M. Day and R. Steele, E.E.T.S. 199 (1936).

St. Erkenwald, ed. R. Morse (Cambridge, 1975).

St. John the Baptist, ed. M. Day, *The Wheatley Manuscript*, E.E.T.S. 155 (1921), pp. 15–19.

St. John the Evangelist, ed. G. G. Perry, *Religious Pieces in Prose and Verse*, E.E.T.S. 26 (1867), pp. 87–94.

St. Katherine, ed. W. Heuser, *Anglia*, xxx (1907), 539–47.

Scotish Ffeilde, ed. J. P. Oakden, *Chetham Miscellanies*, Chetham Society, n.s. 94 (Manchester, 1935).

The Second Burlesque, ed. T. Wright and J. O. Halliwell, *Reliquiae Antiquae* (London, 1841), vol. i, p. 84.

The Siege of Jerusalem, ed. E. Kölbing and M. Day, E.E.T.S. 188 (1932).

Sir Gawain and the Green Knight, ed. J. R. R. Tolkien and E. V. Gordon, 2nd edn. revised by N. Davis (Oxford, 1967).

Summer Sunday, ed. R. H. Robbins, *Historical Poems of the XIVth and XVth Centuries* (New York, 1959), pp. 98–102.

Sum Practysis of Medecyne, by Henryson, ed. H. Harvey Wood, *The Poems and Fables of Robert Henryson* (2nd edn., London, 1958), pp. 155–60.

The Tretis of the Tua Mariit Wemen and the Wedo, ed. W. Mackay Mackenzie, *The Poems of William Dunbar* (London, 1932), pp. 85–97.

Upland's Rejoinder, see *Jack Upland*.

The Wars of Alexander, ed. W. W. Skeat, E.E.T.S. E.S. 47 (1886).

William of Palerne, ed. W. W. Skeat, E.E.T.S. E.S. 1 (1867).

Wynnere and Wastoure, ed. Sir Israel Gollancz (London, 1920; reissued Cambridge, 1974). In passages quoted I have sometimes retained the ms. readings in preference to the editor's emendations.

INDEX